MASCULINE CHRISTIANITY

ZACHARY M. GARRIS

REFORMATION ZION PUBLISHING

Masculine Christianity
© 2020, 2021 Zachary M. Garris
Published by Reformation Zion Publishing
Ann Arbor, Michigan
www.reformationzion.com

All rights reserved. No part of this book may be reproduced, stored in a retrieval system, or transmitted in any form by any means, electronic, photocopy, recording, or otherwise, without the prior written permission of the author, except for brief quotations in reviews and articles.

Unless otherwise indicated, Scripture quotations are from the ESV® Bible (*The Holy Bible, English Standard Version*®), copyright © 2001 by Crossway, a publishing ministry of Good News Publishers. 2016 Text Edition. Used by permission. All rights reserved.

Scripture quoted by permission. Quotations designated NET are from The NET Bible® copyright © 1996, 2019 by Biblical Studies Press, L.L.C. http://netbible.com. All rights reserved.

Published 2021.
First edition published 2020. Revised 2021.
Printed in the United States of America
ISBN: 978-1-7354739-0-1

To Sara,

who is far more precious than jewels (Proverbs 31:10).

Contents

Introduction vii
Chapter 1: The Rise of Feminism and the Erosion of Masculinity. . . . 1
Chapter 2: Sexual Rebellion and Repentance 29
Chapter 3: Complementarianism's Compromise. 55
Chapter 4: Christianity Is Patriarchal 77
Chapter 5: Gender Roles in the Creation Order 103
Chapter 6: Hierarchy and Authority in the Creation Order 119
Chapter 7: Masculine Authority Starts in the Home. 139
Chapter 8: Pastors and Elders Must Be Men (1 Timothy 2 & 3). . . 167
Chapter 9: Women Should Keep Silent in Church (1 Corinthians
 14:34-35) 195
Chapter 10: Masculine Authority in the Church. 225
Chapter 11: Masculine Authority Beyond the Home and Church . . 237
Chapter 12: Leaving a Manly Legacy 269
Scripture Index. 283
Recommended Reading 297

INTRODUCTION

DO WE REALLY need another book on biblical manhood? I obviously think the answer is yes. There are many books available on the subject of biblical manhood, and there are even more debating the Bible's teaching on gender roles. However, these books usually fall into one of two categories: (1) popular-level works focused on practical application with minimal interaction with the biblical text, and (2) academic-level works debating gender roles that are of little interest to the majority of readers.

Bridging the Gap

I myself love to read, sometimes even dense books, yet I was in no rush to dive into the academic literature on gender roles. I read many of these books and articles solely in preparation for this book. How much less likely is it that the average Christian will pick up a book debating 1 Timothy 2? There is certainly a gap here between academia and the church.

Many pastors have *Recovering Biblical Manhood and Womanhood* by John Piper and Wayne Grudem on their bookshelves, and it is a helpful resource in many ways. However, it is a large collection of essays that few will read straight through. And because it is a collection of essays by different authors, it lacks cohesion. Moreover, I think the book deviates from some historic Christian views (as will be shown throughout this book). Most pastors also turn to commentaries when addressing important Bible passages on gender roles, but this task invites problems. For much of modern biblical scholarship, including Bible commentaries, is either outright feminist or at least casts doubt on Scripture's teaching that men have authority in the home, church, and society.

Most Christians, pastors included, are more likely to read a popular-level book on biblical manhood and womanhood. Some of these are truly helpful, though many focus on practical living and the spiritual disciplines. I am not aware of many popular-level books that dig into the important biblical passages on gender roles, especially from a conservative view. This book seeks to bridge the gap between popular-level works and dry academics.

There are times where this book can get technical (especially chapters 8 and 9), including interacting with Greek and Hebrew. This is inevitable when interpreting the Bible. However, those who do not know the biblical languages should be able to follow most of the book just fine. I seek to explain things clearly and make the book interesting and readable. In doing so, I circumvent modern academia, much of which is rotten and filled with unbelieving scholarship. Many conservative academics are unwilling to publish in this area out of fear of controversy, and many publishing companies are unwilling to publish such conservative viewpoints.

Anti-Feminist and Patriarchal

There are two other reasons this book is a useful addition in my opinion. First, it is thoroughly anti-feminist. Many of the books written on gender roles in recent years are from a feminist/egalitarian perspective and attack the historic Christian views that a man has authority in the home and that only men may serve as pastors/elders in the church. This book affirms the historic interpretations and refutes the feminist revisions. It does not deal with critical feminists who dismiss passages of the Bible they do not like, but it engages "evangelical feminists" who claim to embrace the authority and inerrancy of the Bible. I assume the Bible is the inerrant Word of God. If someone rejects the teachings of the Apostle Paul, then that person rejects the God who sent him, and he is not a Christian in any meaningful sense of the term. That being said, evangelical feminism is not any better than critical feminism, as it too rejects the teachings of God's prophets and apostles. Feminism is false teaching that distorts the Bible's instructions for godly living. This is not to be taken lightly as some secondary issue on which we can agree to disagree. God redeems men to live as godly men, and He redeems women to live as godly women. Distorting God's design at creation and His goal in redemption is a grave error.

Second, this book goes further than most "complementarian" works (those defending male headship in marriage and male-only pastors/elders) by affirming some historic teachings that have largely been abandoned today. This includes the teaching that male authority is rooted in the differing natures of men and women and that there is a hierarchy of rank (not value) between the sexes. These terms make many modern people uncomfortable, but they are biblical concepts that are necessary for grounding proper relationships between men and women. This book also affirms the historic interpretation of 1 Corinthians 14:34-35 that women are not to speak publicly in the gathered worship assembly, a view that has been almost entirely rejected by complementarians (in favor of the interpretation that Paul only prohibited women from evaluating prophecy).

This work also contends that many of those holding to complementarianism today do not go far enough in applying gender roles to society, including the areas of civil government and the military. Part of this results from complementarianism's failure to properly and explicitly root gender roles in the differing natures and purposes of men and women. There exists a strong spirit of dichotomy between the church and society, leaving many Christians unwilling to say that sex distinctions and roles apply beyond the family and church. For all its positives, *Recovering Biblical Manhood and Womanhood* was mostly a defense of a narrow version of complementarianism (see chapter 3). The church's failure to speak to gender roles more broadly is fueling society's sexual confusion. So part of this book is a critique of narrow complementarianism, advocating instead for a comprehensive and consistent biblical view of men and women where men rule in the home, church, and society.

Sadly, many complementarians come off as apologetic for holding such "sexist" views by modern standards, so they adopt egalitarian principles while carving out two exceptions because the Bible is just so obvious in these areas (husbands lead in marriage, and only men lead in the church). They also apologize for the abuses of "patriarchy," as if the church has only demeaned women throughout its history rather than give them the highest status in all of human history. Contrary to this timid approach, the church should boldly embrace the Bible's hierarchical and anti-egalitarian teachings as *good* for both men and women and the cure to the unbelieving world's sexual chaos. The church does not need a compromised and watered-down version of biblical teaching on men and women, but a robust, biblical theology.

Gender and Sex

I must make a brief note on the use of the term "gender" that is used throughout this book. A person's "sex" is biologically determined (either male or female), and "gender" is a social expression of this biological basis (masculine or feminine). However, many today misuse the word "gender" to refer to a social construct disconnected from biological reality, thus introducing the concept that a person can identify as a gender different from his or her biological sex (transgenderism).[1] In order to avoid such confusion, I considered only using the phrase "sex roles." But this runs into the problem of being limited only to male and female reproductive roles (such as a woman nursing children), and the Bible is concerned with far more than this.

The Bible speaks to how men and women should behave (gender as a social expression), and it ties such roles to the natural biological differences between men and women (biological sex). Thus, "gender roles" is an appropriate phrase so long as it is properly understood—a man is to act like a man and a woman is to act like a woman. I use the phrase "gender roles" throughout this book, but I also use the words "tasks" and "duties" to help clarify what I mean. The Bible does not give an extensive

---

1. For more on this issue, see Sharon James, *Gender Ideology: What Do Christians Need to Know?* (Great Britain: Christian Focus, 2019).

list of behaviors that are masculine and feminine. But it does teach which primary tasks and duties God has given to men and women, and thus it provides principles for masculine and feminine living. God has assigned different gender roles and duties to humans based on their biological sex. While these roles vary in cultural expression and are subject to distortion as a result of sin, they are rooted in creation, not culture. We must examine what Scripture teaches about such roles in order to conform our lives to God's design for men and women.

Masculine Christianity

As for the title, one may wonder how Christianity can be "masculine" when it is a religion and not a human being. The answer is that masculinity is not limited to biological sex. Though men are given a masculine nature, they still need to act in a masculine manner (and all men fail to do so in some ways as a result of sin). Further, God is not a human, yet He still refers to Himself in masculine terms (He, Him, Father, Son). Masculinity in the Bible is associated with strength, authority, responsibility, and mission. So it is no coincidence that God has put men—and not women—in places of leadership. God appointed men as kings, priests, and elders in the Old Testament, and now He calls men to lead the church, home, and society. The Son of God took on a man's body, and now Jesus is and will forever be a man—and a masculine man at that. There is a masculine bent to Christianity, but sadly, the modern church has become effeminate in many ways.[2] To be "feminine" is a good thing for a woman, but it is not a

---

2. After coming up with the title, I later read that John Piper used the phrase "masculine Christianity" in a conference message he gave on J.C. Ryle in 2012. Piper says, "God has revealed Himself to us in the Bible *pervasively* as King, not Queen, and as Father, not Mother," concluding that "God has given Christianity a masculine feel." He explained, "What I mean by 'masculine Christianity,' or 'masculine ministry,' or 'Christianity with a masculine feel,' is this: Theology and church and mission are marked by overarching godly male leadership in the spirit of Christ, with an ethos of tender-hearted strength, and contrite courage, and risk-taking decisiveness, and readiness to sacrifice for the sake of

good thing for a man. Men who do not act according to God's design are "effeminate," and the church in many ways has likewise become effeminate.

This book urges the church to return to its masculine calling. It does so by starting with the problem, as chapter 1 surveys the rise of feminism and the erosion of masculinity in the West. Chapter 2 issues a call to repentance from sexual rebellion, including the rebellion known as feminism. Chapter 3 shows how the modern church's reaction to feminism, "complementarianism," compromised important points, while chapter 4 shows that Christianity is thoroughly patriarchal. Chapters 5 and 6 demonstrate how gender roles and male rule are rooted in the creation order. Then this book argues for masculine authority and rule in the home (chapter 7), church (chapters 8, 9, and 10), and society (chapter 11). The concluding chapter calls men to leave a godly legacy by loving and leading their families, raising godly children, and building for the future (chapter 12).

One word about my qualifications. I am not a professor, and I do not hold a doctorate in theology. However, I think this may aid my work in some ways. I am not writing as an ivory tower academic, and I am not subject to the pressures to conform to the academy or else lose my job. I also do not write primarily for academics but for everyone living in this increasingly progressive and feminist society. I have a wife and son, I teach in my church, and I interact with people in my work as an attorney. I write so that regular Christians—not just pastors and teachers—can understand the Scriptures and apply them to their lives. I do have academic degrees, including a seminary degree and a law degree. And I have done my work on this subject. This book engages the biblical text in the original languages,

---

leading, protecting, and providing for the community—all of which is possible only through the death and resurrection of Jesus. It's the feel of a great, majestic God, who by his redeeming work in Jesus Christ, inclines *men* to take humble, Christ-exalting initiative, and inclines *women* to come alongside the men with joyful support, intelligent helpfulness, and fruitful partnership in the work." John Piper, "'The Frank and Manly Mr. Ryle'—The Value of a Masculine Ministry" (January 31, 2012), https://www.desiringgod.org/messages/the-frank-and-manly-mr-ryle-the-value-of-a-masculine-ministry.

makes arguments based on that text, and interacts with the relevant academic literature.

My hope is that this book will strengthen Christ's church by furthering the proper interpretation of important texts of Scripture and encouraging God's people to carry out their proper duties in life—for their own good and for the glory of God. I hope this is the kind of book that Christians can recommend to their friends and hand to their pastors. And I hope that it leads to stronger male rule in the home, church, and society. Christianity is and always has been a masculine religion. And by God's grace, this book will lead to the church being more faithful to its masculine calling.

Soli Deo Gloria

Chapter 1

THE RISE OF FEMINISM AND THE EROSION OF MASCULINITY

MASCULINITY IS IN peril. Women are being pushed into roles formerly held by men, which in turn is driving men out of society. Women are pursuing more advanced degrees, working full-time jobs, and sometimes even making more money than their husbands. In other words, women are pursuing careers outside the home. The problem with this is that it comes at the expense of children and family life. Rather than *aiding* men as wives and mothers, women are *competing* with men in the same tasks.

As a result of women displacing them, men are doing quite poorly overall. Fewer men are going to college, and a high number of men are not in the workforce at all. Men are suffering high rates of divorce (often at the instigation of their wives), incarceration, loneliness, alcohol and substance abuse, and suicide. Marriage is in such a sad state that many men have decided to entirely forego traditional marriage and children.

Yet when men suffer, everyone suffers. God has designed men to lead their families, and thus women are also suffering as a result of the decline of men. The erosion of masculinity harms us all. Everyone is aware of the breakdown of the family in the West and its effect on children, many of whom are growing up fatherless or splitting time with their divorced or never-married parents. However, women too are harmed by this breakdown. There are many bad men in the world, and there are now fewer good men doing their job to protect and provide for their wives and children. Women are left vulnerable, and they are being used sexually rather than committed to in marriage.

Of course, it is not only the family that has suffered. The church and state consist of families, and both institutions are weakened by the breakdown of the family unit. The decline of men has coincided with the rise of the welfare state, as civil government seeks to provide financial assistance—and thus fills the provisionary role of the father—for children born outside of wedlock. Such policies have not only rewarded (and thus encouraged) bad practices, but they have also usurped the charity role traditionally reserved for the church.

Women have also sought leadership positions in the church traditionally held by men, with many churches now ordaining women as pastors and elders. Considering the clarity of the relevant biblical passages, as well as the overwhelming historical practice prohibiting such, the acceptance of women church leaders has undermined the authority of both the Bible and church history. There is no question that the church is weaker as a result of female leadership.

Feminism's War on the Family

The major culprit in this societal decline is the ideology known as *feminism*, which is now the default position of most Westerners. However, there is some confusion over the definition of feminism, as many people identify as "feminists" in order to indicate they support "equality" between men and women. But then this term "equality" is also used in a variety of ways. There is a great difference between the affirmation that men and women have equal worth before God and the demand that women carry out the same functions as men in society.[1] The ideology of feminism holds the

---

1. Feminist Estelle Freedman defines feminism in part as "a belief that women and men are inherently of equal worth," but surely this is not the distinguishing feature of feminism, as biblical Christianity affirms such equality. It is Freedman's

latter position that women should carry out the same functions as men in society. In other words, *feminism minimizes sex distinctions, with an emphasis on pushing women away from the home and children and into careers just like men*. Feminism is the belief that men and women are fundamentally the same and thus interchangeable. The feminist movements have been so successful over the years that Westerners live in a post-feminist society, meaning most people today are feminists without the label.

Carolyn Graglia, who left her occupation as a lawyer to become a homemaker, explains that feminists have waged war against the traditional family since the late 1960s, where the "immediate purpose has been to undermine the homemaker's position within both her family and society in order to drive her into the work force." Feminism's "long-term goal" has been to "create a society in which women behave as much like men as possible" so that women will "hold equal political and economic power with men."[2]

Feminist methods have included the promotion of the sexual revolution, as well as the support of no-fault divorce laws and affirmative action requirements, the latter of which has given preference to women in education and job opportunities. Graglia also identifies "the status degradation of the housewife's role" as one of feminism's crucial weapons. While there has been diversity among feminists, "all branches of feminism are united in the conviction that a woman can find identity and fulfillment only in a career."[3] Other things have contributed to the weakening of the family unit, including America's Great Society programs, but feminism is distinguished in that "it has actively sought the traditional family's destruction."[4]

Graglia argues that feminism operates on two flawed assumptions: (1)

---

opposition to male authority (and demand for functional equality) that forms the distinctive feature of feminism, which falls under the "social hierarchies" and male "privilege" that she thinks should be opposed by "social movements." Estelle B. Freedman, *No Turning Back: The History of Feminism and the Future of Women* (New York: Ballantine Books, 2002), 7.

  2. F. Carolyn Graglia, *Domestic Tranquility: A Brief Against Feminism* (Dallas: Spence Publishing, 1998), 1.

  3. Ibid., 2.

  4. Ibid., 3.

Equality means sameness (meaning men and women must do the same things); and (2) Most differences between men and women are imposed by culture.[5] Both of these assumptions will be challenged throughout this book. We will show that "equality" should only be used to speak of men and women having "equal value" before God and man, not equal functions, and we will show that men and women have different natures rooted in God's design, not culture.

First-Wave Feminism and Progressivism

In order to fully understand our modern feminist society, we must understand the various waves of feminism in the 19th and 20th centuries. These movements were so successful that no one today has to argue for a woman's right to vote or hold political office. In fact, to raise an objection against them would be met with utter shock and abhorrence from anyone listening. The same goes for criticizing a woman for placing her children in daycare so she can pursue a career outside the home.

The women's movement as a whole is usually categorized into three waves: (1) the first wave of the 1830s to 1920; (2) the second wave of the 1960s to the 1990s; and (3) the third wave of the 1990s to the present. The first wave at the time was known as the "woman movement" or "women's rights," but the later terms "women's liberation" and "feminism" came to be used to describe even the first wave. While the term "feminism" was not coined until the 1880s in France, it aptly describes all three waves of the women's movement.

First-wave feminism sought to make the economic, political, and social status of women equal to that of men, with its chief goal being the political right for all women to vote. This movement was led by women such as Susan B. Anthony (1820–1906) and Elizabeth Cady Stanton (1815–1902). Stanton helped found the National Women's Rights Convention, an annual series of meetings first held in Worcester, Massachusetts in 1850, at which Anthony eventually became a regular speaker. These meetings

---

5. Ibid., 2.

included speeches on topics such as equal wages, property rights, and marriage rights. However, Stanton and Anthony also took up social causes against alcohol and slavery. They helped form the Women's State Temperance Society in 1852–1853 and then the Women's Loyal National League in 1863 in order to campaign for a constitutional amendment to abolish slavery. The League collected nearly 400,000 signatures on petitions, helping to assist the passage of the Thirteenth Amendment (which abolished slavery) in 1865. The temperance movement later culminated in the Eighteenth Amendment and the Prohibition of the sale of alcohol, which went into effect in 1920.

With slavery outlawed, Stanton and Anthony focused their efforts on women's suffrage, forming the American Equal Rights Association in 1866. The Women's National Loyal League, which was formed in 1863 by Stanton and Anthony, wrote and submitted a proposed amendment to the Constitution in 1878 for women's right to vote. The Wyoming Territory became the first to allow women to vote in 1869, but it was not until 1920 that this right was granted federally with the Nineteenth Amendment—several years after the death of both Stanton and Anthony.

These ties show that first-wave feminism was not an isolated movement pushing for the right for women to vote. Rather, feminism was a *revolutionary movement* with broader goals in mind. It was part of 19th-century progressivism, a movement that came to full fruition in the period known as the Progressive Era (1890–1920). This progressivism is seen in feminism's ties with abolitionism (rather than a more moderate approach of gradual emancipation), which helped spur the War Between the States (1861–1865), and temperance, which resulted in the failed period of Prohibition (1920–1933). Progressivism developed primarily in the Northeastern U.S., among Yankees,[6] and was generally opposed by

---

6. David Hackett Fischer, *Albion's Seed: Four British Folkways in America* (New York: Oxford University Press, 1989), 867: "Progressivism developed mainly in the northern and northeastern states. A large proportion of its leaders were men and women of Yankee stock, who traced their ancestry to the Puritan great migration. Progressivism tended to be rationalist and moralist. Its approach to social

the more conservative South, seen particularly in Southern opposition to the Nineteenth Amendment for women's suffrage.[7]

All three movements—abolitionism, temperance, and women's suffrage—sought to undermine an older order of society. While slavery became outmoded and faded out of use in the world, abolitionism was a radical ideology that fomented sectional division and war in 1861. However, the temperance movement, along with its ultimate legal outcome in Prohibition, was the most explicitly unbiblical. While God forbids drunkenness, He nowhere says the solution is total abstinence, let alone the government banning alcohol. Rather, alcohol is a good gift from God that is to be used properly—including in the Lord's Supper (Psalm 104:14-15; 1 Corinthians 11:21). The movement to ban alcohol punished the godly for the sins of the wicked. Furthermore, it was part of a false gospel, the Social Gospel, that looked to the state for protection from all social ills.

The movement for women's suffrage was also problematic. While the Nineteenth Amendment is assumed by almost everyone today as a positive good, it was controversial at the time. The right of every citizen to vote was not the view of the American Founders, in part because they feared the dangers of democracy and the tyranny of the majority. Voting was not only considered a right, but also a *duty*. In ratifying the Nineteenth Amendment, men voted a new duty upon women—but it was not a duty that every woman wanted. Since government has a protection and military duty taken up only by men, it was argued that the vote in such a government should not be passed on to women.[8] In the end, the desire of *some* women for the vote thrust *all* women into politics and placed on them a new duty outside the home. Thus, we see the logical connection between

---

problems was intellectual; its solutions were institutional. Generally it adopted an idea of ordered liberty which was consistent with New England's Puritan past."

7. Ibid., 868: "Votes for and against leading Progressive measures continued to be primarily regional. A case in point was women's suffrage. The Congressional suffrage resolution of 1919 was strongly supported in the northern states, and strenuously opposed in the south. The suffrage amendment failed of ratification in ten states—all southern."

8. Lyman Abbott, "Why Women Don't Want the Vote," *The Atlantic* (September 1903).

first-wave feminism and its later stages that explicitly called for women to leave the home.

Others argued that universal suffrage assumed an individualism detached from the family unit. Theologian B.B. Warfield (1851–1921), a contemporary of Stanton and Anthony, pointed out that feminism viewed the individual rather than the family as the basic unit of society. Warfield said, "[T]he difference in conclusions between [the Apostle] Paul and the feminist movement of today is rooted in a fundamental difference in their points of view relative to the constitution of the human race. To Paul, the human race is made up of families . . . To the feminist movement the human race is made up of individuals; a woman is just another individual by the side of the man, and it can see no reason for any differences in dealing with the two."[9] Family was the "first government,"[10] of which men were the heads of their households, and thus only men were thought to have the duty to participate in the civil sphere. Women were not permitted to vote because their vote was represented in the vote of their husbands, and wives had significant influence on their husbands. This point was abhorrent to early feminists, especially the unmarried ones, and they thus sought to undermine male headship by advocating for the right for women to vote even *against* their husbands. By giving women the vote, the state did not just enfranchise women, but it also displaced the household's vote.

We should note here that many moderns assume that 19th- and 20th-century men did not care about women because they did not let them vote and that today we are much more enlightened. To borrow C.S. Lewis' phrase, this is "chronological snobbery" of the highest order. Many men of prior "sexist" generations made their decisions, including voting, with their wives, daughters, sisters, and mothers in mind. They cared for the women in their lives far more than the modern effeminate man does. Of course, there were always bad apples. But to assume men of the past cared less

---

9. B.B. Warfield, "Paul On Women Speaking in Church," *The Presbyterian* (October 30, 1919).

10. Ibid.

for women is nonsense. Men's privileges came with great responsibilities. Today, men are less privileged, and they are also less responsible.

Feminism's Egalitarian Roots

Many conservative Christians today praise first-wave feminism and distinguish it from later and even more radical forms, but this is an error. First-wave feminism at its roots was an anti-Christian movement, and its desire for cultural change was driven, not by biblical Christianity, but by secular progressivism. The later forms of feminism built on the first wave's radical philosophical foundation.

First-wave feminism adopted an egalitarian view of men and women that stemmed from the most radical wing of the Enlightenment, that of the Jacobins. The Jacobin party was the political faction of the French Revolution that carried out the Reign of Terror in 1793–1794. Jacobin "equality" stands in opposition to the British tradition of equality before the law. Whereas the British (and thus American) view of equality entailed equal treatment under the law, the Jacobin view meant *sameness*. This is an equality that flattens the world by tearing down hierarchy and role differences. The 18th-century American theologian R.L. Dabney described this as "mechanical equality," and today it is known as "functional equality" or egalitarianism. While the Jacobins of the French Revolution were not feminists, their radical egalitarianism was later applied by feminists to gender roles.

While the British and American legal systems and philosophies were influenced heavily by Christianity, the opposite is true of the Jacobins, who were revolting *against* Christianity. The roots of these two views have relevance for today. Secular progressivism, which is anti-Christian, affirms egalitarianism. Egalitarians despise authority and therefore scorn hierarchy. They begin by rejecting God's authority, and they in turn reject biblical authority structures. On the other hand, biblical, historic Christianity affirms hierarchy. God holds authority over all creation, and He has set certain authority structures in place. Men have authority over their wives in the marriage covenant, parents have authority over their children, elders have authority over the congregation in Christ's church, and civil officials have authority over citizens. Of course, authority can be abused, but this does not change the fact that authority still exists. While all humans are equal in the sense that all are fallen in Adam and are in need of God's grace, God has given different roles to different people in society. Christian equality requires us to treat everyone with love, but it does not undermine the authority structures that God has set in place. Rather, Christian love affirms God's authority structures and those God has placed in authority over us.

Radical Quakers and Heretics

Jacobin equality came to America with its adoption by the radical Quakers and Unitarians. The Quakers, while originating in Britain, abandoned historic Christianity and embraced egalitarianism early on. And it is no surprise that the Unitarians—who rejected the diversity of the Trinity—also embraced egalitarianism regarding human relations. In abandoning orthodox Christianity, the Quakers and Unitarians adopted the egalitarianism of the radical wing of the Enlightenment. And these two groups helped lead the charge for women's rights in America.

The leaders of the first-wave feminist movement were not orthodox Christians but heretics and radicals. Elizabeth Cady Stanton was raised Presbyterian but became an atheist and attacked the Bible's teaching on gender roles. Another feminist leader, Lucy Stone (1818–1893), was a Unitarian. And Susan B. Anthony was a Quaker who most likely became a Unitarian later in life. (Unitarians were also influential in the 19th-century feminist movement in Britain.[11])

Both Elizabeth Cady Stanton and Susan B. Anthony were heavily influenced by the Quakers, also known as the Society of Friends. The Quakers were one of the four major British groups to settle America,

---

11. Kathryn Gleadle, *The Early Feminists: Radical Unitarians and the Emergence of the Women's Rights Movement, 1831–51* (New York: St. Martin's Press, 1995).

coming to the Delaware Valley in the 17th century. However, they were a radical group that embraced egalitarianism and pacifism, followed the "inner light," and rejected the practice of baptism and the Lord's Supper. Quakerism's connections with first-wave feminism can be seen in that it was one of the first groups to allow women to serve as ministers. Many Quakers also embraced abolitionism and temperance.

Stanton became an admirer of Lucretia Mott (1793–1880), a Quaker feminist, and together they formed the Seneca Falls Convention in 1848, the first women's rights convention. As for Anthony, she was born to a Quaker father and attended and taught at a Quaker school. Anthony's family began attending a Unitarian church in 1848, where Anthony also began attending in 1849. She remained there the rest of her life, though she still identified with her Quaker roots. Suffice it to say that neither Stanton nor Anthony was deriving her views from the Bible. Their movement was tied with many anti-biblical teachings, including the ordination of women to the pastorate and loose divorce laws. The National American Woman Suffrage Association, the group founded by Stanton and Anthony, was even led by the Methodist female minister Anna Howard Shaw from 1904 to 1915.

It is worth noting that two religious groups were started by women in the late 19th century—the Seventh Day Adventist church was founded in 1863 by Ellen Gould White (1827–1915), and Christian Science was founded in 1879 by Mary Baker Eddy (1821–1910). While Christian Science is far more radical (and heretical) than the Seventh Day Adventists, both these groups have their roots in the feminism of the 19th century.

The Anti-Christian Roots of Feminism

Elizabeth Cady Stanton, the most radical of the early feminists, drafted a "Declaration of Sentiments" that was adopted by the Seneca Falls Conference of 1848 in New York. This document attacked "mankind" for limiting women's rights in the church—"He allows her in church, as well as state, but a subordinate position, claiming apostolic authority for her exclusion from the ministry, and, with some exceptions, from any public participation in the affairs of the church."[12] Stanton's views on female leadership in the church were made clear in her speech at the first annual meeting of the Woman's State Temperance Society in 1853:

> It has been objected to our Society that we do not confine ourselves to the subject of temperance, but talk too much about woman's rights, divorce, and *the Church* . . . Let it be clearly understood, then, that we are a woman's rights Society; that we believe it is woman's duty to speak whenever she feels the impression to do so; that *it is her right to be present in all the councils of Church and State.*[13]

Thus, we see the connection between temperance and feminism, as well as feminism's explicit demand for women in church leadership. Stanton was not simply concerned with a woman's right to vote—she wanted to overthrow the traditional practices of male leadership in every sphere, including the church.[14]

R.L. Dabney (1820–1898), a contemporary of Stanton, understood the goals of the women's movement. He identified the two claims of first-wave feminism as: (1) The legal disregard of the natural differences between men and women; and (2) The release of women from marital subordination.[15] The latter can be seen in Stanton's unbiblical view of divorce, as she

---

12. Elizabeth Cady Stanton, *A History of Woman Suffrage*, vol 1 (Rochester, NY: Fowler and Wells, 1889), 70–71.

13. Elizabeth Cady Stanton, "First Annual Meeting of the Woman's State Temperance Society," in *The American Nation: Primary Sources* (ed. Bruce Frohnen; Indianapolis, IN: Liberty Fund, 2008), 373–374.

14. Ian J. Shaw, *Churches, Revolutions, and Empires: 1789–1914* (Scotland: Christian Focus, 2012), 345: "An aspect of their protest was the 'subordinate' position afforded to women in the churches, particularly the way they were denied access to higher levels of religious education, and opportunities in professional ministry."

15. Robert Lewis Dabney, "Women's Rights Women," in *Discussions*, vol 4 (Harrisonburg, VA: Sprinkle Publications, 1994), 489: "If we understand the

believed that marriage ought to be held together only for the sake of "love" (a common belief in our own day). This was a rejection of the traditional Christian teaching that divorce is only permissible in the case of adultery or abandonment (Matthew 19:9; 1 Corinthians 7:15). Thus, Stanton was a forerunner to the no-fault divorce laws of the late 20th century. Stanton said the following about divorce and Christianity:

> Any law or public sentiment that forces two immortal, high-born souls to live together as husband and wife, unless held there by love, is false to God and humanity; who shall say that the discussion of this question does not lead us legitimately into the consideration of the important subject of divorce? But why attack the Church? We do not attack the Church; we defend ourselves merely against its attacks.[16]

Stanton's push for looser divorce laws was rejected by most as too radical for her own day. Yet Dabney considered Stanton to be the most consistent among the early feminists—"'Women's Rights' mean the abolition of all permanent marriage ties. We are told that Mrs. Cady Stanton avowed this result, proclaiming it at the invitation of the Young Men's Christian Association of New York. She holds that woman's bondage is not truly dissolved until the marriage bond is annulled. She is thoroughly consistent. Some hoodwinked advocates of her revolution may be blind to the sequence; but it is inevitable."[17]

---

claims of the Women's Rights women they are in substance two: that the legislation, at least, of society shall disregard all the natural distinctions of the sexes, and award the same specific rights and franchises to both in every respect; and that women while in the married state shall be released from every species of conjugal subordination."

16. Stanton, "First Annual Meeting of the Woman's State Temperance Society," in *The American Nation*, 374.

17. Dabney, "Women's Rights Women," in *Discussions*, vol 4, 501. Dabney's quote continues: "It must follow by this cause, if for no other, that the unsexed politicating woman can never inspire in man that true affection on which marriage should be founded. Men will doubtless be still sensual; but it is simply

The point in all of this is that the women's movement, along with its advocacy for women's suffrage, was tied up with a rejection of historic and biblical Christianity. Stanton even went so far as to publish *The Woman's Bible*, a commentary on the Bible that dismissed whatever passages she and her committee considered unfavorable towards women. Stanton herself wrote two-thirds of the work. She identified the teachings of the Bible on woman's subordination as "evil,"[18] and she said in the preface to Part II of the book, "We have made a fetich of the Bible long enough. The time has come to read it as we do all other books, accepting the good and rejecting the evil it teaches."[19] It must be recognized that *The Woman's Bible* was controversial even among feminists in Stanton's day, with some supporting it and others seeking to distance themselves from it. However, these quotations show that *at the root of Stanton's thinking was a rejection of biblical Christianity.*

Overthrowing Male Protection

The same can be seen in Anna Howard Shaw (1847–1919), a Methodist minister and president of the National American Woman Suffrage Association (1904–1915). Shaw was the first ordained woman in the Methodist church (though her ordination was revoked four years later).

---

impossible that they can desire them for the pure and sacred sphere of the wife. Let every woman ask herself: will she choose for the lord of her affections an unsexed effeminate man? No more can man be drawn to the masculine woman. The mutual attraction of the two complementary halves is gone forever."

18. Elizabeth Cady Stanton, *The Woman's Bible* (Mineola, NY: Dover, 2003), 8: "As the position of woman in all religions is the same, it does not need a knowledge of either Greek, Hebrew or the works of scholars to show that the Bible degrades the Mothers of the Race . . . The Old Testament makes woman a mere after-thought in creation; the author of evil; cursed in her maternity; a subject in marriage; and all female life, animal and human, unclean. The Church in all ages has taught these doctrines and acted on them, claiming divine authority therefor. 'As Christ is the head of the Church, so is man the head of woman.' This idea of woman's subordination is reiterated times without number, from Genesis to Revelations; and this is the basis of all church action."

19. Ibid.

MASCULINE CHRISTIANITY

It is clear Shaw sought more than just the right for women to vote, as she also wanted to overthrow male headship and male protection of women. In a June 21, 1915 address, Shaw said:

> Women have been the homemakers while *men have been the so-called protectors, in the period of the world's civilization where people needed to be protected*. I know they say that men protect us now and when we ask them what they are protecting us from the only answer they can give is from themselves. I do not think that men need any very great credit for protecting us from themselves. *They are not protecting us from any special thing from which we could not protect ourselves except themselves*. Now this old time idea of protection was all right when the world needed this protection, but today the protection in civilization comes from within and not from without.[20]

Shaw was seeking to overthrow an entire cultural system of male leadership and male protection of women. According to Shaw, women no longer needed men to protect them. Unfortunately, Shaw seemed unable to foresee the vulnerable position women would be left in when good men no longer protect them from bad men.

It is clear from Shaw's statements that she also wanted women to be able to serve in all positions occupied by men in her day. In response to the argument that women's suffrage would lead to women holding political office, Shaw responded that she did not think this was likely in her day. However, she revealed the connection in her own thinking between women's suffrage and women serving as politicians and even police officers:

> They tell us that if women were permitted to vote that they would take office . . . so long as it is a question of running for office I don't think women have much chance, especially with our present

---

20. Anna Howard Shaw, "The Fundamental Principle of a Republic," in *The American Nation: Primary Sources*, 387.

hobbles. There are some women who want to hold office and I may as well own up, I am one of them. *I have been wanting to hold office for more than thirty-five years . . . I have always wanted to be a policeman* . . . If women vote will they go to war?[21]

Shaw may not have been able to get all the rights she wanted for women in her day, but she knew she had to start somewhere. Women's suffrage was the beginning, and sure enough, women would one day come to hold political office, serve as police officers, and even serve in military combat positions. First-wave feminism threw off the high place of honor and protection that Christian society had given to women in exchange for the "right" to do everything a man does.[22] In his trip to America in the 1830s, prior to first-wave feminism taking root, Alexis de Tocqueville noted, "although the women of the United States are confined within the narrow circle of domestic life, and their situation is in some respects one of extreme dependence, I have nowhere seen woman occupying a loftier position." He added, "and if I were asked . . . to what the singular prosperity and growing strength of that people ought mainly to be attributed, I should reply: To the superiority of their women."[23] Despite the claims of feminism, the fact is that women had a high place in society prior to the feminist movement.

---

21. Ibid., 389.
22. Dabney, "Women's Rights Women," in *Discussions*, vol 4, 503: "In Christian and European society alone has she ever attained the place of man's social equal, and received the homage and honor due from magnanimity to her sex and her feebleness. And her enviable lot among us has resulted from two causes: the Christian religion and the legislation founded upon it by feudal chivalry. How insane then is it for her to spurn these two bulwarks of defense, to defy and repudiate the divine authority of that Bible which has been her redemption, and to revolutionize the whole spirit of the English common law touching woman's sphere and rights? She is thus spurning the only protectors her sex has ever found, and provoking a contest in which she must inevitably be overwhelmed."
23. Alexis de Tocqueville, *Democracy in America*, vol 2 (trans. Henry Reeve; Washington Square Press, 1899), 701.

Second-Wave Feminism and the Sexual Revolution

The second wave of feminism came several generations later in the 1960s, with the focus on women's legal and social equality. This wave fought for a woman's right to initiate divorce proceedings, no-fault divorce, a woman's right to abortion, and equitable wages. The seeds of 1960s feminism had been planted in the first wave of the women's movement, but this second wave was even more radical. This movement was ultimately an all-out attack on marriage, demonstrated in Betty Friedan's 1963 book *The Feminist Mystique*, which called women to trade homelife for the workforce.

Much of second-wave feminism was tied up with the sexual revolution, as women wanted greater independence and sexual freedom. There was an *ideology* behind the second-wave feminism of this period, led by women like Gloria Steinem, who said a woman needs a man "like a fish needs a bicycle." But at the end of the day, what propelled this second wave of feminism was an *invention* in 1950. And that invention was a pill, or rather, "the pill." Prior to 1950, extra-marital sex carried with it a high probability of pregnancy. But this could be significantly reduced as long as a woman took the birth control pill. As the pill became more popular in use, it removed one of the greatest deterrents to extra-marital sex. Men and women could now have "casual" sex with no repercussions, or so it was thought.

The invention of the pill radically changed relationships between men and women and the familial order. As Mary Eberstadt says, "No single event since Eve took the apple has been as consequential for relations between the sexes as the arrival of modern contraception."[24] This is not to say that the pill alone is the culprit for the sexual revolution of the 1960s (a revolution that has continued into our own day). Rather, it is to say that the rebellion against the older order was given a springboard in the birth control pill.

The ideas were already brewing, and men and women were already

---

24. Mary Eberstadt, *Adam and Eve After the Pill: Paradoxes of the Sexual Revolution* (San Francisco: Ignatius Press, 2012), 11.

questioning monogamy and traditional gender roles. But sex results in children, and children get in the way of careers. So when sex and children could be disconnected, traditional roles could be discarded. Women were freed to have sex apart from marriage and jobs apart from children. Enter the modern world.

No-fault divorce was a major goal of this revolution, but so was the "right" to abortion. The distribution of the birth control pill in the 1960s enabled women to have near-consequence-free sex, but women still wanted more—they wanted the right to "terminate" a pregnancy in case they still got pregnant. And this "right" was granted in the 1973 Supreme Court ruling *Roe v. Wade*.

If first-wave feminism can be described as women's desire to *be independent from men*, second-wave feminism can be described as women's desire to *act like men*. The feminists of the 1960s sought to spurn female biology, as they no longer wanted the burden of pregnancy and children. With the invention of the pill, women could have fruitless sex and were therefore able to put off marriage. Most women still did marry, but they began having children later and having fewer of them. In fact, women began to have so few children that the fertility rate in America dropped below the 2.1 children per woman required for population stabilization (and the rate continues to drop), which creates a variety of problems for society.[25] Women wanted careers instead of staying at home and raising children, and many women began to trade the traditional vocation of homemaker for previously male-dominated positions. Children began to be raised by people other than their own parents, with kids spending more time with daycare workers and schoolteachers than their own mothers.

Feminism overall was enabled in part by the Industrial Revolution and technological advancement. Prior to the Industrial Revolution, work and home were intertwined so that the entire family worked together to support the family business and husbands were more involved in childcare. Industrialization in America, especially between 1780 and 1830, drove

---

25. Jonathan Last, *What to Expect When No One's Expecting: America's Coming Demographic Disaster* (New York: Encounter Books, 2013).

many men away from the home to factories in order to provide income for the family. This divided home and work and resulted in fathers being less involved in the raising of their children.[26]

In addition, many of the tasks women had to do at home became much easier (especially in the 20th century) or were handed over to others. Instead of preparing food from scratch, we get food from the grocery store or go to a restaurant. Instead of making clothes, we purchase them from a retail store. Instead of educating children, we send them to schools. And the elderly, who formerly needed to be cared for by their children, are now shipped off to nursing homes. The tasks once required of the wife are now gone, enabling women to join their husbands in working outside the home. Of course, technological improvements have not eliminated all work at home. There is still much to do, including cooking, cleaning, laundry, and caring for and educating children. But the idea of the productive household has become lost. The point is that what once was unthinkable—a mother leaving the home for long hours five days per week—became possible.

We thus see three major revolutions that set the stage for feminism. The French Revolution spread Jacobin egalitarianism, which was used by feminists to undermine male headship in the home. The Industrial Revolution drove men outside of the home in order to provide for their families and made women's domestic work easier. Then the sexual revolution, enabled by the pill, delayed marriage and reduced the number of children women had, thus encouraging women to abandon the home and take up the same tasks as men.

We should also make note of third-wave feminism, which began in the 1990s and was even more radical than the previous waves of the women's movement. While third-wave feminism is not monolithic, it has largely been behind the push for homosexuality and the celebration of sexuality as a means of empowerment. The second-wave feminism of the 1960s did have an element of homosexuality and a rejection of men, but many

---

26. Nancy Pearcey, *Total Truth: Liberating Christianity from its Cultural Captivity* (Wheaton, IL: Crossway, 2008), 327–331.

considered that too radical at the time and thought it would harm the movement. But the taboo of such radicalism slowly eroded over time and has continued to erode. Third-wave feminism has certainly succeeded in accomplishing its goals, with the U.S. Supreme Court legalizing same-sex marriage in all 50 states in the 2015 case *Obergefell v. Hodges*, followed by the extension of anti-discrimination laws to homosexuality and transgenderism in the 2020 case *Bostock v. Clayton County* (both of which are entirely lawless rulings).

These later forms have shown just how anti-Christian feminism is, as it has explicitly attacked God's design for the family. R.J. Rushdoony says that religion "is seen as a projection of the family, and the family must therefore be destroyed in order that religion may also be destroyed."[27] Feminists understood this, and they have thus targeted the family in order to undermine religion.

Feminism Ingrained in Our Laws

As a result of these movements, we now live in a world where feminism is ingrained in our laws in the West. The right to vote was only the start of this moral revolution. Many feminists did not consider suffrage enough and wanted civil government to mandate equality of men and women in every regard. Thus, shortly after the Nineteenth Amendment was ratified, the Equal Rights Amendment (ERA) was introduced in Congress in 1923. However, it was not until 1972 that the ERA passed Congress and was put to the states, where three-fourths of the states needed to ratify the amendment for it to go into law. Thirty-five states ratified the ERA, but thanks in part to the political efforts of anti-feminist Phyllis Schlafly (1924–2016), the amendment was unable to garner the 38 states required for ratification. Those opposed to the ERA argued that it would harm women by leading to them being drafted into the military and losing alimony and custody in divorce cases.

---

27. Rousas John Rushdoony, *The Institutes of Biblical Law* (The Craig Press, 1973), 161.

The sad irony in all this is that although the ERA failed as a constitutional amendment, it was still implemented into law by the courts. We have yet to see the requirement for women to sign up for the draft, though women are now welcome into the military, including combat positions. Other than the draft, sex distinctions have been almost entirely abolished in American law, both at the state and federal levels. Most notably, the federal courts began using the Equal Protections Clause of the Fourteenth Amendment[28] to enforce "gender equality," even striking down things that benefited women. For example, in 1982, the Supreme Court ruled that the Mississippi University for Women was "unconstitutional" because it was state-funded and did not enroll men.[29] Ironically, the majority opinion was written by the first woman on the Supreme Court, Sandra Day O'Connor. (This same Equal Protections Clause was used to strike down state laws discriminating against homosexuals, which eventually led to the 2015 same-sex marriage ruling, *Obergefell v. Hodges*.)

The courts also withdrew legal responsibilities for men, with many states abolishing the common law requirement for a husband to provide for his wife and children (part of what is known as the doctrine of necessaries). In addition, a point often left out of the abortion debate is that the *Roe* decision entirely cut men out of the equation. *Roe v. Wade* (1973) not only granted women the "right" to abort their children, but it also permitted women to make this decision without the father's consent—even if the mother and father are married. Thus, *Roe* legally bastardized children by

---

28. The Supreme Court has understood "equal protection" and "due process" in the Fourteenth Amendment as elastic phrases, but these were precise legal terms with narrow meanings. "Equal protection of the laws" applied to the legislature and was intended to secure black Americans the same rights as whites. "Due process" referred to judicial procedure, not a legislative act. Legal historian Raoul Berger summarizes the original intention of the Fourteenth Amendment as follows: "In lawyers' parlance, the privileges or immunities clause conferred *substantive* rights which were to be secured through the medium of two *adjective* rights: the equal protection clause outlawed statutory, the due process clause judicial, discrimination with respect to those substantive rights." Raoul Berger, *Government by Judiciary: The Transformation of the Fourteenth Amendment* (2nd ed.; Indianapolis: Liberty Fund, 1997), 235.

29. *Mississippi University for Women v. Hogan*, 458 U.S. 718 (1982).

taking away the father's authority over them. The mother is the only one who can decide whether her child lives or dies.

The changes in law did not stop with the courts. Divorce laws were loosened when California became the first state to pass a no-fault divorce law in 1969, meaning either spouse could file for divorce without any evidence of fault by the other party. By 1983, every state adopted some form of no-fault divorce except South Dakota and New York (and they adopted it by 2010). Prior to no-fault laws, the person initiating a divorce had to show fault, such as adultery or abandonment. No-fault divorce only requires an assertion by one party that there is a "breakdown" in the marriage. Divorce thus became much easier for people to attain, and the rates of divorce skyrocketed.

Yet worse than easy divorce, courts have increasingly trended towards not factoring fault at all into the division of property and child custody following a divorce. This means a man or woman can commit adultery, file for divorce, and still take 50% of the marital property (and split child custody and parenting time). Apart from egregious behavior, most states permit a spouse to breach the marriage contract with no penalty.[30] A contract with no penalty for breach raises the question—why even have a contract at all? It is no wonder such breach (divorce) has become commonplace and why many couples have decided to completely forego the unenforceable marriage "contract" and instead cohabitate.

State and federal anti-discrimination laws were also passed to protect women in the workforce. The push for equal wages for women was solidified in the Equal Pay Act of 1963, which made it illegal for companies to pay different wages to men and women for comparable work. Companies could no longer discriminate on the basis of sex "for equal work on jobs the performance of which requires equal skill, effort, and responsibility, and which are performed under similar working conditions."[31] Where these

---

30. In the United States, states issue a marriage "license," which is a state-issued contract with default terms set by each state, though this can be modified in some ways with a prenuptial agreement.

31. Equal Pay Act of 1963, section 206(d), http://www.eeoc.gov/laws/statutes/epa.cfm.

laws became problematic is not in pay requirements but in the prohibition of employers favoring men over women in hiring—even though young women are bound to be less efficient and take more time off due to pregnancy and childbirth. Thus, government has removed a natural advantage of men in the workforce. While this may seem good to many today, the result is that women are now taking up careers in spite of biology, and they are competing with men for breadwinner jobs.[32] This has further spurred the decline in the birthrate, the availability of domestic-oriented women, and the number of men making enough money to support a stay-at-home wife.

The rise of feminism in Western society has also coincided with the rise of statism. Government has displaced fathers, and many people now look to the state to provide for their needs, from cradle to grave. It is hard to say whether the rise of government has caused the decline of men or whether the decline of men has led to the rise in government. It probably works both ways. However, bad government policies have certainly contributed to the breakdown of the family, such as no-fault divorce, financial handouts for unmarried mothers, the decriminalization of adultery and homosexuality, and now state-recognized same-sex "marriage." Laws incentivize behavior, especially those that involve money. This is seen most clearly in the government incentivizing women to have children out of wedlock by paying them to do so (regardless of the intention to help such women). This policy has undoubtably contributed to America's out-of-wedlock birthrate surpassing 40%. Even for those not seeking government

---

32. Women entering the workforce increased available labor and thus drove down wages in some fields (unless the number of jobs increased proportionately). While it may be argued that women entering the workforce created more jobs for both men and women, two things must also be taken into account: (1) Many women fill traditional breadwinner jobs (such as those in law, medicine, and business) that do not necessarily grow in proportion to the number of jobs created; and (2) Many of the jobs created as a result of women entering the workforce are not breadwinning jobs, such as those in the areas of childcare (e.g. daycare, after-school programs), cleaning, food services, and education (many schoolteacher jobs do not pay breadwinner money). Furthermore, higher-income women tend to marry higher-income men, concentrating wealth among the upper classes.

money, the availability of welfare benefits introduces what is known as "moral hazard," as it reduces the risks of out-of-wedlock sex by alleviating the consequences.

The displacement of the family is also seen in the growth of socialistic programs. In prior ages, those in need looked to family members, friends, churches, and private charities for financial help. But not today. The government taxes productive citizens at an absurd rate and then gives handouts with little discretion or means-testing. Among these programs in the United States are food stamps, Supplemental Security Income, Social Security Disability, Medicaid, Medicare, and the Affordable Care Act.

Feminism Infecting the Church

Cultural decline never leaves the church unaffected, and culture is often a reflection of the church. Christians live under the same laws as everyone else, and they are often exposed (unfortunately) to the same media and schools. So when feminism has infected society, it should come as no surprise that feminism has also spread to the church. In fact, in some ways feminism was *promoted* by the church. It started with the push for women pastors in the 19th and 20th centuries (some of whom participated in the women's rights movement) and then came into full force in the mid-1970s.

Debate over gender roles in the church took off in the 1980s, and two opposing groups were formed—the Council on Biblical Manhood and Womanhood (CBMW) in 1987 and Christians for Biblical Equality (CBE) in 1988. The feminist group (they prefer the term "egalitarian"), CBE, argued for women pastors and against male headship in the home, while CBMW reacted against the feminist movement in the church.

It cannot be said that the egalitarians won the war over women's roles, but they certainly won the battle. Mainline liberal denominations succumbed to feminism and are now overrun with women pastors. Even some so-called "conservative" churches, which affirm the authority and inerrancy of the Bible, ordain women to the ministry. These are known as "evangelical feminists," in contrast to the critical feminists found in mainline liberal churches. We now live in a day where a strong number of Protestant churches are functionally egalitarian, if not theologically so. Most pastors are afraid to preach on passages teaching that men have authority in marriage and that only men can hold church office, let alone condemn the sin of effeminacy that plagues the modern church. The result is that many marriages in "conservative" churches are functionally egalitarian and more churches cave to women pastors (and women preaching to men) every year.

Furthermore, it has become commonplace for women in the church to pursue careers instead of children and homemaking. Christian parents have fully bought into the feminist mindset and thus train their children accordingly—and pastors refuse to address this problem. Like the culture at large, the church is full of women who want to marry men who make more money than they do (hypergamy), a perfectly reasonable desire. Yet these women are left with a smaller group of suitors due to their career pursuit, as they now make more money than many men. And since they spent all that time in school and probably have significant debt, they justify taking on a career outside the home even if they do marry. Yet wives working full time means home life is not properly cared for—there are fewer family meals together, daycare and public schools become more appealing, and technological devices are given to children as a substitute for parental attention. Further, many men are foregoing marriage because they do not want to marry a woman who acts like a man. They want to marry a woman who will take care of the home and bear children.

Thus, feminism is ruining the West, and it is ruining the Western church. Feminism tears down authority structures, with a particular focus on the family unit. The goal of feminism is to push women out of the home and into the workplace, making them more like men. Feminism is the twisted idea that a woman is free when serving an employer but a slave when serving her family. And this has all been to woman's detriment. As German theologian Werner Neuer says, "The tragedy of feminism is that it propagates precisely the opposite of the real interests of women. Instead of helping women to develop their femaleness to its optimum, it tends to encourage them to imitate men. Women should participate to the same extent as men in careers, in society, and in politics."[33]

The church has not effectively pushed back against this trend and has in many circumstances outright embraced it. It is hard to deny the conclusion that the modern Western church has become feminist. And in adopting feminism, the church has become weak and impotent. It has traded its masculine calling for effeminacy. The church has abandoned God's design and thus cannot live out God's calling to lead the world.

The distortion of biblical gender roles has had other consequences. When women act like men and men act like women, it should not surprise us that we are now facing the advocacy of homosexuality in the church. It is the logical outcome of the breakdown of gender roles. For when the sexes behave like one another, the differences become less apparent and confusion sets in. And sexual confusion fans the flame of unnatural desire for members of the same sex. Unfortunately, some "conservative" churches have not fully rejected homosexuality but have permitted Christians to "identify" as homosexuals as long as they do not "practice" homosexuality (thus driving a wedge between desire and act).

What we are dealing with is the triumph of progressivism. The political and social left rules the West, and its evangelists have infiltrated the church. They are undermining the family by pushing a distortion of marriage (same-sex "marriage") and the mass murder of children (abortion). What is supposed to be the conservative wing of the church (sometimes called "evangelicalism") has also succumbed to such progressivism and is now too weak and soft to fend off the onslaught. The effeminacy of the church explains why so many Christians have embraced leftist views, often defending such things on the basis of distorted biblical doctrines. Progressive Christians reason that since God is loving, we must accept the behavior of all people (rather than call them to repentance). One of the best ways to describe the feminist movement as a whole is a rebellion *against* historic Christian society and its authority structures. Yet the

---

33. Werner Neuer, *Man and Woman in Christian Perspective* (trans. Gordon J. Wenham; Wheaton, IL: Crossway, 1991), 166.

church has embraced its very enemy. Feminism is no longer just an enemy without, but also an enemy within.

When it comes down to it, there are two major dividing lines between conservatism and leftist progressivism. The first is that progressives view the individual as the central unit in society, while conservatives view the family as central. The second is that progressives are egalitarians. I am here speaking of egalitarianism in the broad sense, with feminism being a particular form. Progressives demand that women must serve in all positions that men do, while conservatives hold that the world is inevitably hierarchical. Christianity has never been egalitarian. It recognizes that God made the world hierarchical and that everyone will look somewhere for authority. Scripture gives us instructions on how to live in this hierarchical world, and thus progressives reject the Scriptures.

The Church's Failure

Though feminism has influenced men and women, it is the women in particular who are not following their natural role. The majority of men today are still seeking to get a job and provide for a family. However, the women are seeking to carry out this same task, and in doing so they abandon the pursuit of children and domesticity. This leaves both sexes frustrated.

Feminism is a colossal failure, and I am going to point the finger primarily at men. Men have failed to lead women, including their wives and daughters, to the detriment of us all. Women still deserve blame, but responsibility ultimately goes to the men—that is how God has ordered society. As rulers, men have to take responsibility. Both men and women have rebelled against God's design, but it is the men who have allowed it. Men, including Christian men, have stood by and failed to respond biblically. They have been passive and effeminate rather than strong and masculine. Women have been misled by bad actors, and those bad actors have left us with an effeminate church.

Christian fathers have allowed their daughters to go the way of the world rather than point them to the Scriptures and train them to seek children and domesticity. This includes Christian pastors. But pastors bear additional guilt, as they have failed to address this sin in their congregations. Many Christian pastors are faithful to proclaim that Jesus died for our sins and was raised from the dead, yet they say nothing of the Lord's demands for gender roles and sexuality. They have not preached against unlawful divorce, promiscuous dating culture, egalitarian marriage practices, effeminate male behavior, the idolatrous pursuit of career and materialism over children, and homosexuality. They have failed to preach "the whole counsel of God" (Acts 20:27) and so protect the flock from ravenous wolves.

The point of this book is that Christianity is a masculine religion. Men have authority, and as go the men, so go the women and children. Yet we are facing a crisis of masculinity in the church. Men have failed to lead, including our pastors, and now our women are acting like men and our men like women. To recover from this crisis of masculinity, we must start with God the Father. We must start with worship. Christianity has a masculine message of a husband who laid down His life for His bride. But we have an effeminate church preaching an effeminate gospel, proclaiming Jesus as Savior while ignoring His command for male rule in His kingdom.

In 2005, author Mary Kassian said, "Feminism is a watershed issue. It is to the evangelical church of the new millennium what liberalism was to the church in decades past."[34] I agree with Kassian, but we have the additional concern that the church has been far too late—and weak—in addressing the problem. Dabney predicted in 1871 that feminism "will destroy Christianity and civilization in America."[35] Its threat is that serious. It is never too late for repentance, but it must come soon. Repentance starts by looking to the Word of God. And that is where we will now go.

---

34. Mary Kassian, *The Feminist Mistake: The Radical Impact of Feminism on Church and Culture* (Wheaton, IL: Crossway, 2005), 288.

35. Dabney, "Women's Rights Women," in *Discussions*, vol 4, 498.

Chapter 2

SEXUAL REBELLION AND REPENTANCE

THERE IS WIDESPREAD apostasy in the West. Apostasy is the act of abandoning the Christian faith, and that is exactly what is happening in large numbers among formerly Christian nations. Having an established state church can make a nation a Christian nation, but it is not the only thing. A nation can also be described as Christian when a majority of its people identify as Christian and live out the Christian faith.

The United States of America prohibited an official federal church in the First Amendment, though some states had official churches into the 19th century, with Massachusetts being the last to disestablish in 1833. (This is because the First Amendment did not apply to the states—"*Congress* shall make no law respecting an establishment of religion . . .") Yet there are reasons to describe the United States as a Christian federation, particularly based on the early history of the colonies/states. All four major groups in early America were religious—the Puritans in the Northeast, the Cavaliers in the Tidewater region, the Scotch-Irish in the backcountry, and the Quakers in the Delaware Valley (though they were unorthodox, to say the least).

Yet things are changing. The West is no longer majority Christian, at least not in practice. The majority of Westerners are still baptized and thus are at least nominally Christian. But often little is done after baptism to teach children the faith. Parents do not catechize, and pastors fail to faithfully preach and teach the Scriptures. Instead, most baptized children are trained in secular public schools and catechized by television and popular music. Then when they grow up and leave the faith or live in sin, few churches carry out discipline and call apostates to repentance. This spiritual negligence has led to the West's capitulation to radical secularism. Secularism is a monster that swallows up everything that gets in its way. It has hijacked courts and law schools, universities and public schools, and media and entertainment industries.

One of the chief doctrines of secular progressivism is "equality"—not equality before the law or equality of worth before God—but the Jacobin equality that tears down authority structures. In applying this Jacobin equality to the sexes, secularists minimize all differences between men and women and reject role distinctions. This twisted view of equality has not only undermined biblical gender roles, but it has also led to the abandonment of heterosexual marriage.

Rebellion Against God's Design for the Sexes

What we are witnessing in the West is not just confusion but *rebellion* against God's design. The difference is that people know better. They have a knowledge of God in creation and therefore are "without excuse" (Romans 1:20). Similarly, people *know* that husbands have authority over their wives. They *know* that women cannot be pastors. They *know* that women should have children and care for them. They *know* that women should not serve in combat. They *know* that homosexuality is contrary to nature. And they *know* that a man is not a woman. Yet they act otherwise.

How do we know that they know better? Because they have Scripture passed down through the generations, and it addresses all these issues. And if that were not enough, they have a conscience—"They show that the work of the law is written on their hearts, while their conscience also bears witness" (Romans 2:15). God has written His law on the hearts of men. And He has given us eyes to see and minds to comprehend the ways of the world. It does not take a genius to understand that men and women have complementary sexual organs and that this fact alone rules out homosexuality and transgenderism as acceptable practices.

And while many churches have not caved to the homosexual/transgender revolution, many of those same churches have caved on gender roles. Even for the "conservative" churches who only have male pastors and elders, few would dare to speak against women in the military or women pursuing careers instead of children.

A new dispute has even arisen among churches holding that homosexual practice is sinful, with some claiming that homosexual desire is not sinful. Seeing that this debate has arisen among my fellow Presbyterians, I must point out that our Westminster Standards clearly state that "unnatural lusts" fall under the prohibitions of the Seventh Commandment—"You shall not commit adultery."[1] Romans 1:24-27 is cited for the forbidding of unnatural lusts, and this passage refers to homosexual desire. Paul says,

> For this reason God gave them up to dishonorable passions. For their women exchanged natural relations for those that are contrary to nature; and the men likewise gave up natural relations with women and were consumed with passion for one another, men committing shameless acts with men and receiving in themselves the due penalty for their error (Romans 1:26-27).

Three times this passage mentions "nature/natural"—the women gave up the "natural function" [τὴν φυσικὴν χρῆσιν] for that which is "contrary to nature" [εἰς τὴν παρὰ φύσιν] (1:26), and the men abandoned "the natural function of the female" [τὴν φυσικὴν χρῆσιν τῆς θηλείας] and "burned in their passion toward one another" (1:27).

What does "nature" mean here? The Greek word translated "nature" is φύσις (*phusis*), which the Greek dictionary BDAG defines as "the regular or established order of things."[2] Some commentators argue that Paul used

---

1. Westminster Larger Catechism, Q & A 139.
2. Walter Bauer, F. W. Danker, W. F. Arndt, and F. W. Gingrich (BDAG), *A*

the word to appeal to a mere custom in 1 Corinthians 11:14-15 (regarding women having longer hair than men), and this meaning is then imported into Romans 1:26-27 by those wanting to justify homosexual activity. However, an appeal to custom does not mean something has no basis in the created order,[3] and "the underlying moral logic of 1 Corinthians 11:14 is not merely an appeal to custom but to what Paul and the Corinthians understood to be a physiological difference between male and female."[4] Moreover, "the term [φύσις] is normally used to mean exactly the opposite of custom: that which is innate in the order of things, which cannot be acquired."[5]

There is a natural order of things based on God's design, from which we derive an ontology of men and women. (Ontology is the branch of philosophy dealing with the nature of being.) Marriage is a creation ordinance, and creation itself teaches that only a man and woman as different beings can form this sexual bond. Reproduction requires a man and a woman, and thus any sexual activity beyond this relationship is a deviation from nature, God's design for humans. Hence, Paul says that men abandoned the "natural function of women" in exchange for "shameless acts with men," clearly referring to male homosexuality.

The Bible certainly prohibits homosexual *behavior* (see also Leviticus

---

Greek-English Lexicon of the New Testament and other Early Christian Literature (3rd ed.; Chicago: The University of Chicago Press, 2000), 1070.

3. Paul says that nature "teaches" that long hair is a "disgrace" for a man but the "glory" of a woman (1 Corinthians 11:14-15). It is almost a universal custom for women to have longer hair than men, and Paul is arguing that this practice is rooted in God's design. Some will argue against this by pointing to the Nazirite vow where men had long hair (Numbers 6:5). However, the Nazirite vow only required that "no razor shall touch his head until the time [of the vow] is completed." This was a temporary practice instituted by God that signified separation, not effeminacy. The very fact that it required men to refrain from cutting their hair recognizes that this was a deviation from the norm.

4. Branson Parler, "Hair Length and Human Sexuality: The Underlying Moral Logic of Paul's Appeal to Nature in 1 Corinthians 11:14," *Calvin Theological Journal* 51 (2016): 112–113.

5. Craig S. Keener, *Paul, Women & Wives: Marriage and Women's Ministry in the Letters of Paul* (Peabody, MA: Hendrickson, 1992), 43.

18:22; 20:13). But it also prohibits homosexual *desire*. Paul in Romans 1 not only describes homosexual practice but also the desire that gives birth to such behavior. As seen above in Romans 1:27, the men burned in "passion" or "desire" [τῇ ὀρέξει, *te orexei*].[6] Three verses earlier, Paul condemned evil "lust" or "desire" using the word ἐπιθυμία (*epithumia*)—"Therefore God gave them up in the lusts [ἐπιθυμίαις] of their hearts to impurity, to the dishonoring of their bodies among themselves" (Romans 1:24).

God cares not only about our actions but also our desires. Just as the desire to commit adultery is sin (Matthew 5:27-28), so too the desire for homosexual relations is sin. Both involve the desire for prohibited acts, and the desire is rooted in a sinful heart. A person with such a desire should repent and ask God to change his or her desires. As Paul elsewhere says, we must "put to death . . . evil desire" [ἐπιθυμίαν κακήν] (Colossians 3:5).

Returning to Christ's Design for the Sexes

What we need is to return to Christ and His ways for our lives. This means we need repentance, the turning away from sin and turning to Christ. Jesus demands obedience, including to His design for gender. He has given us male and female natures, yet we must live these out according to His commands. And we know our Lord's teaching through searching the Scriptures. We are to look to the Hebrew Old Testament (Matthew 5:17-19), as well as the writings of the apostles and prophets in the Greek New Testament (Ephesians 2:20).

However, as we examine the teaching of Scripture on gender roles, we find some things that may surprise Christians. One thing we learn is that our behavior as men and women impacts whether we will attain eternal life. Yes, we are justified only through faith in Jesus (Romans 3:28; Galatians 2:16). But genuine faith will bring forth good works. Bad works are evidence of bad faith. As our Lord says, "every healthy tree bears good fruit, but the diseased tree bears bad fruit" (Matthew 7:17).

---

6. BDAG, 721–722: ὄρεξις is "a condition of strong desire."

God made man as male and female (Genesis 1:27; 5:2), so it is only right that He tells us what it means to live as male and female. And since humans were made male and female "from the beginning of creation" (Mark 10:6), we know this is a good feature of humanity that God is redeeming through Christ. The goal of salvation, the *telos*, is that we become godly men and women. Scripture not only commands men and women to *fulfill* their proper roles, but it also forbids *confusing* roles. Men are not to act like women, and women are not to act like men. To do so is "contrary to nature" (Romans 1:26) and such rebellion against God's design may in fact be evidence that a person is not a genuine believer in Christ.

While there are cultural influences upon masculinity and femininity, culture has a limited role. Scripture teaches there are natural distinctions between men and women that are rooted in creation. As Dutch theologian Herman Bavinck (1854–1921) says, "Culture can surely bring about some changes, but it can do so only within specific limits and on the foundation of nature itself. People and nations were very different from each other in various times and circumstances, but the man has always been a man and the woman has always been a woman. There is nothing mutable about this fact; we have only to accept it. It is not a work of the devil to be destroyed, but a work of the Father to be acknowledged."[7]

Bavinck says there are two dangers here—"we can both underestimate and overestimate this distinction" between men and women.[8] Throughout history some have overestimated the distinction by denying woman "the status of being fully human."[9] Yet Scripture affirms that both men and women are made in God's image and thus are both fully human. Bavinck says, "[W]oman can be a helper suitable for the man only because she is his equal and reflects God's image just as much as he does."[10] But as we will see, our modern society is far more prone to underestimating the distinction between men and women.

---

7. Herman Bavinck, *The Christian Family* (trans. Nelson D. Kloosterman; Grand Rapids, MI: Christian's Library Press, 2012), 65.
8. Ibid.
9. Ibid., 66.
10. Ibid.

Effeminate Men Will Not Enter the Kingdom (1 Corinthians 6:9-10)

The Apostle Paul sometimes uses strong language regarding gender roles. At the end of his first letter to the Corinthians, he commands men to "act like men" [ἀνδρίζεσθε, *andrizesthe*] (1 Corinthians 16:13). This is the only use of the verb ἀνδρίζομαι (*andrizomai*) in the New Testament, but it is also used in the Septuagint, the Greek Old Testament, for the command to "be strong and courageous" [Ἰσχυε καὶ ἀνδρίζου]—which is used by Moses (Deuteronomy 31:6-7), Joshua (Joshua 10:25), David (1 Chronicles 28:20), and God (Deuteronomy 31:23; Joshua 1:6 [LXX]). The verb ἀνδρίζομαι can mean "conduct yourself in a courageous way"[11] and in this sense also has application for Paul's female readers. However, not only does the prefix of the *ver*b [ἀνδρ-, andr-] have an "emphasis on maleness,"[12] but courage in Scripture is often associated with masculine behavior (Judges 20:22; 1 Samuel 4:9; also the above commands to Moses, Joshua, and Solomon). Men in particular are to express courage because it is a masculine virtue.

More explicitly, Paul says that "effeminate" men "will not inherit the kingdom of God":

> [9] Or do you not know that the unrighteous will not inherit the kingdom of God? Do not be deceived: neither the sexually immoral, nor idolaters, nor adulterers, nor men who practice homosexuality, [10] nor thieves, nor the greedy, nor drunkards, nor revilers, nor swindlers will inherit the kingdom of God (1 Corinthians 6:9-10).

Paul boldly declares that the "unrighteous" will not inherit God's kingdom, and he then goes on to tell us exactly who these unrighteous persons are. These are not just people who occasionally sin. Rather, these are people

---

11. BDAG, 76.
12. Ibid.

who partake in these sins enough that they are identified with their sin. A Christian who gets drunk once can repent and ask for forgiveness, but the person who gets drunk every day is a "drunkard" who will not enter God's kingdom.

Paul's list is not exhaustive, but he does highlight sexual sins—"fornicators" [πόρνοι, *pornoi*; "sexually immoral" in the ESV], "adulterers" [μοιχοί, *moichoi*], "effeminates" [μαλακοί, *malakoi*], and "sodomites" [ἀρσενοκοῖται, *aresenokoitai*]. All sexual sinners will be excluded from God's kingdom, whether heterosexual or homosexual. However, we will give particular attention here to Paul's reference to homosexuals.

The ESV unfortunately translates the two words for homosexuals in 1 Corinthians 6:9 as "men who practice homosexuality," combining the Greek words μαλακοί (*malakoi*, "effeminates/catamites") and ἀρσενοκοῖται (*arsenokoitai*, "homosexuals/sodomites"). The singular forms of these words are μαλακός (*malakos*) and ἀρσενοκοίτης (*arsenokoites*), respectively. The ESV does at least add the following footnote—"The two Greek terms translated by this phrase refer to the passive and active partners in consensual homosexual acts." This footnote is correct, as the words together condemn both partners in a homosexual relationship. Roman society only condemned the passive partner, as Roman men considered it morally acceptable to use non-Roman male slaves and boys as homosexual objects.[13] But Paul went further and condemned *all* homosexual behavior, including the active partner.

Contrary to the ESV, it is best to keep these two Greek terms separate in translation, as the word μαλακός (*malakos*) conveys more than mere homosexual behavior. To see this point, let us first discuss the second word Paul uses, ἀρσενοκοίτης (*arsenokoites*), which is best translated as "homosexual" or "sodomite." BDAG defines it as "a male who engages in sexual activity w. a pers. of his own sex . . . of one who assumes the dominant role in same-sex activity, opp. μαλακός."[14] While the translation

---

13. Bruce W. Winter, *After Paul Left Corinth* (Grand Rapids, MI: Eerdmans; 2001), 110.
14. BDAG, 135.

"homosexual" is accurate, the term "sodomite" best expresses the meaning of the dominant or active partner. (The NKJV and NRSV translate it as "sodomite.") The only other place ἀρσενοκοίτης is used in the New Testament is 1 Timothy 1:10, as part of Paul's list of sinners. This list in 1 Timothy 1:9-10 mentions violations for the Fifth through Ninth Commandment, with ἀρσενοκοίταις following πόρνοις (*pornois*, "fornicators") and clearly falling under the Seventh Commandment—"You shall not commit adultery" (Exodus 20:14). The word might have been used in the ancient world, but because it is otherwise unknown, it is thought that Paul invented ἀρσενοκοίτης by combining two Greek words used in the Septuagint in both Leviticus 18:22[15] and 20:13[16] for "male" [ἄρσην] and "bed" [κοίτη]. Paul's use of ἀρσενοκοίτης should also be understood in light of his condemnation of "men committing shameless acts with men [ἄρσενες ἐν ἄρσεσιν]" in Romans 1:27.

The other word Paul uses, μαλακός (*malakos*), has the general meaning of "soft." This is seen in its only other New Testament uses in Matthew 11:8 and Luke 7:25 [μαλακοῖς ἱματίοις] to describe "soft" or "fancy" clothing. Jesus makes the point that John the Baptist did not wear such clothing, as it was reserved for those who live among kings. In the Septuagint, μαλακός is used twice to describe soft speech (Proverbs 25:15; 26:22 [LXX]). Thus, the word in Scripture is associated with "soft" or "effeminate" behavior.

Other Greek writers also used the word μαλακός to refer to "soft" or "effeminate" men and not just homosexuals. Herodotus in his *Histories* says that "soft lands breed soft men [μαλακούς]."[17] In his *History of the Peloponnesian War*, Thucydides speaks of a warning given to a man "not to let himself be shamed down, for fear of being thought a coward [μαλακός]

---

15. Leviticus 18:22: "You shall not lie with a male as with a woman; it is an abomination." [LXX: καὶ μετὰ ἄρσενος οὐ κοιμηθήσῃ κοίτην γυναικός· βδέλυγμα γάρ ἐστιν.]

16. Leviticus 20:13: "If a man lies with a male as with a woman, both of them have committed an abomination; they shall surely be put to death; their blood is upon them." [LXX: καὶ ὃς ἂν κοιμηθῇ μετὰ ἄρσενος κοίτην γυναικός, βδέλυγμα ἐποίησαν ἀμφότεροι· θανατούσθωσαν, ἔνοχοί εἰσιν.]

17. Herodotus, *Histories* (trans. A.D. Godley; Cambridge, MA: Harvard University Press, 1920), 9.122.

if he do not vote for war."[18] And Josephus, writing in the early 90s A.D., uses a form of the word to describe the Israelites—"After this, the Israelites grew effeminate [μαλακῶς] as to fighting any more against their enemies, but applied themselves to the cultivation of the land, which producing them great plenty and riches, they neglected the regular disposition of their settlement, and indulged themselves in luxury and pleasures."[19] (Notice the connection between effeminacy and luxury.) [20]

Thus, the word μαλακός does not literally refer to a homosexual but is used to describe a soft/effeminate man, and the ultimate expression of such effeminacy is that of the passive partner in male homosexual behavior. When paired with ἀρσενοκοίτης ("homosexual/sodomite"), μαλακός certainly makes reference to the passive male homosexual or "catamite." BDAG defines μαλακός as "pert. to being passive in a same-sex relationship, *effeminate* esp. of *catamites*, of men and boys who are sodomized by other males in such a relationship, opp. ἀρσενοκοίτης."[21]

Some argue that μαλακοί in 1 Corinthians 6:9 must only have a sexual meaning because it is sandwiched between "adulterers" [μοιχοί] and "sodomites" [ἀρσενοκοῖται]. However, "idolaters" [εἰδωλολάτραι] is also sandwiched between the two sexual terms "fornicators" [πόρνοι] and "adulterers" [μοιχοί], and though idolatry can be tied with sexual sin (e.g. 1 Corinthians 10:7-8), Paul is likely condemning all idolaters here. In fact, Paul uses the word "idolaters" [εἰδωλολάτραι] in the prior chapter in a similar list of sins, and it is distinguished from sexual immorality—"I wrote to you in my letter not to associate with sexually immoral people—not at all meaning the sexually immoral of this world, or the greedy and swindlers, or idolaters, since then you would need to go out of the world"

---

18. Thucydides, *History of the Peloponnesian War* (trans. Richard Crawley; New York: E.P. Dutton, 1910), 6.13.

19. Josephus, *The Antiquities of the Jews* (trans. William Whiston; Nashville, TN: Thomas Nelson, 1998) 5.2.7.

20. For more examples, see Tim Bayly, Joseph Bayly, and Jürgen von Hagen, *The Grace of Shame: 7 Ways the Church Has Failed to Love Homosexuals* (Bloomington, IN: Warhorn Media, 2017), 33–44.

21. BDAG, 613.

(1 Corinthians 5:9-10). Thus, neither εἰδωλολάτραι nor μαλακοί should be limited to its sexual meaning in 1 Corinthians 6:9, but both should be understood to include broader behavior.

Some liberal scholars who seek to justify homosexual behavior have attempted to argue that μαλακοί in 1 Corinthians 6:9 has nothing to do with sexual behavior and only means "soft," while some conservative scholars have overreacted by arguing that μαλακοί only means homosexual behavior to the exclusion of softness. Both are incorrect. Paired with ἀρσενοκοῖται ("homosexuals/sodomites"), Paul is certainly using μαλακοί to condemn "catamites" in 1 Corinthians 6:9. But in using the word μαλακοί, Paul is also condemning all effeminate behavior, some of which is associated with homosexuality.[22] This is how both the King James Version and New American Standard Bible translate the word ("effeminate"), and it is also how many older commentators understood it, including John Calvin (see below).

Why does this matter? Because Paul not only condemns male homosexual behavior and those who practice it, but he also uses the word "soft" to condemn *male effeminate behavior in its entirety*. Male homosexuality, particularly that of the passive partner, is the ultimate expression of male effeminacy, but such actors also often engage in effeminate "appearance and manner" so as to attract homosexual partners.[23] The sinful sexual act

---

22. Robert A. J. Gagnon, *The Bible and Homosexual Practice: Texts and Hermeneutics* (Nashville, TN: Abingdon, 2001), 338: "In 1 Cor 6:9, the term *malakoi* has most in view males who actively seek to transform their maleness into femaleness in order to make themselves more attractive as receptive or passive sexual partners of men; *arsenokoitai* has most in view men who serve as the active partners of the *malakoi*." Whereas Gagnon argues that Paul's use of μαλακοί includes only effeminate behavior that is tied with homosexuality, I am arguing that it refers to all effeminate behavior with an emphasis on homosexuality. Gagnon's understanding is seen when he says, "[I]n 1 Cor 6:9, *malakoi* should be understood as the passive partners in homosexual intercourse, the most egregious case of which are those who also intentionally engage in a process of feminization to erase further their masculine appearance and manner." Ibid., 312.

23. Robert A. J. Gagnon, "A Comprehensive and Critical Review Essay of Homosexuality, Science, and the 'Plain Sense' of Scripture, Part 2": 229, http://www.robgagnon.net/articles/homoBalchHB TReview2.pdf: "The word *malakoi*

cannot be separated from the associated effeminate behavior. Therefore, we conclude that effeminate men—and not just homosexuals—will be excluded from the kingdom of God. Christian men must act like men and forsake soft behavior and effeminacy.

As for the translation of 1 Corinthians 6:9-10, we conclude that μαλακοί should be translated as "effeminates" and ἀρσενοκοῖται as "sodomites." Paired together, these words certainly make reference to the passive and active partners in male homosexual behavior. However, "effeminates" is a better translation of μαλακοί than "catamites" because the word is metaphorical and has a broader meaning of "soft" men. Thus, my suggested translation of 1 Corinthians 6:9-10 is almost identical to the NASB (1995), but I contend that ἀρσενοκοῖται has the more specific meaning of "sodomite" than the NASB's more general "homosexual":

> Or do you not know that the unrighteous will not inherit the kingdom of God? Do not be deceived—neither fornicators, nor idolaters, nor adulterers, nor effeminates, nor sodomites, nor thieves, nor the greedy, nor drunkards, nor revilers, nor swindlers, will inherit the kingdom of God.

Of course, we should not overlook Paul's words of repentance that follow—"And such were some of you. But you were washed, you were sanctified, you were justified in the name of the Lord Jesus Christ and by the Spirit of our God" (1 Corinthians 6:11). Paul speaks harshly for those who live in rebellion against God's design, but he also proclaims God's

---

and its Latin equivalent *molles* (and their cognates) were often employed in antiquity in a restrictive sense; namely, to refer to adult males who were biologically and/or psychologically disposed to desire penetration by men and who actively feminized their appearance and manner as a means to attracting such partners. Given the context issues already cited, Paul probably intended *malakoi* in this restrictive sense." However, Gagnon also recognizes that μαλακός "has a broad range of meaning in Greek literature," and says, "In my own reading, the meaning of malakoi in 1 Cor 6:9 probably lies somewhere in between 'only prostituting passive homosexuals' and 'effeminate heterosexual and homosexual males.'" Gagnon, *The Bible and Homosexual Practice*, 307–308.

gracious offer of forgiveness to those who repent. Some Christians are former adulterers, effeminates, and sodomites. But in becoming Christians, they repented and now live according to God's commands, and they will enter God's kingdom. That hope is set before all who are sinning against God in these ways.

Men Must Act Like Men

This still leaves the question—what does it mean for a man to be effeminate other than engage in homosexual behavior? Paul does not elaborate on this point. But most of us have a good idea of what it means for a man to be soft. Soft men do not act like men. They act like women (who are supposed to be soft!). Paul is not saying men may not have any feminine traits or may never partake in activities considered feminine by culture. But he is saying a man should not act like a woman. That obviously includes not being the passive partner in homosexual sex. But it also includes the failure to carry out the duties God has given to men.

We know from the rest of Scripture that a man is supposed to protect, provide, and lead. A man who does not do these things is effeminate. He is not acting like a man. A man who refuses to work and provide for his family and leaves that task to his wife is effeminate. A man who does not protect his wife and children from harm is an effeminate man. A man who leaves spiritual leadership to his wife is effeminate. Such men will not inherit God's kingdom.

Older commentators associated luxury and decadence with effeminacy. In commenting on 1 Corinthians 6:9, John Calvin says, "By effeminate persons I understand those who, although they do not openly abandon themselves to impurity, discover, nevertheless, their unchastity by blandishments of speech, by lightness of gesture and apparel, and other allurements."[24] Calvin makes a similar comment on Deuteronomy 22:5,

---

24. John Calvin, *Commentary on the Epistles of Paul the Apostle to the Corinthians*, vol 1 (trans. John Pringle; Edinburgh: Calvin Translation Society, 1848), 208–209.

which prohibits women from wearing a "man's garment" and a man from wearing a "woman's cloak" (more on this in chapter 11):

> This decree also commends modesty in general, and in it God anticipates the danger, lest women should harden themselves into forgetfulness of modesty, or men should degenerate into effeminacy unworthy of their nature. Garments are not in themselves of so much importance; but as it is disgraceful for men to become effeminate, and also for women to affect manliness in their dress and gestures, propriety and modesty are prescribed, not only for decency's sake, but lest one kind of liberty should at length lead to something worse.[25]

Matthew Henry makes a similar point in his commentary on Deuteronomy 22:5—"It forbids the confounding of the dispositions and affairs of the sexes: men must not be effeminate, nor do the women's work in the house, nor must women be viragos, pretend to teach, or usurp authority."[26]

This is how many Christian theologians throughout history have understood effeminacy. Apart from sexual immorality, effeminacy can be expressed in a variety of other behaviors, including speech and dress. This applies to many Western men today who have been corrupted by luxury and decadence. The pleasures of entertainment have made them content, unwilling to risk discomfort and pain for greater pursuits. They have become effeminate and weak, and they refuse to fight for anything.

Effeminacy is the opposite of masculinity. Effeminacy is when men do not act like men. Contrast this with masculinity, where men act according to God's design. Douglas Wilson says of masculinity, "Simply put,

---

25. John Calvin, *Commentaries on the Four Last Books of Moses*, vol 3 (trans. Charles W. Bingham; Grand Rapids, MI: Baker, 2003), 110.
26. Matthew Henry, *Commentary on the Whole Bible*, vol 1 (Christian Classics Ethereal Library), https://ccel.org/ccel/henry/mhc1/mhc1.Deu.xxiii.html.

masculinity is the glad assumption of sacrificial responsibility."[27] Men are to model themselves after Jesus, who sacrificed Himself for His bride, the church (Ephesians 5:25). This is the masculine pattern men must follow. It is wrapped up in God-given authority. Wilson again says, "Masculinity is authoritative, and the Scriptures teach that authority flows to those who take responsibility, and it flees from those who seek to evade it."[28] Christian men must therefore embrace masculinity and reject effeminacy.

In discussing masculinity and effeminacy, it is appropriate to address a problem that plagues modern man—the sin of "niceness." Many men, especially Christian men, just want to be nice to people—nice in the sense of being agreeable and not wanting anyone to dislike them. However, the Bible does not call for men to be nice. Men should be *kind* and *gentle* at appropriate times, as these are fruit of the Spirit (Galatians 5:22-23). But kindness and gentleness are not the same thing as niceness. Niceness is weakness. It is people-pleasing. Niceness is men trying to keep peace when there is no peace.

This is a life of conflict, and there is a time to fight and a time to confront. Nice men are yes-men in a world that needs to be told no. No one fears nice men, but nice men are full of fear. The best example of this today is when men apologize for something just because someone was offended. But when a real man does nothing wrong, he does not apologize just to appease critics. Niceness avoids conflict and for that reason it can never overcome challenges. Nice men produce nothing of lasting value. Niceness is a form of effeminacy and is at odds with biblical masculinity.

This attitude of niceness and effeminacy has also plagued Christian worship services. Many churches would rather sing love songs to Jesus

---

27. Douglas Wilson, *Father Hunger: Why God Calls Men to Love and Lead Their Families* (Nashville, TN: Thomas Nelson, 2012), 41.

28. Ibid., 42. I think Wilson's definition of masculinity is preferable to that of John Piper, who uses "lead" instead of "authority" and focuses on a man's obligations towards women. While men should "lead, provide for, and protect women," masculinity should not be restricted to relations with women. John Piper and Wayne Grudem, eds., *Recovering Biblical Manhood and Womanhood: A Response to Evangelical Feminism* (Wheaton, IL: Crossway, 2006), 35–36.

instead of Psalms or hymns that proclaim Christ's reign over the earth. Churches have forsaken the Old Testament because it is too violent and patriarchal. And they have traded wine in the Lord's Supper for grape juice, which is symbolic of the weakness and effeminacy of the modern church.

Women Must Act Like Women (1 Timothy 2:15)

Paul also gives a warning against women not acting like women. While Paul has many specific teachings for women, including submission to husbands and childrearing (Titus 2:4-5), his words in 1 Timothy 2:15 make the point that *Christian women must behave like women*. Similar to Paul's exclusion of effeminate men from the kingdom in 1 Corinthians 6:9, Paul ties womanly behavior to salvation:

> Yet she will be saved through childbearing—if they continue in faith and love and holiness, with self-control (1 Timothy 2:15).

This verse poses some challenges, but with a little work we can arrive at Paul's intended meaning. It comes in the context of Paul's requirement that women be "quiet" in church and not "teach" or "exercise authority" over men (1 Timothy 2:9-15). In prohibiting women from these tasks, Paul appeals to the creation order—Adam was formed prior to Eve, and Eve was the one who was deceived (2:13-14). (This section is given a detailed treatment in chapter 8.)

Based on the context of womanly roles, it makes sense that Paul's reference to "childbearing" is literal. He is speaking of women getting pregnant and bearing children. Of course, this makes modern Christians uncomfortable because Paul put the word "saved" in front of it.

One way out is to take "saved" [σωθήσεται, *sothesetai*] as "preserved," in the sense of physical preservation, which is the view of the NASB and Cynthia Long Westfall.[29] However, it is hard to see in what sense this

---

29. Cynthia Long Westfall, *Paul and Gender: Reclaiming the Apostle's Vision for*

promise holds true. Women are not preserved through childbearing, and even many faithful Christian women die in the process of giving birth. Moreover, preservation in childbearing does not fit the context. Westfall argues that "the reference to childbirth would be most naturally understood as an allusion to Genesis 3:16" and the judgment of pain in childbearing.[30] However, while Paul does reference Eve becoming a "transgressor" in 2:14, there is no reference to God's judgment for the fall in 1 Timothy 2. In fact, becoming a "transgressor" perfectly fits the context of needing *spiritual* salvation. Further, Genesis 3:16 concerns "pain" in childbearing, not death (as only Adam was told he would die; Genesis 3:19), and it is uncertain how godly women would be preserved from pain in childbirth.

Spiritual salvation also makes better sense of the context of women carrying out their proper roles and doing "good works," as Paul commands women to learn submissively and prohibits them from teaching or exercising authority over men (1 Timothy 2:10-12). Paul even speaks of spiritual salvation a few verses earlier when he says that God "desires all people to be saved and to come to the knowledge of the truth" (2:4). Thus, Westfall's assertion that the "focus on a woman's spiritual salvation is random and off-topic" and has "little relevance to the issues raised" is patently false.[31] She claims that "a reference to women's God-given role would neither be understood nor be consistent with the pejorative associations with the process of childbirth," as if childbirth (or, more accurately, the whole process of "childbearing") was only associated with pain and judgment in the ancient world and not also life and blessing.

Alternatively, Andreas Köstenberger takes "saved" to mean "spiritual preservation from falling into error (specifically, Satan's deception),"[32] appealing to a possible usage in 1 Timothy 4:16—"Keep a close watch on yourself and on the teaching. Persist in this, for by so doing you will *save*

Men and Women in Christ (Grand Rapids, MI: Baker Academic, 2016), 129–140.
  30. Ibid., 131.
  31. Ibid.
  32. Andreas J. Köstenberger and Margaret E. Köstenberger, *God's Design for Man and Woman: A Biblical-Theological Survey* (Wheaton, IL: Crossway, 2014), 219.

both yourself and your hearers." Köstenberger argues, "Timothy won't literally save his hearers; it's Jesus who saves them,"[33] and thus he concludes that "save" must mean spiritual preservation in 1 Timothy 4:16. However, though it is Jesus who saves directly, He also uses preachers such as Timothy as the means of guarding His flock and helping His people remain faithful unto death. Thus, a pastor's teaching is a means of his flock's salvation. Moreover, a possible meaning of "save" as "spiritual preservation from error" in 1 Timothy 4:16 does not mean that is how Paul is using the word in 2:15.

Köstenberger does correctly take "childbearing" to refer to woman's domestic sphere. Combined with his "spiritual preservation" view, he concludes that "women will be spiritually preserved if they devote themselves to their God-given role in the domestic and familial sphere."[34] His case rests strongly on a parallel between 1 Timothy 2:15 and 1 Timothy 5:14-15—"So I would have younger widows marry, bear children, and give the adversary no occasion for slander. For some have already strayed after Satan." However, while there may be a parallel between the two passages, not straying after Satan and being spiritually saved are not mutually exclusive. If Paul in 1 Timothy 2:15 is referring to salvation more broadly, this would also include preservation from spiritual deception. In the end, the reference to straying after Satan in 1 Timothy 5:15 cannot be imported into 1 Timothy 2:15 just because both mention childbearing. The immediate context of 1 Timothy 2:15 is most important, and it concerns spiritual "transgression" (2:14), not mere deception.

Therefore, the view that "saved" in 1 Timothy 2:15 means "preserved," either physically (Westfall) or spiritually (Köstenberger), should be rejected. As Porter states, "[I]n virtually all authentically Pauline contexts σῴζω denotes a salvific spiritual act, perhaps eschatological in consequence."[35] While σῴζω (*sozo*) can mean "delivery" from danger,[36] the immediate

---

33. Ibid., 215.
34. Ibid., 216.
35. Stanley E. Porter, "What Does It Mean to Be 'Saved by Childbirth,'" *Journal for the Study of the New Testament* 49 (1993): 93.
36. Westfall, *Paul and Gender*, 152.

context is determinative. And the preceding verse in 1 Timothy 2:14 concerns Eve's fall into "transgression" [παράβασις], which requires spiritual salvation—salvation from sin and God's wrath—not mere preservation from false teaching or death.

Is the Childbearing About Jesus? (1 Timothy 2:15)

Another way out of the connection between women bearing children and salvation is to take 1 Timothy 2:15 as a reference to the birth of Jesus. George Knight advocates this view, taking the verse to refer to Eve since she is the preceding reference ("the woman") in 2:14 and Paul uses a singular verb to start 2:15—"*she* will be saved through childbearing" [σωθήσεται δὲ διὰ τῆς τεκνογονίας]. The "childbearing" is then understood as a reference to Mary's bearing of Christ, the promised Messiah of Genesis 3:15 who would crush the head of the serpent. In addition to the context of 1 Timothy 2:14 referring to Eve's fall in Genesis 3, Knight argues that the vocabulary (passive σῴζω plus διά) indicates the instrumental use of διά (*dia*), in the sense that "salvation is brought through these elements, not by them." Knight cites the similar construction found in Acts 15:11; Romans 5:9; 1 Corinthians 15:2; 1 Peter 3:20; and 1 Corinthians 3:15 (this latter verse having a different construction with the addition of ὡς).[37]

However, there are several problems with this Messianic interpretation. First, τεκνογονία (*teknogonia*, "childbearing") refers to the *process* of childbirth—"the bearing of children"—and not the children produced.[38] Thus, this could not refer to Jesus but only Mary's bearing of Him. Some advocates of the Messianic interpretation appeal to the presence of the article [τῆς] in front of the word—"*the* childbearing." But this does not change the meaning of τεκνογονία, nor does it require that only one act of childbearing is in view. Second, the context of 1 Timothy 2:13-15 deals

---

37. George W. Knight III, *The Pastoral Epistles: A Commentary on the Greek Text* (The New International Greek Testament Commentary; Grand Rapids, MI: Eerdmans, 1992), 146–147.

38. BDAG, 994.

with Eve, and there is no reference to Mary. The Messianic view merely assumes Mary and Jesus must be in view because the word "saved" is used in reference to "childbearing." Third, Paul uses a plural verb in the second clause of 2:15—"if *they* continue [μείνωσιν, *meinosin*] in faith and love and holiness, with self-control." This shift to the plural makes it more likely that Paul uses the singular verb "saved" to refer to "woman" in general in 2:15 (and not Eve).[39] In other words, Paul was using Eve ("the woman") as a springboard to refer to "woman" as the entire sex. Fourth, the future verb ("will be saved") makes better sense if it refers to woman in general and the role of childbearing. Eve had been long dead and the birth of Jesus had already taken place when Paul wrote 1 Timothy. Fifth, there is nothing in the verse or context that suggests this is a reference to Jesus. Surely women (and men) are saved by Christ, but why would Paul be so cryptic here? Sixth, the following interpretation that "childbearing" refers to a woman's proper roles fits well with the context of Paul forbidding women from carrying out men's roles of teaching and exercising authority (2:12), as they are instead to carry out "good works" (2:10).

Knight may be correct that the vocabulary (passive σῴζω plus διά) indicates the instrumental use in that salvation is brought "through" childbearing. BDAG lists διά in 1 Timothy 2:15 under "marker of instrumentality or circumstance whereby someth. is accomplished or effected, *by, via, through*." However, BDAG lists this reference specifically under the subcategory "of attendant and prevailing circumstance."[40] Thus, διά may

---

39. Some argue "they" refers to Adam and Eve in 1 Timothy 2:13. Alternatively, Westfall argues "they" could refer to both the woman and man mentioned in 2:12. Westfall, *Paul and Gender*, 138. However, it makes little sense to now bring Adam or man in general into the picture in 2:15 when Paul only spoke of Eve's deception and transgression in 2:14 and used the singular for only woman's salvation ("she will be saved") in 2:15. The context of 2:8–15 is about the proper behavior of women—women are to perform "good works" (2:10), "learn quietly with all submissiveness" (2:11), not teach or exercise authority over men (2:12), and "remain quiet" (2:12). Paul is dealing with women and their proper behavior here, not men. Further, 2:15 says "they" must practice "self-control" [σωφροσύνη], which is previously mentioned only in connection with women in 2:9.

40. BDAG, 224. A.3.c.

show "attendant circumstance," in the sense of "with" or "accompanied by" (see Romans 2:27; 1 Corinthians 2:4; 1 Timothy 4:14). In this case, 1 Timothy 2:15 is understood as women's salvation being "accompanied by" childbirth. It is not that the act of bearing children merits anything before God, but rather that women are saved by faith in Christ and such faith produces womanly behavior, exemplified by the bearing of children. However, even if salvation is "through" childbearing as an instrument, this still fits with the teaching that Christians are "saved" through good works—not meriting salvation by our actions, but "working out" our salvation in obedience to God (Philippians 2:12). Christians are justified by faith in Christ, but salvation cannot be attained apart from good works (see below).

Childbearing as Representative of Woman's Role

Thus, Paul is using "childbearing" as a synecdoche (a part representing the whole) for godly, womanly behavior. Women are not to "teach or exercise authority over a man," but they are to instead "remain quiet" (1 Timothy 2:12) and fulfill their feminine role as exemplified by motherhood (2:15). "Childbearing" in 2:15 elaborates on the "good works" that Paul calls women to perform in 2:10. In other words, *godly women must act like women*. Thus, Paul is saying in 1 Timothy 2:15 that women acting according to God's design is part of the process of salvation—not justification but salvation more broadly, including sanctification. As Thomas Schreiner says, "When Paul says that women will be saved by childbearing, he means, therefore, that they will be saved by adhering to their ordained role."[41] Or as J.N.D. Kelly remarks, woman "will achieve this [salvation], not through performing masculine tasks like teaching in church, but through

---

41. Thomas R. Schreiner, "An Interpretation of 1 Timothy 2:9-15: A Dialogue with Scholarship," in *Women in the Church: An Interpretation & Application of 1 Timothy 2:9-15* (eds. Andreas J. Köstenberger and Thomas R. Schreiner; 3rd ed.; Wheaton, IL: Crossway, 2016), 222.

child-bearing . . . If she sticks to this instead of usurping masculine functions, and fulfills it in the right spirit, she will obtain salvation."[42]

Bearing children is the most unique part of womanhood, and it is a task worthy of high praise. It is a fulfillment of the Cultural Mandate given to Adam and Eve to "be fruitful and multiply and fill the earth" (Genesis 1:28), though now childbirth is subject to pain as part of God's judgment (Genesis 3:16). Thus, Paul is saying godly women will do what God has designed women to do, a large part of which is to bear children. This interpretation fits with the prior context of prohibiting women from doing manly tasks, namely teaching and exercising authority (1 Timothy 2:12). It also fits with the immediate context, as Paul elaborates that women bearing children must "continue in faith and love and holiness, with self-control" (2:15). This understanding connects back to a few verses earlier, where Paul said women must adorn themselves with "what is proper for women who profess godliness—with good works" (2:10). It also fits with Paul's instructions for younger widows three chapters later—"So I would have younger widows marry, bear children, manage their households, and give the adversary no occasion for slander. For some have already strayed after Satan" (5:14-15). Women following God's design keeps them doing good works and protects them from the devil. Thus, womanly behavior is part of their salvation.

Two qualifications should be noted. First, Paul is not saying a woman must have children in order to be saved by Christ. If a woman cannot bear children because of infertility, that is not a sign of God's condemnation. Rather, she is to seek God in prayer, and He may open her womb as He did the wives of the patriarchs (Genesis 29:31; 30:22). But if she cannot bear children, she can still live a godly life by keeping God's commands. (And, of course, adoption is always an option.) However, women who *intentionally* reject God's design for them to marry and bear children should repent of such rebellion.[43]

---

42. J.N.D. Kelly, *A Commentary on the Pastoral Epistles: I & II Timothy, Titus* (Black's New Testament Commentaries; London: Adam & Charles Black, 1963), 69–70.

43. Surely someone will bring up the gift of celibacy in response. However,

Second, Paul is not saying women are saved by good works apart from faith in Christ and His death and resurrection. Rather, Paul is saying Christian women must exhibit godly behavior as those who belong to Christ. They must do good works—as the fruit of their faith—to be saved ("good works" are mentioned in 2:10). And those good works include acting like women (1 Timothy 5:14; Titus 2:3-5). This is part of holy living—"the holiness without which no one will see the Lord" (Hebrews 12:14). One could add to this the Old Testament prohibition of women wearing men's clothing (including dressing like a soldier) in Deuteronomy 22:5, but that exegesis will have to wait (see chapter 11). It is an error to always equate salvation with justification. God declares sinners to be righteous ("justified") through faith (Romans 3:28), but good works are necessary to our salvation in the broader sense[44] (Matthew 7:21; Philippians 2:12). Thus, Westfall is wrong to say that the spiritual salvation view of 1 Timothy 2:15 "contradicts Paul's teaching on salvation by faith."[45] As Calvin says, "The Apostle does not argue here about the cause of salvation, and therefore we cannot and must not infer from these words what works deserve; but they only shew in what way God conducts us to salvation, to which he has appointed us through his grace."[46]

---

marriage is normative for humans, and the only people who should not marry are those whom God has gifted with celibacy for ministry purposes, like the Apostle Paul (1 Corinthians 7:7). This is not the gift of "singleness," but celibacy, meaning the person is in a position where he or she does not struggle with sexual impurity and is content being unmarried and celibate (1 Corinthians 7:8-9).

44. Francis Turretin, *Institutes of Elenctic Theology*, vol 2 (ed. James T. Dennison, Jr.; trans. George Musgrave Giger; Phillipsburg, NJ: Presbyterian and Reformed, 1994), 143 [11.20.6]: "Hence arises the necessity of good works to glory; not of merit, but of means. No one can be glorified in heaven who has not been sanctified on earth by the pursuit of holiness and obedience to the law." Turretin devotes an entire question to the "necessity of good works," affirming that they are "required as the means and way for possessing salvation." Ibid., 702 [17.3.3].

45. Westfall, *Paul and Gender*, 131.

46. John Calvin, *Commentaries on the Epistles to Timothy, Titus, and Philemon* (trans. William Pringle; Edinburgh: Calvin Translation Society, 1856), 71.

Acting Like Men and Women

These warnings about effeminate men and anti-domestic women have great relevance for our day. We live in a culture that is increasingly rebelling against God's design for men and women, and this is affecting the church. Women are forsaking motherhood, and men are forsaking authority and responsibility. Women are acting like men, and men are acting like women. This has created what is known as androgyny, ambiguous sex characteristics. But that is not how the Bible portrays the sexes. There are manly and womanly characteristics. For example, the Apostle Paul associates gentleness and affection with motherhood, and he associates exhortation and authority with fatherhood:

> [7] But we were gentle among you, like a nursing mother taking care of her own children. [8] So, being affectionately desirous of you, we were ready to share with you not only the gospel of God but also our own selves, because you had become very dear to us . . . [11] For you know how, like a father with his children, [12] we exhorted each one of you and encouraged you and charged you to walk in a manner worthy of God, who calls you into his own kingdom and glory (1 Thessalonians 2:7-8, 11-12).

It is not that men should never be affectionate and women should never exhort. Rather, the Apostle Paul recognizes that showing affection is primarily a feminine quality and engaging in exhortation is primarily a masculine quality. There are God-designed differences between men and women.

Men are the source of authority and strength. And the home, church, and society are all authority structures. Thus, a home, church, and society led by women will fail. This is why our current authority structures are failing. Marriage is deteriorating. The church is weak. And our society is crumbling. We need men to lead, not women. When it comes to the church as a whole, what we are primarily dealing with is the sin of *effeminacy*. What is supposed to be a masculine church is starting to look effeminate. Not a feminine church, as there is a difference. Women who act like women are feminine. But *men who act like women* are effeminate.

While both sexes are rebelling against God and His design for them, it is the men who deserve most of the blame. This is because God has put men in authority. A man has authority in the home, and the authorities in the church are men. Though women are rebelling against God's design for them—and they certainly deserve some blame—they would not be doing so to this extent if men were not complicit. Every rebellious woman has a father who failed in some regard. Effeminate men enable womanly rebellion. Women who reject marriage and children do so because they do not have fathers and pastors around telling them to do otherwise. A godly man raises his daughters to act like women.

Of course, there have been reactions to such effeminacy, some good and some misguided. The lack of masculinity in modern society has led to distortions and overreactions. This includes machoism, such as body-building (a gross exaggeration of the male physique, relying on hormonal supplementation and/or extreme dieting) and extremely violent sports (like MMA, where men beat each other to death). Such distortions have also taken place in the church. John Eldridge's *Wild at Heart* was a popular men's book that encouraged men to be outdoorsy and take chances in life. While not entirely off the mark, this is not what Scripture says makes a biblical man. Biblical men exercise godly authority, take responsibility, and fulfill the mission God has for them.

Everyone has either a male or female nature, but we can rebel against nature. It is not enough to have a man's body or have a woman's body. Women must act like women, and men must act like men. This is part of holy living and thus part of our salvation in Christ. Practicing God's design for the sexes is part of how we fulfill His purpose for our lives—both for God's glory and for our happiness.

Chapter 3

COMPLEMENTARIANISM'S COMPROMISE

FEMINISM HAD LONG made its way through the Western church by the time a formal resistance movement was organized in 1987. This resistance movement came to be known as "complementarianism," and it emphasized two points: (1) Husbands hold a leadership role in marriage; and (2) Pastors and elders must be men. The organization behind this movement was the Council on Biblical Manhood and Womanhood (CBMW), founded in 1987, with its core beliefs outlined in the Danvers Statement of that same year. These complementarian views were advanced by the 1991 book, *Recovering Biblical Manhood and Womanhood: A Response to Evangelical Feminism*, a collection of essays edited by John Piper and Wayne Grudem.

What's in a Name?

While complementarianism has had a positive influence in many ways, it also set itself up for problems from the start. One of these problems was that the leaders of the movement opted for the clunky title "complementarianism" instead of something simpler and more descriptive, such as "patriarchy." The desire to avoid the negative connotations of a word like patriarchy is somewhat understandable, but with its root words meaning "father rule," patriarchy aptly describes the Bible's teachings. Further, any word for male rule will likely develop negative connotations in a hostile feminist society, and misunderstandings can be shed through proper teaching. But instead of seeking to redeem a more descriptive word, the leaders of this movement sought to promote the newly-invented "complementarianism."

Unfortunately, most Christians still do not know what the word means, and worse, feminists have used the word to describe their own views. This great irony is seen in that egalitarians responded to *Recovering Biblical Manhood and Womanhood* with the 2004 book entitled, *Discovering Biblical Equality: Complementarity without Hierarchy*. Thus, feminists embraced for themselves the very word that was supposed to set their adversaries apart. Did the complementarian leaders not realize that everyone affirms that men and women complement each other in *some* sense? The leaders of the complementarian movement chose a name that does not even distinguish their position from that of feminists. This would not have been possible with the bolder and more historic term "patriarchy," which feminists would never affirm.

The Inconsistencies of Complementarianism

While the name has been problematic, it is the theology that is at issue. Unfortunately, complementarianism has been plagued by inconsistency among its adherents. Many who have affirmed the label have held compromising positions that let feminism in the back door. Most notably, the vast majority of complementarian theologians have adopted the novel interpretation of 1 Corinthians 14:34-35 that limits Paul's prohibition of women speaking in church to the weighing of prophecy. This interpretation has opened the door to women speaking publicly in church, and it has weakened the complementarian case by limiting its arguments against women preaching to 1 Timothy 2:8-15 (the parallel passage of 1 Corinthians 14:34-35). D.A. Carson adopted this innovative position in his chapter on 1 Corinthians 14:34-35 in *Recovering Biblical Manhood and*

Womanhood, and it has been complementarian canon ever since. Contrast this with the historic view of this passage that women cannot speak publicly in church (see chapter 9).

Further, while some complementarians take 1 Timothy 2:12 to prohibit women from preaching or teaching the Bible and theology to men, others take this passage to only prohibit women from holding the office of pastor/elder. In combination with the weighing of prophecy view of 1 Corinthians 14:34-35, this narrow interpretation of 1 Timothy 2:12 opens the door to women preaching sermons and teaching Sunday school to men, reading Scripture and leading prayer in public worship, leading co-ed Bible studies, and even teaching Bible courses to men at a Christian college or seminary.

Even leading complementarian theologians Thomas Schreiner and Wayne Grudem, who take the prohibition in 1 Timothy 2:12 more broadly, have stated that they think women can lead prayer and read Scripture in public worship (and even administer the sacraments).[1] Some complementarians, such as John Frame and Tim Keller, have even adopted the saying, "a woman may do anything a non-ordained man may do."[2] In seeking to maximize what women can do in public ministry, these men have adopted the feminist ethos (see chapter 10 for more on this issue).

Complementarians also tend to water down male headship in the home, preferring to speak only of a husband's "leadership" instead of "authority" and "rule" (see below). No wonder egalitarians have charged complementarians with being "functionally egalitarian." As egalitarian Ronald Pierce said of complementarianism, "In theory its proponents argued for male authority, while in practice many of them bore a striking

---

1. Thomas R. Schreiner, "A Response to Craig Blomberg," in *Two Views on Women in Ministry* (ed. James R. Beck; Grand Rapids, MI: Zondervan, 2005), 190; Wayne Grudem, *Countering the Claims of Evangelical Feminism: Biblical Responses to the Key Questions* (Colorado Springs: Multnomah, 2006), 62.

2. John Frame, *The Doctrine of the Christian Life* (Phillipsburg, NJ: P&R Publishing, 2008), 640; Kathy Keller, *Jesus, Justice, and Gender Roles* (Grand Rapids, MI: Zondervan, 2012), 21, 29. Kathy is the wife of Tim Keller, and she stated that this was the position of the church that Tim pastored.

resemblance to their egalitarian counterparts. In other words, while 'authority' was theoretically at the center of their argument, in actual practice it was often at the margins."[3]

As if this were not enough, the majority of complementarians limit the Bible's teaching on men and women to the home and church, in what is known sometimes as "narrow" complementarianism. (There are some notable exceptions, such as John Piper,[4] who hold to a "broad" complementarianism applying to all of society. But this seems to be the minority position.) Narrow complementarians either do not think God's differing design of men and women has implications for other spheres of life (such as civil government) or they do not wish to say so in public. Either way, men and women carry their masculine and feminine natures with them in all aspects of life, and this narrow complementarianism creates a dichotomy between the church and society at large. Narrow complementarianism was enshrined in complementarianism's foundational documents, as the Council on Biblical Manhood and Womanhood did not formally affirm male rule as the standard for all of society. While many complementarians do not think women should serve as soldiers and while CBMW does publish some articles saying such, the 1987 Danvers Statement makes no mention of the civil sphere or broader society. In fact, its first stated "purpose" is to "set forth the Biblical view of the relationship between men and women, especially in the home and in the church." This emphasis on home and church—to the neglect of society at large—has been characteristic of complementarianism. CBMW has even included women on its "council" rather than reserve such authority for men, which serves as an example of this very problem.

Further, the book *Recovering Biblical Manhood and Womanhood* explicitly sought to avoid addressing the issue of women in societal leadership, as the authors collectively note that they "question whether the prohibitions"

---

3. Ronald W. Pierce, "Contemporary Evangelicals for Gender Equality," in *Discovering Biblical Equality: Complementarity Without Hierarchy* (eds. Ronald W. Pierce and Rebecca Merrill Groothuis; Downers Grove, IL: Intervarsity Press, 2005), 67.

4. See John Piper, *What's the Difference?* (Wheaton, IL: Crossway, 2001).

in 1 Timothy 2:11-14 (including women having authority over men) "can rightly be applied outside that framework"[5] to things like government or business. Instead, the authors state that "when it comes to all the thousands of occupations and professions, with their endlessly varied structures of management, God has chosen not to be specific about which roles men and women should fill. Therefore we are not as sure in this wider sphere which roles can be carried out by men or women in ways that honor the unique worth of male and female personhood. For this reason we focus (within some limits) on how these roles are carried out rather than which ones are appropriate."[6] The authors thus dodge a significant issue and permit feminism to take root outside the church unopposed. The authors also ignore the fact that the Bible does speak to the question of women in combat and in civil office (see chapter 11).

Complementarianism's Discomfort with Hierarchy

All of these inconsistencies stem from the fact that complementarianism compromised foundational principles of the historic Christian teaching on men and women. This compromise can be seen in two points: (1) Complementarianism expresses discomfort in using the terms "authority" and "hierarchy" for its position, while introducing confusion in its use of the word "equality;" and (2) Complementarianism fails to explicitly root gender roles in the differing natures of men and women. These two compromises of complementarianism gave too much ground to their egalitarian counterparts and left room for confusion and inconsistencies among complementarian adherents.

While some complementarians would acknowledge their views are hierarchical (something egalitarians charge them with), we are here focusing on the foundational complementarian writings, primarily the 1987 Danvers Statement and the 1991 book *Recovering Biblical Manhood and*

---

5. *Recovering Biblical Manhood and Womanhood*, 187.
6. Ibid., 89.

Womanhood. In the preface to the book, editors John Piper and Wayne Grudem explicitly state:

> [W]e certainly reject the term "hierarchicalist" because it overemphasizes structured authority while giving no suggestion of equality or the beauty of mutual interdependence.[7]

These leaders of complementarianism reject using the term "hierarchicalist" to describe their views because hierarchy does not convey "equality." Let us define these terms so as to see the problem with this statement. "Hierarchy" refers to "a group of persons or things arranged in order of rank, grade, class, etc."[8] This aptly describes the biblical teaching that a man has authority over his wife and thus in some sense ranks above her. The term "equality" is vague and often loaded with references to societal rights, and we must be careful not to let modern notions of "equality" dictate our reading of Scripture. The root word "equal" is more helpful here, meaning "of the same quantity, size, number, value, degree, intensity, quality, etc." or "having the same rights, privileges, ability, rank, etc."[9] The first definition for "equal" is only accurate for men and women if used to affirm the biblical teaching that men and women have "equal value" before God. However, the second definition for "equal" flatly contradicts the definition of "hierarchy," as it defines "equal" to mean two things are the "same" in "rank." A later author in *Recovering Biblical Manhood and Womanhood* defines "equality" to mean that "Man and woman are equal in the sense that they bear God's image equally."[10] This is accurate, but it does not clarify what Piper and Grudem mean.

Thus, we see the problem of Piper and Grudem rejecting the description of their position as "hierarchical" because it does not account for

---

7. Ibid., 15.
8. *Webster's New World College Dictionary* (4th ed.; Cleveland, OH: Wiley Publishing, 2007), 671.
9. Ibid., 480.
10. Raymond C. Ortlund, Jr., "Male-Female Equality and Male Headship: Genesis 1–3," in *Recovering Biblical Manhood and Womanhood*, 95.

"equality." The term "equality" introduces confusion because of its wide range of meaning, with one of its common definitions contradicting "hierarchy." Piper and Grudem rightly want to affirm that men and women are "equal" in worth and that women are not less valuable because they are helpers who are to submit to their husbands. This qualification is good to make so as to prevent misunderstanding. However, the term "hierarchy" should not be rejected because of this qualification. Their language leaves open the possibility that Piper and Grudem actually reject that man and woman have a different rank in authority.

Contrary to Piper and Grudem, the Bible clearly affirms "hierarchy," and we should embrace the term for the sake of clarity. The Bible commands wives to "submit" to husbands because the husband is the "head"—the authority—of his wife (Ephesians 5:22-24; Colossians 3:18). The Greek word used for a wife's "submission" in these passages is ὑποτάσσω (*hupotasso*), which certainly encompasses hierarchy. This is clear from the Greek dictionaries—"Every NT use" of ὑποτάσσω "involves some sense of hierarchy,"[11] and, "Originally it is a hierarchical term which stresses the relation to superiors."[12] Authority and submission entail "hierarchy," and Christians should not reject this biblical concept. As German theologian Werner Neuer says, "The equal worth of men and women according to Genesis 2:18 and other passages is not to be confused with their equal rank, but it includes a super/subordination of equally valuable partners."[13] Thus, egalitarians are accurate in describing the complementarian position as "hierarchical," and those who reject egalitarianism should gladly affirm their position as "hierarchicalist."

Noting their discomfort with hierarchy, it should not surprise us that complementarians are also timid in expressing male authority in the home. This is seen in that Piper and Grudem say they "prefer" to speak of a man

---

11. *New International Dictionary of New Testament Theology: Abridged Edition* (ed. Verlyn D. Verbrugge; Grand Rapids, MI: Zondervan, 2000), 583.

12. Gerhard Delling on ὑποτάσσω, *Theological Dictionary of the New Testament*, vol 8 (eds. Gerhard Kittle and Gerhard Friedrich; trans. Geoffrey W. Bromiley; Grand Rapids, MI: Eerdmans, 1972), 41.

13. Werner Neuer, *Man and Woman in Christian Perspective*, 79.

having "leadership" rather than "authority" over his wife.[14] Appealing to texts such as 1 Corinthians 7:3-4 (which is limited in scope to marital sexual relations), they conclude that "authority" in marriage has been transformed in Christ to mean "responsibility" rather than "right" and "power"—"The transformation of authority is most thorough in marriage. This is why we prefer to speak of leadership and headship rather than authority."[15] This discomfort with "authority" is also expressed in the 1987 Danvers Statement of the Council on Biblical Manhood and Womanhood, which speaks of the husband's "leadership" four times and his "authority" only once, while the term "hierarchy" is absent from the document.

While "leadership" is a proper term to use for a man's role, it should not be used to shy away from the biblical language of authority and submission. The Apostle Paul uses the word "head" to mean "authority" and commands wives to "submit." And while a husband's authority in marriage certainly includes responsibility, he still possesses actual authority. Why do complementarians undercut their position by abandoning biblical language and concepts? Christ has authority over the church, and Paul compares the husband as "head" of the wife to Christ as "head" of the church (Ephesians 5:23). Would complementarians also prefer to speak of Christ as only having "leadership" over the church? Of course not. Christ has authority over the church, and a husband has authority over his wife.

Complementarianism's Failure to Root Gender Roles in Nature

The second compromising position of complementarianism is that it fails to explicitly root gender roles in the differing natures of men and women.[16] Both men and women are made in the image of God, and they are equal

---

14. *Recovering Biblical Manhood and Womanhood*, 88.
15. Ibid., 78.
16. Dan Doriani is one of the few complementarians to explicitly use the language of man and woman having a different nature. Dan Doriani, *Women and Ministry: What the Bible Teaches* (Wheaton, IL: Crossway, 2003), 145: "The *Congruent Creation* approach asserts that men and women are equal in value but different in nature."

in value before God and man. However, as noted above, this term "equal" introduces confusion and should not be used without explanation. It is essential that we distinguish between male and female natures and that we root gender roles in these differing natures. In this we are dealing with the issue of *ontology*, the nature of being. From these ontological differences flow God's purposes and duties for men and women, in what are often called "gender roles." God's laws regarding men and women reflect their natures, as He did not give divine commands detached from His design of their entire being. A man is to exercise authority because God wired him to exercise authority, and a woman is to submit because God wired her to submit.

Though complementarians seem to hold that gender roles are rooted in the differing natures of men and women, this point is not made as explicitly or as clearly as it should be. Affirmation 1 of the Danvers Statement says, "Both Adam and Eve were created in God's image, equal as persons and distinct in their manhood and womanhood." It then follows this by speaking of "masculine and feminine roles" that are "part of the created order" (Affirmation 2). By saying man and woman are "distinct" in "manhood and womanhood," the Danvers Statement seems to be saying that men and women have different male and female "natures" without using the word. It then roots gender "roles" in the "created order," which is certainly proper (e.g. 1 Timothy 2:13). However, the Danvers Statement does not elaborate on this point and instead introduces confusion with the statement that men and women are "equal as persons" (Affirmation 1).

Piper and Grudem speak more clearly of men and women having different natures, and they even say that role is rooted in nature. Piper says, "Masculinity and femininity are rooted in who we are by nature."[17] Then Piper and Grudem together state, "We are concerned not merely with the behavioral roles of men and women but also with the underlying nature of manhood and womanhood themselves,"[18] and, "One of the theses of this book is that the natural fitness of man and woman for each other in

---

17. *Recovering Biblical Manhood and Womanhood*, 44.
18. Ibid., 60.

marriage is rooted in something more than anatomy. There is a profound male or female personhood portrayed in our differing bodies."[19] These are sound statements, and they should be made up front so as to emphasize this important point.

Unfortunately, when we look at Grudem's own writings on this subject—and they are voluminous—we see that he can be confusing on the relation of "role" and male and female "nature." In his popular *Systematic Theology*, Grudem affirms that men and women share "equality in personhood" but are "different in role."[20] By "equal" in "personhood" he means that men and women have equal "importance" and "worth."[21] But is "personhood" really the best way to express this point? It introduces a term that could be confused with "nature." Further, Grudem in this work does not distinguish between male and female natures and comes across as if "role" can be separated from the very being of a man and woman.

In a later work, Grudem uses the phrase "equal value,"[22] which is a major improvement from his earlier use of the phrase "equal personhood." He even says that "Women's submission to male headship is based on their having a differing being, not an inferior being."[23] Assuming "being" is understood to refer to the woman's "nature," Grudem makes a strong point. But again, this should be made explicitly up front. Grudem was essentially forced to state that a woman's role to submit is rooted in her having a "differing being" (nature) in response to criticism from egalitarian Rebecca Groothuis. Unfortunately, a reader has to dig deep to find this point and is instead introduced early to the confusing distinction between "personhood" and "role."

---

19. Ibid., 87.
20. Wayne Grudem, *Systematic Theology: An Introduction to Biblical Doctrine* (Grand Rapids, MI: Zondervan, 1994), 454.
21. Ibid., 456.
22. Grudem, *Countering the Claims of Evangelical Feminism* (2006), 68.
23. Ibid., 255.

An Egalitarian Forces Their Hand

The criticisms from egalitarians on this point pushed some complementarians into stating what they should have said from the outset. In the 2005 egalitarian book, *Discovering Biblical Equality*, Rebecca Groothuis wrote a chapter accusing complementarians (whom she calls "patriarchalists") of holding that women are inferior ontologically because "woman's unequal 'role' entails woman's unequal being."[24] She explained how the distinction between ontology and function is "fundamental to the doctrine of male leadership today."[25] She then critiqued the phrase "equal in being but unequal in role" (which summarizes the view of many complementarians) as a "historically novel claim."[26]

Groothuis argued that complementarian "roles" are "not just about function but are fundamentally a matter of ontology or being."[27] Woman's "subordination to male authority is thus a moral necessity, rooted in ontology—in the way God made man and woman to be from the beginning."[28] The following point is key:

> Patriarchy involves different functions, to be sure, but the different functions are grounded in supposed differences in the nature, meaning and purpose of manhood and womanhood. To describe as merely "roles" the different functions that follow from these ontological/teleological differences is to equivocate and obfuscate.[29]

Groothuis concluded, "Woman's inferior 'role' cannot be defended by the claim that it is ontologically distinct from woman's equal being. In female subordination, being determines role and role defines being; thus

---

24. Rebecca Merrill Groothuis, "'Equal in Being, Unequal in Role': Exploring the Logic of Woman's Subordination," in *Discovering Biblical Equality*, 304.
25. Ibid., 303.
26. Ibid.
27. Ibid., 305.
28. Ibid., 308.
29. Ibid., 315.

there can be no real distinction between the two."³⁰ Thus, Groothuis critiqued complementarianism for seeking to disconnect role and being/nature (ontology), and in this I am in full agreement with her.

In his response to Groothuis in a 2009 article in the CBMW journal, complementarian Steven Cowan said, "I will grant (and I think most other complementarians will grant) that woman's subordination is ontological, being grounded in women's femaleness. As Ortlund writes, 'A woman, just by virtue of her womanhood, is called to help [i.e., be subordinate to men] for God.' Yet I will not grant, and I think that no complementarian need grant, that women's subordination is either permanent or comprehensive."³¹ Cowan went on to say, "While I agree that woman's subordination is ontologically grounded, it does not appear that it is either permanent or comprehensive. Moreover, even if woman's subordination were essential, I have offered reasons to think that this would not entail that women were inferior in value to men."³²

Cowan cogently argued that wifely submission does not mean women are inferior in the sense of having less value or worth. But in doing so, notice that Cowan "granted" that "woman's subordination is ontological, being grounded in women's femaleness." This is the point I have been making, and Cowan is entirely correct. However, I question Cowan's claim that "most other complementarians" grant this. And even if his claim is correct, it is noticeable that Cowan had to "grant" this rather that state it up front in the first place. *It took an egalitarian critique for Cowan to state what complementarians should have been saying from the beginning*—that male authority is rooted in male nature and female submission is rooted in female nature. Gender roles are rooted in the differing natures of men and women.

---

30. Ibid., 333.

31. Steven B. Cowan, "The Metaphysics of Subordination: A Response to Rebecca Merrill Groothuis," *The Journal for Biblical Manhood and Womanhood* 14/1 (Spring 2009): 45–46; citing Raymond C. Ortlund, Jr., "Male-Female Equality and Male Headship: Genesis 1–3," in *Recovering Biblical Manhood and Womanhood*, 102.

32. Ibid., 51.

Embracing Hierarchy and Nature

Thus, we see that complementarians have expressed discomfort with the terms "authority" and "hierarchy" even though hierarchy is necessary to the Bible's teaching of male headship, and they have used the word "equality" loosely and introduced confusion over their position when they should limit the term to the phrase "equal value." Moreover, complementarians have failed to explicitly root male and female roles in the differing male and female natures. It is therefore unsurprising that most complementarians today refuse to apply the differing roles of men and women to the civil sphere and instead relegate gender roles to the home and church. Complementarianism sought to defend the Bible from feminist attacks, and the Bible gives the most explicit commands for gender roles in the home and church. Since the nature in which the role is rooted is ignored, many complementarians feel they cannot (or at least should not) speak on gender roles outside the home and church.

Contrary to complementarianism, we should start with the foundational truth that men and women have *different natures* and that there is a *hierarchy of rank* between the sexes. This hierarchy is rooted in nature. This is not to say that all men have authority over all women, but rather that women are not to hold authority over men. A husband has authority over his wife, and only men are to hold positions of authority over men in the church and society. Woman is not made to rule.

It should be obvious that men and women have unequal natures. As Herman Bavinck says, "Nature teaches this distinction, and no science or philosophy is needed to acquaint oneself with this. Man and woman differ in physical structure and physical strength, in psychological nature and psychological strength; thereby they naturally enjoy different rights and are called to different duties."[33] Establishing the differing male and female natures is important because role differences and duties flow from these differing natures. This can be seen in the words of Southern Presbyterian theologian Benjamin Morgan Palmer (1818–1902), who explicitly ties

---

33. Herman Bavinck, *The Christian Family*, 25.

gender roles to these differing natures—"Woman is led to this submission by the instinct of her nature . . . Man is endowed with attributes which qualify him for his more obtrusive position. He is strong, forceful, massive, fond of adventure, full of dash and courage. The woman is not less equipped for her station by the qualities which distinguish her. She is endued with grace and beauty, to win rather than subdue . . . above all, crowned with that sense of dependence out of which submission springs as an instinct."[34]

Theologians of old spoke of man having superiority over woman—not in the sense of man being more valuable, but holding authority over woman. In commenting on 1 Corinthians 11:7-10, John Calvin says that God conferred upon man "superiority over the woman" with woman being "inferior in rank."[35] Commenting on 1 Timothy 2:12, Calvin says that woman "by nature (that is, by the ordinary law of God) is formed to obey" and thus Paul "bids them [women] be 'quiet,' that is, keep within their own rank."[36]

The parallel passage of 1 Timothy 2:12 is 1 Corinthians 14:34—"the women should keep silent in the churches. For they are not permitted to speak, but should be in submission." Commenting on this verse, Calvin says, "the office of teaching is a superiority in the Church, and is, consequently, inconsistent with *subjection*. For how unseemly a thing it were, that one who is under subjection to one of the members, should preside over the entire body! It is therefore an argument from things inconsistent—If the woman is under subjection, she is, consequently, prohibited from authority to teach in public. And unquestionably, wherever even natural propriety has been maintained, women have in all ages been excluded from

---

34. B.M. Palmer, *The Family in its Civil and Churchly Aspects* (Richmond, VA: Presbyterian Committee of Publication, 1876), 55.

35. John Calvin, *Commentary on the Epistles of Paul the Apostle to the Corinthians*, vol 1, 357.

36. John Calvin, *Commentaries on the Epistles to Timothy, Titus, and Philemon*, 68.

the public management of affairs. It is the dictate of common sense, that female government is improper and unseemly."[37]

Calvin certainly discusses gender roles in these passages, but he does so by rooting role in nature and sexual hierarchy. God has designed the nature of woman to obey and be submissive, and this is inconsistent with holding authority over men. Calvin expresses the historic Christian position that roots gender roles in the differing natures of men and women, yet it seems most complementarians would be uncomfortable with these words of Calvin.

In his survey of Christian thought on this issue, Daniel Doriani argued that in addition to this ontological view of gender roles (what he terms the Thomist view), Duns Scotus (1265–1308) held that gender roles are only rooted in God's decree and not the differing natures (what he terms the Scotist view). Writing in 1995, Doriani thought many complementarians at that time took a "mediating position"[38] between gender roles being rooted merely in God's command (Scotist) and in nature (Thomist). Yet Doriani also identified a "Scotist tendency in recent complementarian thought"[39] and claimed that "recent conservative theologians have shied away from ontological arguments for male headship."[40] He said, "natural law or Thomistic arguments based on size, bearing, and rationality have virtually disappeared from serious discourse."[41]

Doriani cited some exceptions in *Recovering Biblical Manhood and Womanhood*, including John Piper, and interestingly he noted that "two of the strongest advocates of ontological differences" in the book were a sociologist and biologist.[42] Doriani's survey supports our conclusion that

---

37. John Calvin, *Commentary on the Epistles of Paul the Apostle to the Corinthians*, vol 1, 468.

38. Daniel Doriani, "History of the Interpretation of 1 Timothy 2," in *Women in the Church: A Fresh Analysis of 1 Timothy 2:9-15* (eds. Andreas J. Köstenberger, Thomas R. Schreiner, and H. Scott Baldwin; 1st ed.; Grand Rapids, MI: Baker, 1995), 263.

39. Ibid., 264.
40. Ibid., 259.
41. Ibid., 257–258.
42. Ibid., 259, 261.

complementarianism departed from the historic Christian position. As he stated, "Perhaps many complementarians believe there are no ontological differences between men and women; perhaps they are reluctant to state unpopular ideas. Either way, few traditionalists [complementarians] explain God's reasons or explore how he may have etched his decree in nature."[43]

Thus, we see that *complementarianism was actually something new*. It was not a continuation of the historic Christian teaching on men and women but was a deviation in many ways. While complementarianism affirms many biblical truths, it has also softened the position and practice of earlier generations. Many complementarians would certainly argue this is a good thing and that the church was unbiblical in some of its prior views. That is a premise I will seek to critique throughout this book. I think it is complementarianism, particularly in its narrow form, that has departed from Scripture's teachings.

Since I have critiqued the CBMW and the Danvers Statement, one may fairly ask how I would word a statement on biblical manhood and womanhood. Thus, I propose the following affirmations:

1. All men and women share human nature made in God's image, and Christian men and women are joint heirs with Christ.
2. Yet men and women have distinct sexual natures that determine their roles, purposes, and duties in life.
3. God designed men to provide, protect, and lead, and He designed women to bear children, care for the home, and serve as helpers to their husbands.
4. There is hierarchy in rank between the sexes, whereby God has designed men to rule in the home, church, and society.
5. Though men and women have differing natures, roles, and rank, they are both equally valuable before God and man.

---

43. Ibid., 260–261.

The Error of Rooting Gender Roles in the Trinity Instead of Nature

While not my primary criticism of complementarianism, I must make mention of the eternal functional subordination of the Son (known as ESS or EFS). The failure to explicitly root male and female roles in the differing male and female natures has introduced a problem that has earned criticism across the board, even from non-feminists. This problem is that many complementarians seek to root gender roles in the Trinity. Men like Wayne Grudem appeal to the Trinity to defend the concept that a person can "submit" to another person while they both are "equals." This is known as the eternal functional subordination of the Son (ESS), the view that God the Son was functionally subordinate to the Father prior to the incarnation.

Grudem describes this position as the "orthodox doctrine that the Son is eternally subordinate to the Father in role or function."[44] He distinguishes between ontological subordination and functional subordination, arguing that the Son has always been ontologically equal but functionally subordinate to the Father. Grudem then seeks to ground a wife's functional subordination to her husband in the Son's subordination to the Father.[45] (This argument was first put forth by George W. Knight III in his 1977 book, *The New Testament Teaching on the Role Relationship of Men and Women*.[46])

---

44. Wayne Grudem, *Systematic Theology*, 244–245.

45. While Grudem says that a wife's submission "reflects" the Son's subordination and that the Trinity serves as an analogy for marriage, he also uses stronger language that grounds the concept of marital submission in the Son's eternal subordination: "[T]he idea of headship and submission existed *before creation*. It began in the relationship between the Father and Son in the Trinity." Grudem, *Evangelical Feminism & Biblical Truth: An Analysis of More than 100 Disputed Questions* (Sisters, OR: Multnomah, 2004), 47.

46. George W. Knight III, *The Role Relationship of Men and Women: New Testament Teaching* (Phillipsburg, NJ: Presbyterian and Reformed, 1985), 43–44. This revised edition states: "Although Christ the Son's submission is expressed in the areas of action and of incarnation (the areas of service and of the accomplishment of salvation; cf. also 1 Cor. 15:24-28), it is also an expression of the ontological relationship of preincarnate, submissive Sonship (cf., e.g., John 15:18-23, 30).

Many theologians have criticized Grudem's position and charged him with heresy. Without entertaining such a charge, it should be stated that the Bible's teaching that Jesus submitted to the Father refers to the *incarnate* Son who took on a created body. When Scripture speaks of Jesus submitting to the Father (e.g. John 4:34; 6:38; 1 Corinthians 15:28), it refers to His submission to the Father as a human being.[47] Though the Father and Son relate to each other eternally as Father and Son (eternal generation) and there is an order (*taxis*) of relationship, the Bible does not teach an eternal subordination in function. Such a teaching calls into question the classical doctrine that there is one will of God. Whereas Christ (a person) has two wills because He has two natures (human and divine),[48] God (a being) has one will because He has one divine nature (*ousia*). The will is a property of nature, and since the Father and Son share one nature (the Son is *homoousion*), they must share one will. Thus, the Son cannot eternally submit to the Father in His divinity.[49]

The ontological relationship analogous to that between man and woman, writes Paul, is that between Father and Son (1 Cor. 11:3). That Christ submits as Son and as incarnate—that is, because of certain ontological aspects—does not mean that He is therefore inferior to the Father." Knight here affirms even an ontological submission of the Son to the Father, surely in reference to the person (not nature) of the Son in eternal generation (as a submission of nature would be the heresy of subordinationism). There is an order (*taxis*) of relationship, not rank, among the persons of the Trinity, and in this sense, the Son is subordinate to the Father. This is how some older theologians used the word "subordinate." As Letham says, the "submission or obedience of the Son in the Trinity is in terms of the order, the relations of the person, and is *such as is fully compatible with their unity and equality*." Robert Letham, *The Holy Trinity: In Scripture, History, Theology, and Worship* (Phillipsburg, NJ: P&R, 2004), 492. However, this language of "eternal subordination/submission" causes confusion and should thus be avoided.

47. D. Glenn Butner, Jr., "Eternal Functional Subordination and the Problem of the Divine Will," *Journal of the Evangelical Theological Society* 58/1 (2015): 145. Butner critiques the ESS interpretation of 1 Corinthians 15:28, arguing that 15:20-23 refers to Christ in His humanity and that Psalm 8:6 and 110:1 are cited (15:25, 27) to refer to Christ's role as human mediator.

48. Monothelitism held that Jesus has two natures but only one will. This view was rejected at the Third Council of Constantinople in 681.

49. Butner, "Eternal Functional Subordination and the Problem of the Divine Will," *JETS* 58/1 (2015): 137: "If a will is a property of nature, then the Trinity

Contrary to some recent critics, ESS and complementarianism should be distinguished as two different views, as not all complementarians agree with Grudem and ESS. However, some complementarians seek to base their views on ESS (and some egalitarians seek to base their views on a rejection of ESS). My position is that the relationship of the persons of the Trinity should not be used to ground the gender roles of *created* beings. The Bible never roots gender roles in the Trinity or even makes a male headship analogy based on the Trinity. Rather, biblical gender roles are rooted in God's design at creation in putting the man in authority over his wife. In Ephesians 5, the husband's authority over his wife is compared to Christ's authority over *the church*, not the Father's authority over the Son.

I think many complementarians have appealed to ESS because they have a faulty theological foundation for male and female roles. As noted above, many complementarians ignore the differing natures of men and women, if not outright claim men and women are "ontologically equal." However, men and women are only equal in value, not equal in being. A man has a male nature, not a female nature. And a woman has a female nature, not a male nature. The similarities and differences between men and women are not comparable to those of the Father and Son who share one divine nature.

The Failure of Complementarianism

The inconsistencies of complementarianism have caused problems in many conservative churches, as it is commonplace for churches that do not permit women pastors to still allow women to teach Sunday school to men, read Scripture and lead prayer in public worship, and sometimes even preach sermons from the pulpit. Complementarianism's inconsistencies have also created problems for institutions that do not explicitly fall

---

only has one will and thus one person of the Trinity cannot *qua* divinity eternally 'obey' or 'submit' to another." See also D. Glenn Butner, Jr., *The Son Who Learned Obedience: A Theological Case Against the Eternal Submission of the Son* (Eugene, OR: Pickwick, 2018).

under the term "church," such as seminaries, Bible colleges, parachurch ministries (including CBMW), and Christian book publishers. This is in part because complementarians have failed to root gender roles in male and female natures and have thus removed the rationale for prohibiting women from exercising authority outside of the narrow scope of public worship.

A sad fact is that Christian educational institutions today are by and large egalitarian. Academia as a whole has become effeminate, with women taking men's teaching jobs and women now making up the majority of university students. Academia has become more emotional and less logical, and men do not want to be part of such a system. And this is no less true for Christian academics. Even many Christian educational institutions that would identify as complementarian have adopted egalitarian practices, such as hiring women to teach Bible courses to men in college and seminary. Broader evangelical institutions are a lost cause in this area, with seminaries (such as Trinity Evangelical Divinity School) and colleges (such as Wheaton College) filled with women teaching biblical studies. Many of these institutions even favor women in their PhD programs and faculty hiring. It does not concern them that there are limited positions for PhD programs and professorships (thus leaving fewer breadwinner jobs for men in ministry), nor does it concern them that seminaries are pastoral-training institutions and they permit women to train men for a position (pastor) that the women teachers cannot themselves hold.

Parachurch ministries have also embraced egalitarianism. Many campus ministries allow women to preach and teach the Bible to male college students. And Christian publishing houses, many of which are run by women, have been pushing feminism for years. Many academic commentaries are filled with feminist interpretations of important passages (as will be seen throughout this book), and formerly conservative publishers are printing books that push back against biblical concepts of authority and submission. Even the once conservative P&R published such a book in 2019, *Beyond Authority and Submission* by Rachel Green Miller.

It has gotten to the point where many complementarian institutions and churches are pushing for women in as many positions as possible to cover for their lack of opportunity to serve as pastors and elders. Thus, they invent all sorts of new "women's ministries" and women-targeted teachings (instead of supporting ministries that aid motherhood). While we should support women studying Scripture and theological doctrine, it is of note that there are few comparable men-only teachings series.

It is hard to avoid the conclusion that complementarianism has failed. Complementarianism was an unstable position from the start, and it is no surprise to see it unraveling before our eyes. It has been inconsistent in its treatment of hierarchy in the natural order and has failed to explicitly root male and female roles in their differing natures. Complementarianism has been timid, failing to confront the culture head on regarding the issues of gender and sexuality. It has opted for an approach limited to the church and family instead of one that applies the Bible's teaching to all of life. But what the world needs is not a middle way between feminism and biblical Christianity. The world needs biblical Christianity, and that means something more comprehensive and robust. The world needs Christian patriarchy.

Christianity is patriarchal. It is about a God who has authority over all of creation. God sent His Son to redeem His church, and in doing so, He restores the order of creation. God has put authority structures in place in this world, and He is at the top. Christianity is hierarchical, and since it puts man in authority over woman, it is also patriarchal.

Rejecting patriarchy means rejecting not only God's revelation of male-female relationships, but also God Himself—the ultimate Patriarch. It is not a matter of *whether* men will rule, but *which* men will rule. It is not whether patriarchy, but which patriarchy. The ancient world practiced a patriarchy full of abuses. In the modern, secular world, a patriarchy of a different sort reigns, consisting mostly of self-absorbed playboys who use women and do not take responsibility for their actions. Christian patriarchy is not like these distortions, yet it is patriarchy nonetheless. God made men to rule. Complementarians need not shy away from such a truth.

Chapter 4

CHRISTIANITY IS PATRIARCHAL

PATRIARCHY IS A bad word today, associated with all history prior to modern enlightened man. And by enlightened man, I mean everyone born after 1970. Before that, men treated women like dirt. Or so it is thought. In reality, patriarchy simply means "father rule," from the Greek word πατριάρχης (*patriarches*), formed from the words for "father" [πατήρ, *pater*] and "rule" [ἄρχω, *archo*]. It describes the practice of men providing for and protecting women and children, as well as men leading in the church and society. Does that really sound that bad?

God Our Patriarch

God designed men to rule, and we see this point from God's own revelation of Himself. Though God is spirit (John 4:24) and is neither male nor female, God has revealed Himself in masculine terms. God is our heavenly Father who holds authority over us (Matthew 5:48; 6:9), provides for our needs (Matthew 5:25-26), and gives us good gifts (Luke 11:13). Sometimes God is compared to a woman (Deuteronomy 32:18; Isaiah 49:15; Psalm 123:2) and is said to comfort like a mother (Isaiah 66:13). Men too are compared to women at times (Galatians 4:19). Yet both men and God are never referred to in feminine terms. Men are still men, not women. And

God always reveals Himself in masculine terms. God is a He, not a "she" as some liberal theologians surmise.

Why has God revealed Himself in masculine terms? Because God has authority over us as our Lord and King, and *masculinity connotes authority*. Femininity does not. God does not rule over us as mother but as Father. God is our patriarch. And God the Father has made human fathers to rule. It is part of nature. Not every father rules well, but every father does rule. Men always rule, for either good or bad. An absent father will leave his children destitute and in need. An emotionally-distant father will leave his children longing for more. But a good father leaves his children thriving, being loved and led well.

This is not to say that God has no feminine qualities. While God is never portrayed as being feminine, both masculine and feminine qualities find their origin and example in Him.[1] We know this because both man and woman are made in God's image (Genesis 1:27; 5:1-2). Thus, God has revealed Himself in masculine terms, while possessing both masculine and feminine qualities. In the same way, men should still have some feminine qualities and women some masculine qualities. As theologian Herman Bavinck says, "No man is complete without some feminine qualities, no woman is complete without some masculine qualities."[2]

God has revealed Himself in masculine terms, and throughout the Scriptures God reveals that men are to rule—in the home, church, and society. Thus, the word "complementarian" does not go far enough. While it is true that men and women complement each other, even egalitarians can affirm this in some sense (e.g. sexual complementarity). We must speak more forcefully than this, and thus we need a word that communicates male rule better. Enter patriarchy. It has the word "rule" in it (*archo*),

---

1. Herman Bavinck, *The Christian Family*, 66: "God is never portrayed or presented as being feminine. But if the woman is said to be created along with man in the image of God, then that includes the fact that the uniqueness and richness of feminine qualities no less than those of the masculine capacities find their origin and example in the divine Being. God is a Father who takes pity on his children, but he also comforts like a mother comforts her son."

2. Ibid., 8.

which tells us something about male authority. But it is also gentle, as it includes the word "father." This speaks of more than just a man. This rule is by a father, a man who has children that he is to care and provide for. Yes, some men are bad fathers, but that does not take away from what a father is *supposed* to be.

It should not be controversial to describe the Bible as patriarchal. It was historically understood this way, and opponents of the Bible certainly view it this way. Critical feminist scholars recognize the patriarchal nature of Christianity—they just happen to hate it. We saw this with the suffragette Elizabeth Cady Stanton, who wrote her *Woman's Bible* in order to tear down the Bible's references to patriarchal rule and "demeaning" teaching about women. The only people that object to the Bible being called patriarchal are the Christians who do not want to be labeled as "sexists" by the modern culture. But as we will see below, the Bible most certainly demonstrates and prescribes father rule. To deny that Christianity is patriarchal is to deny the teaching of Scripture.

Patriarchy in the Old Testament—the Patriarchs

Let us begin in the Old Testament. The first man, Adam, was created prior to his wife Eve. He was made to work and keep the garden, with Eve as his helper (Genesis 2:15, 18). God named mankind after the man, not the woman (Genesis 5:1-2). And even though Eve sinned first and gave Adam the fruit to eat, *God called for Adam first*, saying "Where are you?" ("you" is singular in the Hebrew) (Genesis 3:9). Adam ruled and had authority over his wife. Thus, God held Adam accountable for Eve's sin. Yet God also held Adam accountable *for the entire human race*. Adam brought sin and death upon all humans—"sin came into the world through one man . . . many died through one man's trespass . . . because of one man's trespass, death reigned through that one man" (Romans 5:12, 15, 17). Eve did not bring this about, as Adam had covenantal authority in the garden. Adam was responsible for all his descendants and thus passed sin and death on to all his posterity (see chapters 5 and 6 for more).

Then we have the men who are known as the "patriarchs"—Abraham, Isaac, and Jacob. All three of these men ruled their families. God called Abraham and promised to make of him a great nation, to make his name great, and to bless all families of the earth in him (Genesis 12:2-3). God promised Abraham offspring and land (15:4-5, 16-21; 17:4-8), and He gave him the covenant of circumcision, a sign only applied to males in the household (17:9-14). These promises were passed down to all of Abraham's descendants, and they were specifically inherited by Abraham's son Isaac (17:19-21) and Isaac's son Jacob (28:13-15).

The Apostle Paul likely includes Abraham, Isaac, and Jacob as "patriarchs" when he speaks of Christ becoming a servant to Jews to "confirm the promises given to the patriarchs" (Romans 15:8; cf. 9:5). The author of Hebrews explicitly calls Abraham "the patriarch" (Hebrews 7:4). However, the term "patriarch" is used more broadly than this in Acts. Stephen says that Jacob became father of the "twelve patriarchs" (Acts 7:8-9), and Peter refers to "the patriarch David" (Acts 2:29). Thus, Scripture uses the term "patriarch" more broadly to include important male leaders in the Old Testament.

Patriarchy in the Old Testament—Elders, Prophets, Judges, Priests, and Kings

Israel was organized into 12 tribes named after Jacob's 12 sons (not daughters). And it was the sons who received Jacob's blessings (Genesis 49). Israel's tribes consisted of clans and families, with heads of each group. Out of this we see civil government arise with elders in Israel (Exodus 3:16; 4:29).[3] As Bavinck says, "The entire organization of the nation was along

---

3. While Israel's "elders" sometimes appear to be described as distinct from the "heads of tribes" (Deuteronomy 5:23; 29:10; Joshua 24:1), elsewhere these groups are described as one and the same (Numbers 11:16; Deuteronomy 31:28; 1 Kings 8:1; 2 Chronicles 5:2). It is likely that in the former passages the phrases "elders," "heads," "judges," and "officers" are listed separately but all refer to the same group. The most able men were chosen as "chiefs" and "heads" who "judged" Israel (Exodus 18:21-26).

patriarchal lines, arranged in terms of the principle of genealogical descent. The twelve tribes, among whom Judah was preeminent, were divided into clans, the clans into extended families, and these extended families into households. Each of those groups had its own head, representative, or prince; and all these heads or princes together formed the 'members of the assembly.' When they gathered, the 'congregation' of Israel was gathered."[4]

God called Moses to lead Israel out of Egyptian slavery, and the prophet Moses served in both ecclesiastical and civil leadership. This position was passed down to the man Joshua (Deuteronomy 31:1-8). God then sent 12 judges to "save/deliver" Israel (Judges 2:16). All of these judges were men, except Deborah, who is described as both a prophetess and judge (Judges 4:4-5). However, Deborah is not described in the same way as the men judges, and she did not serve as a military leader, which was the primary role of the judges. Instead, Deborah urged Barak to fight (Judges 4:6-9), and it is Barak who is mentioned alongside the judges later in Scripture (1 Samuel 12:11; Hebrews 11:32). Thus, Deborah is not a model for female civil or ecclesiastical leadership. (This issue is addressed more in chapter 11.)

Yahweh then raised up Samuel to lead and judge Israel (1 Samuel 7:6, 15-17). God gave Israel a king because they wanted to be like the other nations (1 Samuel 8). Every king was a man, and there was no queen except the usurper Athaliah the mother of King Ahaziah (2 Kings 11:1-20; 2 Chronicles 22:10–23:15). The priests of Israel were also all men. All the male Levites had priestly duties and had a teaching role (Deuteronomy 21:5; 33:10; 2 Chronicles 17:7-9; 35:3; Nehemiah 8:7-9; Malachi 2:4-7). But only the sons of Aaron served as priests in the tabernacle/temple (Exodus 28:1; Numbers 3:3).[5]

---

4. Bavinck, *The Christian Family*, 30.

5. Sometimes the Bible uses language that seems to identify all male Levites as "priests" (e.g. Joshua 18:7). However, technically only Aaron's male descendants were priests and offered sacrifices in the tabernacle (Exodus 28–29; Leviticus 8–10). The rest of the Levites assisted the priests (Numbers 3:5-9). This distinction is particularly clear in the story of Korah's rebellion, as Korah was a Levite who coveted the role of the priests (Numbers 16:8-10). Yet while there is a technical

Thus, we see that God's leaders in the Old Testament were men. The patriarchs were men, the kings were men, the elders were men, and the priests were men. Abraham, Jacob, Moses, David, and Samuel provide us with examples of godly men. They were men devoted to Yahweh and demonstrated great courage throughout their lives. We see this in Abraham's rescuing of Lot (Genesis 14:1-16), Jacob's wrestling with God (Genesis 32:22-32), Moses' defending his fellow Israelite from an Egyptian (Exodus 2:11-15),[6] David's defeat of Goliath (1 Samuel 17:1-54), and Samuel's execution of Agag (1 Samuel 15:33).

The only apparent exception to the rule of male leadership in the Old Testament is that there were women prophetesses, including Miriam, Moses' sister (Exodus 15:20), Deborah (Judges 4:4), Huldah (2 Kings 22:14; 2 Chronicles 34:22), and Noadiah (Nehemiah 6:14). However, the role of prophetess can be explained in two ways.

First, female prophetesses exercised a different role than male prophets. While God revealed His Word to some women to speak as prophetesses, none of these women had a formal leadership position in Israel. Moreover,

---

distinction between the priests and Levites, it is also useful to speak of all the male Levites as priests because they all had a special role in guarding and serving the tabernacle and later temple.

6. Moses is often charged here with being a murderer since he killed the Egyptian who was beating a fellow Hebrew (Exodus 2:11-12), but the Exodus text does not provide a clear interpretation of these events. That Moses "looked this way and that" before striking the Egyptian does not mean this was an unjustified killing but only that Moses sought to avoid punishment—and hence he fled once he thought his deed was known (Exodus 2:14-15). At most, Moses committed manslaughter, not murder, since he was defending another man from a beating. The Egyptian was not innocent. However, Exodus 2:14 can be read as the Israelites rejecting Moses' attempt to deliver them ("Who made you a prince and a judge over us?"). This is how Stephen interprets things—"This Moses, *whom they rejected*, saying, 'Who made you a ruler and a judge?'" (Acts 7:35). Stephen also says of Moses, "When he was forty years old, it came into his heart to visit his brothers, the children of Israel. And seeing one of them being wronged, he defended the oppressed man and avenged him by striking down the Egyptian. *He supposed that his brothers would understand that God was giving them salvation by his hand, but they did not understand*" (Acts 7:23-25).

as Origen noted,[7] women prophetesses never prophesied publicly but only prophesied to individuals and small groups. For example, Huldah prophesied to a small group of messengers from the king (2 Kings 22:14). Public prophecy was reserved for men, which is why the majority of the prophets were men and why Bible books are named after male prophets. In addition to the prophet Moses authoring the Torah, the books of the Bible in the section known as the Prophets are all named after men. Joshua and Samuel were prophets, as well as the "Latter Prophets" of Isaiah, Jeremiah, Ezekiel, and the Twelve minor prophets (Hosea, Joel, Amos, Obadiah, Jonah, Micah, Nahum, Habakkuk, Zephaniah, Haggai, Zechariah, Malachi).

Second, prophecy itself differs from the authoritative tasks of teaching and ruling. Prophecy is a "revelatory gift" where the prophet "is the instrument through which God speaks His Word to the church."[8] This differs from the public teaching of God's Word, where the teacher does not just reveal but also explains God's Word to His people. While God has revealed His word through women prophetesses, He does not permit them to publicly teach His Word.

The leaders in the rest of the Old Testament were all men. Daniel was a prophet, and Ezra and Nehemiah led Israel in their return to the Promised Land after captivity. This is not to say women did not play an important role in the Hebrew Bible. They did, mostly as wives and mothers. Some women even protected the covenant against male folly. This is a theme throughout the Old Testament, seen in Rebekah deceiving Isaac in order to make sure he followed God's promise (Genesis 25:23; 27:1-40) and Moses' wife Zipporah circumcising their son in order to prevent death because Moses failed to do so (Exodus 4:24-26). And of course, there are Bible books named after great women—Ruth and Esther.

---

7. See footnote 7 in chapter 9.
8. Guy Prentiss Waters, *How Jesus Runs the Church* (Phillipsburg, NJ: P&R Publishing, 2011), 110.

Patriarchy in the Old Testament—the Household

Men also played an important leadership role at the family level. Israel had patriarchal laws recognizing a man's authority and responsibility as father and husband. As for husbands, the Tenth Commandment assumes male headship—"You shall not covet your neighbor's house; you shall not covet your neighbor's wife, or his male servant, or his female servant, or his ox, or his donkey, or anything that is your neighbor's" (Exodus 20:17; cf. Deuteronomy 5:21). It is often charged that a wife was the "property" of her husband, as if the wife had the same status as an animal or slave. This is incorrect. Rather, the wife was under the husband's covenantal headship, and this meant the husband had obligations toward his wife, including to protect her and provide for her (Exodus 21:10).

As for fathers, they had authority over their unmarried daughters, just as husbands had authority over their wives (Numbers 30). This covenantal authority was transferred from father to husband at marriage. This authority gave a father the power to annul the acts of his unmarried daughter, including her vow—"If a woman vows a vow to the LORD and binds herself by a pledge while within her father's house in her youth . . . if her father opposes her on the day that he hears of it, no vow of hers, no pledge by which she has bound herself shall stand" (Numbers 30:3-5). A husband could do likewise for his wife (Numbers 30:6-8).

A father also had the authority to annul a marriage that would otherwise be created by his daughter's sexual union—"If a man seduces a virgin who is not betrothed and lies with her, he shall give the bride-price for her and make her his wife. If her father utterly refuses to give her to him, he shall pay money equal to the bride-price for virgins" (Exodus 22:16-17). This law deals with the case where a man seduces an unbetrothed[9] virgin and has sexual intercourse with her ("lies with her").[10] The man

---

9. Betrothal was similar to engagement, though divorce was required in order to break a betrothal (Matthew 1:18-19).

10. There is a question of how the similar law in Deuteronomy 22:28-29 relates to Exodus 22:16-17. The Exodus 22 law seems to be consensual on the woman's part (the man "seduces" her), whereas Deuteronomy 22 uses stronger

was required to marry the woman with whom he had sex, unless the woman's father "utterly refuses" the marriage. In such a case, the marriage is *annulled* and the man must still pay the bride-price for the woman as compensation, as the woman's marriage value has diminished since she is no longer a virgin.

In both the case of a vow and seduction, the father had the authority to render his daughter's actions null and void. The Mosaic law assumes the authority of a father over his unmarried daughters—an authority that carried with it the responsibility to *protect* his daughters. Brothers also played an important role in protecting their sisters and thus aided their father in this covenantal task (Genesis 34; Song of Songs 8:8-10).

Jesus Our Patriarch

But that was the Old Testament. Things have changed since then, right? Not exactly. The New Testament fulfills the Old Testament, and as such, it continues the practice of male rule. Jesus today is portrayed as an effeminate, long-haired hippy in many pictures and films, but this could not be further from the truth. Modern effeminate men have made Jesus into their own image. Jesus not only had shorter hair like other Jewish men of His day, but He was authoritative. He was the ideal man. Jesus taught "as one who had authority" and not like their scribes (Matthew 7:28-29), and He exercised godly authority when He turned over tables near the temple out of zeal for God's house (Mark 11:15-18).

Jesus—the central figure of the entire Bible—was a man. Thus, male rule in the New Testament begins with the God-man who took on human flesh. God took on a male body, not a female body. This must mean *something*. This is the Son of God (Mark 1:1), not the daughter of God. This is the Son of Man (Matthew 9:6; cf. Daniel 7:13), not the daughter of man. Jesus took on a body like ours. He was born a baby boy and grew in wisdom and stature (Luke 2:52), becoming a full-grown man. And

---

language ("seizes her," "violated her") and may refer to rape (though the phrase "they are found" suggests otherwise).

Jesus still has His resurrected body as He reigns in heaven (Luke 24:31, 39; Acts 1:9-11). He will forever be the Son of God in male form. This demonstrates that manhood and womanhood are not temporary, but we will be men and women for eternity in the new heavens and earth.

Why did God take on not just human flesh, but a man's flesh? Yes, it would have been culturally unthinkable for the Messiah to be a woman. But there is more to it. God's people expected a male Messiah because the prophecies of the Messiah were all about a man[11] and because God's leaders had always been men.[12] But why were God's leaders men? Because God made man to rule. The cultural expectation was based in nature and God's design.

So we see that Jesus is greater than all the great men who came before Him. Jesus is a second and better Adam, who perfectly obeyed the Father (Romans 5:18-19). Jesus is a better Moses, who intercedes for His people (Hebrews 3:1-6). He is our Great High Priest (Hebrews 7:26-28; 8:1), following in the line of the man Melchizedek (Hebrews 5:6, 10; 6:20; 7:17). Jesus is the promised offspring of David (2 Samuel 7:12-13), our King who exercises rule over heaven and earth (Matthew 28:18-20). Kings and priests were men, so it is only right that Jesus, our Great High Priest and King, is a man. It could not be any other way. Like the God-appointed leaders of old, *the Son became a man to lead and rule His people forever*. This role would not befit a woman.

Jesus was the truest of men, who suffered and laid down His life for His people. As the Roman soldiers mocked Jesus and put a purple robe on Him and a crown of thorns on His head, Pilate said to the crowd, "Behold the man" (John 19:5). Though he uses the more generic word

---

11. For a list of Scripture texts requiring a male savior, see Bruce A. Ware, "Could Our Savior Have Been a Woman? The Relevance of Jesus' Gender for His Incarnational Mission," *The Journal for Biblical Manhood and Womanhood* (Spring 2003): 33–38.

12. Köstenberger and Köstenberger, *God's Design for Man and Woman*, 83: "Jesus continues the pattern of male leadership that ranges all the way from Adam to the patriarchs, and from kings and priests to the Messiah . . . In light of the pervasive male pattern of leadership in both Testaments, it is virtually inconceivable that Jesus might have been incarnated as a woman."

for human, ὁ ἄνθρωπος (*ho anthropos*), this is clearly a reference to a man (just as ἄνθρωπος is used for Jesus in 1 Corinthians 15:21 and 1 Timothy 2:5). Pilate did not realize all that he was saying. Jesus was *the man*, the ultimate man. And Jesus the man takes a bride for Himself, the church, which He has redeemed with His blood. He did the manliest thing of all, laying down His life for His bride (Ephesians 5:25). In doing so, Jesus conquered sin, death, and the devil. He is the knight on a white horse who struck down the dragon to rescue His bride in the greatest love story of all time (Revelation 19:11–20:15).

Patriarchy in the New Testament—Apostles

Yet the church is also described in masculine terms, as the goal of the church is to grow up "into Christ," to "mature manhood" [ἄνδρα τέλειον, *andra teleion*] (Ephesians 4:13, 15). Jesus gave the church apostles, prophets, evangelists, pastors, and teachers to "equip the saints" and build up "the body of Christ"—"until we all attain to the unity of faith and of the knowledge of the Son of God, to mature manhood, to the measure of the stature of the fullness of Christ" (Ephesians 4:11-13).

Jesus first called the 12 apostles, all of whom were men (Matthew 10:2). The apostles correspond to the 12 tribes of Israel, which came from the 12 sons of Jacob. Thus, Jesus is a new Israel with 12 apostles. His apostles went forth preaching the gospel and discipling the nations (Matthew 28:18). These 12 apostles will judge the 12 tribes of Israel (Matthew 19:28), and their 12 names will be written on the foundations of the heavenly city (Revelation 21:14).

It is not certain how many other apostles there were. We know Matthias replaced Judas (Acts 1:26), and only "men" [ἀνδρῶν] were in consideration for this office (Acts 1:21-22). We also know the Apostle Paul was added to this group of apostles, as Jesus called him on the road to Damascus (Acts 9:3-8) and Paul identifies himself as an apostle (e.g. Romans 1:1; 11:13). However, Paul tells us there were more apostles than just the 12 when in

1 Corinthians 15:5-7 he says that Jesus appeared to "the twelve . . . then to all the apostles." As to whom this group of apostles included is unclear.

Paul considers James, the brother of Jesus, to be an apostle—"But I saw none of the other apostles except James the Lord's brother" (Galatians 1:19; cf. 1 Corinthians 15:7). Barnabas is called an "apostle" [ἀπόστολος] along with Paul in Acts 14:4 and 14:14, but this could be a non-technical term referring to a messenger (cf. Acts 13:2-4).[13] Paul may have included Apollos in the category of apostle (1 Corinthians 4:6-9). He may also have included Silvanus and Timothy as apostles (1 Thessalonians 1:1; 2:6-7), though this may only include Silvanus since Timothy is never called an apostle elsewhere when Paul includes him in his letters (2 Corinthians 1:1; Philippians 1:1; Colossians 1:1).[14]

Regardless of these additions, Jesus originally chose 12 men to be His apostles—"the Twelve." These men formed a leadership group in distinction from "disciples," a group that included women. Jesus' choice of 12 men was not merely a cultural decision, for Jesus was not shy about overturning cultural errors. If Jesus wanted to choose women apostles, He could have done so. Yet He did not.[15] Rather, Jesus chose men as apostles

---

13. John Calvin, *Acts* (The Crossway Classic Commentaries; eds. Alister McGrath and J.I. Packer; Wheaton, IL: Crossway, 1995), 237–238: "When Luke called Barnabas an apostle together with Paul, he was extending the meaning of the word beyond the primary order that Christ appointed in his church, just as Paul made Andronicus and Junias 'outstanding among the apostles' (Romans 16:7). Properly speaking, Paul and Barnabas were evangelists and not both apostles— unless perhaps because Barnabas was Paul's colleague we give them both the same official rank; in that case he may appropriately be called an apostle." Alternatively, Galatians 2:9 and 1 Corinthians 9:6 support Barnabas being understood as holding the office of apostle.

14. Gene L. Green, *The Letters to the Thessalonians* (The Pillar New Testament Commentary; Grand Rapids, MI: Eerdmans, 2002), 126.

15. Köstenberger and Köstenberger, *God's Design for Man and* Woman, 93: "If Jesus had wanted to include women leaders in his apostolic circle out of principle, he would have done so. He was the Messiah, the Son of God, God's representative to humanity. If there had been a new pattern of leadership that God wanted to establish with regard to gender roles, Jesus would have established it."

because God designed men and not women to rule His church, as seen in all the leadership positions in biblical history.

Feminists argue that there was a woman apostle named Junia mentioned by Paul—"Greet Andronicus and Junia ['Ιουνιᾶν], my kinsmen and my fellow prisoners. They are well known to [or among] the apostles" (Romans 16:7). However, there are far too many uncertainties in this verse to assert that there was a woman apostle. First, 'Ιουνιᾶν (*Iounian*) is in the accusative form, so it is not clear what the first name was, whether the female Junia or the male Junias (a contraction of Junianus or the Hellenized form of the Hebrew Yehunni).[16]

Second, the phrase ἐπίσημοι ἐν τοῖς ἀποστόλοις (*episemoi en tois apostolois*) could mean Junia/Junias was "well known to the apostles" (the exclusive view) or "well known among the apostles" (the inclusive view—meaning Junia was a member of the group of "apostles"). Some scholars have argued that comparisons in biblical and patristic Greek show that when ἐν (*en*) is followed by a personal noun in the dative case, as in Romans 16:7, this indicates the exclusive view, while the inclusive view is expressed for personal nouns by ἐν plus a genitive.[17] In addition to the grammatical argument, the exclusive view that Junia/Junias was "well known to the apostles" fits the context, as Paul describes Andronicus and Junia/Junias here as "kinsmen" and "fellow prisoners," terms used for other non-apostles (Romans 16:21; Colossians 4:10). It makes sense that these godly Christians were known by the other apostles and not numbered among them.

---

16. Albert Wolters, "ΙΟΥΝΙΑΝ (Romans 16:7) and the Hebrew Name Yehunni," *Journal of Biblical Literature* 127 (2008): 397–408.

17. Michael Burer and Daniel B. Wallace, "Was Junia Really an Apostle? A Re-examination of Rom 16.7," *New Testament Studies* 47 (2001): 76–91. Burer and Wallace argue that J.B. Lightfoot's 1865 commentary heavily influenced scholars toward the inclusive view because he had a legendary reputation as a grammarian, but that he provided no support for this view other than that it was held by the Greek fathers. Burer later responded to critics and provided additional information in Michael Burer, "ἐπίσημοι ἐν τοῖς ἀποστόλοις in Rom 16:7 as 'Well Known to the Apostles': Further Defense and New Evidence," *Journal of the Evangelical Theological Society* 58/4 (2015): 731–755.

Third, even if Romans 16:7 refers to a woman named Junia who is identified as an "apostle" (as one "among the apostles"), this could mean she was an apostle in the non-technical sense of "messenger" or "representative"[18] (the word ἀπόστολος is related to the verb "to send") or it could refer to a church planter or missionary.[19] This is how Paul described others who did not hold the office of apostle—"And as for our brothers, they are messengers [ἀπόστολοι] of the churches, the glory of Christ" (2 Corinthians 8:23), and "I have thought it necessary to send to you Epaphroditus my brother and fellow worker and fellow soldier, and your messenger [ἀπόστολον] and minister to my need" (Philippians 2:25). Moreover, why would Paul put a woman in the same category as himself, the Twelve, and James? (1 Corinthians 15:7; Galatians 1:19). Paul does not even put Epaphroditus in that esteemed group. Andronicus and Junia/Junias are only mentioned here in Romans 16:7, and it does not make sense to say they were prominent or "well known" apostles—a description that would be reserved for apostles such as Peter and John.

In the end, it cannot be held with any confidence that there was a woman apostle named Junia. The text is ambiguous, and there is nothing else in the New Testament indicating that a woman could hold the office of apostle. In fact, everything outside of Romans 16:7 teaches that only men could be apostles. Considering Jesus' practice of only appointing men as apostles, there is a significant burden on those claiming Junia was a woman apostle. And that burden simply has not been met.

Patriarchy in the New Testament—Elders and Deacons

In addition to Jesus calling only men as apostles, Paul instructed the church to appoint only men as elders.[20] Like elders in the Old Testament, New

---

18. BDAG, 122, cites Philippians 2:25 and 2 Corinthians 8:23 under the definition *"delegate, envoy, messenger."*
19. Köstenberger and Köstenberger, *God's Design for Man and Woman*, 155: "In all probability, then, Andronicus and Junia were a distinguished missionary couple."
20. I am assuming here that there is only one office of elder, composed of two

Testament elders are men. Paul plainly says an elder must be a "man" [ἀνήρ, *aner*] (1 Timothy 3:2; Titus 1:6). Yes, this was part of his requirement that an elder is a "man of one woman" [μιᾶς γυναικὸς ἄνδρα], and yes, this certainly prohibits polygamous men from serving as elders and requires elders to be faithful to their wives. But Paul still requires elders to be men. This is not his way of using a masculine singular to include both men and women. Later in 1 Timothy 5:9, Paul uses the exact opposite phrase in the requirement for enrolling widows in the church—a widow must be the "wife of one husband" [ἑνὸς ἀνδρὸς γυνή]. There is a parallel between 1 Timothy 3:2 and 1 Timothy 5:9. A widow has to be a "woman," and an elder has to be a "man." Furthermore, Paul prohibits women from teaching and exercising authority over men, and he bases this on the creation order (1 Timothy 2:11-14). Elders are to be "able to teach" (1 Timothy 3:2), and women are not allowed to publicly teach Christian doctrine to men. Thus, women cannot be elders. (See chapter 8 for an elaboration of this argument for male-only pastors/elders.)

Paul also instructed the church to appoint deacons, a new office in the New Testament focused on the task of service. Some of the same arguments apply to male-only deacons as to male-only elders, as Paul follows with similar requirements for both—"Deacons *likewise* must be . . ." (1 Timothy 3:8-13). Like elders, Paul requires a deacon to be a "man" who "manages" his household well—"Let deacons each be the husband of one wife [μιᾶς γυναικὸς ἄνδρες], managing their children and their own households well" (3:12). This requirement certainly refers to men, as the word "manage" [προΐστημι, *proistemi*] means "to exercise a position of leadership, *rule, direct, be at the head (of)*."[21] This household management requirement is similar to that for elders, except for elders Paul gives the additional comment that the household management is the basis for measuring the elder's care for the church—"for if someone does not know

---

orders—teaching elders (pastors/ministers) and ruling elders. This is known as the two-office view (elders and deacons), in contrast to the three-office view that distinguishes between pastors and elders. For more on this issue, see footnote 1 in chapter 8.

21. BDAG, 870.

how to manage his own household, how will he care for God's church?" (1 Timothy 3:4-5). Paul might have left out the subsequent question for deacons simply to avoid repetition. If this is the case, then deacons also carry some authority in the church, and therefore the prohibition of women exercising authority over men in 1 Timothy 2:12 would also prohibit women from serving as deacons. This is further supported by Philippians 1:1, where Paul addresses his letter to both the elders and deacons, suggesting both carry authority in the church.[22]

However, there is difficulty in 1 Timothy 3 because, unlike with elders, Paul inserts a requirement for "women/wives" [Γυναῖκας, *gunaikas*]— "Their wives likewise must be dignified, not slanderers, but sober-minded, faithful in all things" (1 Timothy 3:11). The Greek has no article and can mean either "women" or "wives." The ESV takes it to refer to the elders' wives and thus adds the possessive "their." That Paul speaks of "women" as a separate group ("women likewise") shows that he only speaks of men in 3:8 as "deacons" (also 3:12-13). Just as Paul distinguishes deacons from elders (3:8), so here in 3:11 he distinguishes women from deacons. The question thus arises who these "women" are. While some hold that Paul here establishes a separate office of deaconess, it is odd that Paul only provides one verse for women in the middle of five other verses about men deacons (3:8-10, 12-13). If Paul meant to include women as deaconesses, one would expect him to list their complete qualifications as he did for the men deacons and not only reserve one verse with four qualifications for them (3:11). Paul also could have used the masculine word "deacon" with the feminine definite article ("the") to explicitly describe these women as deaconesses, but he does not. Instead, he uses the word for "women/wives" [Γυναῖκας] to distinguish this group as non-deacons. Paul does not include these "women/wives" in the office of "deacon," nor does he

---

22. Clarence DeWitte Agan III, "Deacons, Deaconesses, and Denominational Discussions: Romans 16:1 as a Test Case," *Presbyterion* 34/2 (Fall 2008): 102: "the pairing of 'deacons' and 'elders' at Philippians 1:1 and 1 Timothy 3 suggests that the διάκονος was one who served in authority over a congregation but under the authority of elders/overseers."

establish a separate office for them. Rather, the comment on "women/wives" in 3:11 is a parenthesis.

Why then does Paul only mention the wives (or women assistants) for deacons and not elders? Unlike elders, deacons have the role of service, and "diaconal ministry would involve the deacons intimately in the lives of female members of the congregation."[23] So it makes sense that women serve along with the deacons to other women (inside and outside church), whether these assistants are the deacons' wives or other women in the church. "Wives" is a preferable interpretation because that is how γυνή (*gune*) is understood in 1 Timothy 3:2 and 3:12, and it would be fitting with Paul's concerns for sexual propriety. The wives of deacons will serve alongside them in some way.

Advocates of women deaconesses also appeal to Romans 16:1, where Phoebe is called a διάκονος (*diakonos*) "of the church at Cenchreae."[24] This view requires διάκονος here to refer to the office of deacon, but διάκονος can merely mean "servant" or "minister." This is seen in that Epaphras is also called a διάκονος in Colossians 1:7 and Timothy is called a διάκονος in 1 Timothy 4:6, yet neither are known as "deacons." Further, Paul uses the participle form διακονῶν (*diakonon*) and the noun διακονία (*diakonia*) to describe his own ministering and ministry to Jerusalem in Romans 15:25 and 15:31. Thus, like Epaphras and Timothy, Paul might have been describing Phoebe as a servant or messenger of the church of Cenchreae.[25] The argument that Phoebe must have held the office of deacon because her specific church is mentioned (Cenchreae)[26] is not conclusive.

Further, Acts 6:1-7 probably explains the origin of deacons in the New Testament, and all of them were men. The 12 apostles appointed seven

---

23. Guy Prentiss Waters, *How Jesus Runs the Church*, 115.
24. B.B. Warfield, "Presbyterian Deaconesses," *The Presbyterian Review* 10/38 (1889): 283–293. Warfield relies heavily on the argument that the post-apostolic church permitted deaconesses. He thinks Acts 16:1 "likely" refers to a deaconess but that 1 Timothy 3:11 does not.
25. Agan III, "Deacons, Deaconesses, and Denominational Discussions": 105–107.
26. Jamin Hübner, *A Case for Female Deacons* (Eugene, OR: Wipf & Stock, 2015), 20.

"men" (ἄνδρας, *andras*) to serve tables so that the apostles could focus on "prayer and the ministry of the word" (Acts 6:4). The word "deacon" is not used here, but the verb διακονεῖν (*diaokonein*, "to serve") is used in 6:2 and the noun διακονίᾳ (*diakonia*, "service") in 6:1. This passage probably establishes the office of deacon[27] (or at least provides an example of proto-deacons), men serving so the apostles could preach, similar to the way deacons free up elders to preach and rule.

Thus, Paul requires deacons to be men. Like elders, deacons must be men who manage their households well (1 Timothy 3:2, 4-5, 12). Both elders and deacons hold office in the church (Philippians 1:1). There are no clear examples of women deacons in the New Testament, and the probable origin of the diaconate involved only men (Acts 6:1-7). There is certainly a role for women serving with the deacons, seen in 1 Timothy 3:11, but women do not hold the office of deacon.

There has been some confusion over this issue in church history, and even some conservative churches have allowed women to hold the office of deacon. However, this is to confuse the gift of service with the office of deacon.[28] Having the gift of teaching or ruling does not make one an elder. In the same way, having the gift of service does not make one a deacon. An office is not merely a name for a person who has a particular gift, but it is an official church position. The office of deacon carries authority related to service in the church, and a deacon is called and ordained by the

---

27. C.N. Willborn argues the "consensus" Reformed view is that Acts 6:1-6 concerns the origin of the office of deacon, a view held by John Calvin, John Owen, and Louis Berkhof. C.N. Willborn, "The Deacon: A Divine Right Office with Divine Uses," *Confessional Presbyterian* 5 (2009): 185–186.

28. Hübner argues that it is possible for a person "to be *functioning* as a deacon without being *officially recognized* as a deacon," and he includes Phoebe in this category. Jamin Hübner, *A Case for Female Deacons*, 24. However, this misses an important distinction between gifting and office. A man may preach a sermon to a church, and he may even be gifted in teaching, but that does not make him an elder. He may not meet all the requirements for an elder. In the same way, even if Phoebe served the church similarly to how a man does who holds the office of deacon, that does not mean Phoebe would meet the qualifications for the office of deacon.

church.²⁹ (Ordination of deacons is seen in the laying on of hands in Acts 6:6.) While such authority differs from elders, it is authority nonetheless. Some women have an important role in serving alongside the deacons, and churches should appoint men and women to assist the deacons. But women are not to hold the office of deacon (and in order to avoid confusion, such assistants should not be called "deaconesses").

Patriarchy in the New Testament—Prophets

Feminists make many leaps in their arguments with less clear passages of Scripture, such as Paul's greetings in Romans 16:1-3. In addition to arguing Phoebe was a deaconess, they argue she was also a leader in the church as a "patron" [προστάτις, *prostatis*] (Romans 16:2). However, while the masculine noun προστάτης (*prostates*) could refer to a leader (e.g. 1 Chronicles 29:6 [LXX]), the feminine προστάτις used to describe Phoebe refers to "a woman in a supportive role, *patron, benefactor*."³⁰ Phoebe may have been a widow who inherited her husband's estate and opened her home to fellow Christians.³¹ Paul was using a play on words, telling the Roman Christians they should *parastete* [παραστῆτε, "assist"] Phoebe because she was a *prostatis* [προστάτις, "helper"] of others. This verse does not teach that Phoebe was a church leader of any sort. There were women who were "fellow workers" [συνεργούς] with Paul, such as Priscilla in Romans 16:3. But one cannot conclude these were apostles or that such women performed apostle-like tasks, as is sometimes asserted. There were many women who aided Paul in his work, and he was praising them for their godly actions.

Just like the Old Testament, there were women prophetesses in the New Testament. Peter quotes Joel 2:28-29 as finding fulfillment in the new

---

29. For more detail on this issue, see the *Report of the Committee on Women in Church Office Presented to the Fifty-fifth (1988) General Assembly of the Orthodox Presbyterian Church*, http://www.opc.org/GA/women_in_office.html.
30. BDAG, 885.
31. Köstenberger and Köstenberger, *God's Design for Man and Woman*, 150.

covenant, which speaks of God pouring out His Spirit so that "your sons and your daughters shall prophesy" (Acts 2:17). Anna was a "prophetess" (Luke 2:36-38), and Philip had "four unmarried daughters who prophesied" (Acts 21:9). This continues the practice of the Old Testament, where God gifted some women as prophetesses but restricted all other offices to men. There is continuity between the Old and New Testaments.

Some have argued New Testament prophecy differs from Old Testament prophecy in that it is less authoritative and now must be evaluated. However, this does not fit the evidence. New Testament prophets held a high position in the church (1 Corinthians 12:28; Ephesians 2:20; 3:5), and testing/evaluating prophecy was a continuation of the practice in the Old Testament (Deuteronomy 13:1-5; 18:20-22).[32] So what sets prophetesses apart from prophets? Women prophetesses in the New Testament did not prophesy publicly, just as the prophetesses in the Old Testament did not. Prophetesses only prophesied privately to small groups or individuals, not in public worship. Furthermore, prophecy was a revelatory gift and does not involve the public teaching of God's Word.

Patriarchy in the New Testament—the Household

The New Testament also continues the Old Testament practice of male covenantal headship in the home. The apostolic letters, particularly those of Paul, make clear that the husband is the "head" of the household, meaning he has authority over his wife (1 Corinthians 11:3; Ephesians 5:23). This includes the obligation to lead, provide for, protect, and honor his wife (Ephesians 5:25; 1 Peter 3:7). The wife is commanded to "submit" to her husband (Ephesians 5:22, 24; Colossians 3:18; 1 Peter 3:1). Just as a father had covenantal headship over his daughters that was transferred to a woman's husband in marriage (Numbers 30), so Paul teaches that a husband has covenantal authority over his wife. The New Testament teaching on the family emphasizes the man's leadership role.

---

32. For a fuller treatment of this issue, see the discussion of 1 Corinthians 14:34-35 in chapter 9.

Paul even says that the family unit comes from God the Father—"For this reason I bow my knees before the Father, from whom every family in heaven and on earth is named" (Ephesians 3:14-15). This is a play on words, as Paul declares that every "family" [πατριά, *patria*] in heaven and on earth is named after God the "Father" [πατέρα, *patera*]. This word for "family" is used only two other times in the New Testament, to refer to the house and "lineage" [πατριᾶς] of David (Luke 2:4) and in the quotation of God's promise to Abraham, "And in your offspring shall all the families [αἱ πατριαί] of the earth be blessed" (Acts 3:25). Interestingly, Peter here quotes the Septuagint of Genesis 22:18 but uses the word πατριά instead of ἔθνος (*ethnos*, "nations"). This makes sense, as nations are but collections of families. God is the source of all peoples, all families, and all nations.

The New Testament also uses the important language of sonship for believers. God is our Father, and we are His sons. As Paul says, "[F]or in Christ Jesus you are all sons [υἱοί, *huioi*] of God through faith" (Galatians 3:26). And because we are sons, God has given us the "Spirit of his son" and made us heirs (Galatians 4:6-7; cf. Romans 8:14; 9:26). Though Christians are also "children" of God (John 1:12; Philippians 2:15), sonship in particular emphasizes the firstborn status we have in Christ. The ancient world practiced primogeniture, where the firstborn son received all the inheritance rights from the father. That is what Christians receive from God the Father.

The Historical Witness of Patriarchy

It is sometimes asserted that women held positions of leadership in the early church. For example, former U.S. president Jimmy Carter (1977–1981) claimed, "During the years of the early Christian church women served as deacons, priests, bishops, apostles, teachers and prophets. It wasn't until the fourth century that dominant Christian leaders, all men, twisted and distorted Holy Scriptures to perpetuate their ascendant positions within the religious hierarchy." [33]

---

33. Jimmy Carter, "Losing My Religion for Equality," *The Age* (July 15, 2009),

As we have seen, this could not be further from the truth. The apostles were all men, and the Bible explicitly forbids women from serving as teachers and pastors/elders. So the early church could only have had women leaders if they abandoned Paul's teachings. Further, this was just not the case that women were church leaders in the first three centuries. Jimmy Carter assumes the erroneous claims of feminist "scholarship."

While the Scriptures are our highest authority, proper interpretation and practice can be aided by the history of the church. And the fact is that the church practiced patriarchy up until the modern era. The early church inherited the teachings of the apostles, and this was passed on through the medieval church and the Reformers. No major theologian of the early church, medieval, and Reformation periods endorsed female clergy or argued against male headship in the home. Male headship and male clergy were assumed, in large part because of the clarity of the Bible on these matters.

The great theologians affirmed gender hierarchy and spoke of men having superiority.[34] Keep in mind that they use the terms "superior" and "inferior" to refer to authority and rank, just as the Westminster Larger Catechism of 1647 does to speak of authority under the Fifth Commandment, including the marriage relationship.[35] Man having "superiority" does not mean he has greater value or worth than woman. The Patriarch of Constantinople, John Chrysostom (c. 349–407), commenting on 1 Timothy 2:11-14, says the fact that God made man first and woman for man shows man's "superiority," as God "wishes the man to have the preeminence in every way."[36]

---

https://www.theage.com. au/politics/federal/losing-my-religion-for-equality-20090714-dk0v.html.

34. While I do not support all his conclusions, for a survey of Christian thought on patriarchy, see Kevin Giles, *The Trinity and Subordinationism: The Doctrine of God and the Contemporary Gender Debate* (Downers Grove, IL: InterVarsity, 2002), 145–155.

35. See WLC 123–133. WLC 118 refers to "governors of families" as "superiors," and WLC 129 implies marriage is a superior-inferior relationship when it speaks of "protecting" and "providing."

36. John Chrysostom, *The Homilies of John Chrysostom, Archbishop of*

The great Reformer John Calvin (1509–1564), commenting on 1 Corinthians 11:7-10, says that Paul in 11:7 speaks "of the distinction, which God has conferred upon the man, so as to have superiority over the woman. In this superior order of dignity the glory of God is seen, as it shines forth in every kind of superiority." Commenting on 11:8-9, Calvin says, "He establishes by two arguments the pre-eminence, which he had assigned to men above women. The first is, that as the woman derives her origin from the man, she is therefore inferior in rank. The second is, that as the woman was created for the sake of the man, she is therefore subject to him, as the work ultimately produced is to its cause. That the man is the beginning of the woman and the end for which she was made, is evident from the law."[37] In requiring women to cover their heads in 1 Corinthians 11:10, Calvin says that Paul looks "to God's eternal law, which has made the female sex subject to the authority of men. On this account all women are born, that they may acknowledge themselves inferior in consequence of the superiority of the male sex."[38]

The Scottish Reformer John Knox (1513–1572), citing 1 Corinthians 11:8-10, says of women rulers, "It is manifestly repugnant that any woman shall reign or bear dominion over man. For God first by the order of his creation, and after by the curse and malediction pronounced against the woman, by the reason of her rebellion, has pronounced the contrary . . . woman in her greatest perfection was made to serve and obey man, not to rule and command him."[39]

William Gouge (1575–1653), an English Puritan minister and member of the Westminster Assembly, taught that the husband's authority is rooted in natural law and that such authority must be embraced by

---

Constantinople, on the Epistles of St. Paul the Apostle to Timothy, Titus, and Philemon (ed. Philip Schaff; Oxford, 1843).

37. John Calvin, *Commentary on the Epistles of Paul the Apostle to the Corinthians*, vol 1, 357–358.

38. Ibid., 358.

39. John Knox, *The First Blast of the Trumpet Against the Monstrous Regiment of Women* (ed. Edward Arber; London, 1880), 18. I modernized the old English spelling here.

the wife. In his book *Of Domesticall Duties* (1622), he says, "Nature has honored the male over the female, so that where they are linked together in one yoke, it is given by nature that he should govern, and she obey. This the pagans observed by light of nature . . . Until a wife is fully instructed there and truly persuaded of it, no duty can be performed by her as it ought, for submission has relation to higher rank and authority."[40]

Matthew Henry (1662–1714), the renowned Bible commentator, says in his commentary on 1 Corinthians 11:3 that man has "superiority and headship" and woman should be "in subjection and not assume or usurp the man's place." Thus "she should have a mind suited to her rank, and not do any thing that looks like an affection of changing places."[41]

Even C.S. Lewis included male headship in marriage as a Christian essential in his 1952 book *Mere Christianity*, saying, "The need for some head follows from the idea that marriage is permanent . . . If marriage is permanent, one or other party must, in the last resort, have the power of deciding the family policy." As to why the man is the head, he asks, "[I]s there any very serious wish that it should be the woman? . . . There must be something unnatural about the rule of wives over husbands, because the wives themselves are half ashamed of it and despise the husbands whom they rule."[42]

Embracing Patriarchy

The Bible is a patriarchal book. Scripture teaches that a man rules his family—a husband has authority over his wife, and a father has authority over his children. The passages are really quite clear. And the church has recognized this throughout its history, at least until the modern period.

---

40. William Gouge, *Building a Godly Home: A Holy Vision for a Happy Marriage*, vol 2 (eds. Scott Brown and Joel R. Beeke; Grand Rapids, MI: Reformation Heritage Books, 2013), 101–102. This book is a modernization of Gouge's words found in *Of Domesticall Duties*, treatise 3.

41. Matthew Henry, *Commentary on the Whole Bible*, vol 6, https://ccel.org/ccel/henry/mhc6/mhc6.iCor. xii.html.

42. C.S. Lewis, *Mere Christianity* (New York: HarperSanFrancisco, 1980), 113.

Christian feminists will do anything they can to wiggle their way out of these passages, but their attempts are futile. The Bible speaks plainly that a husband has God-given authority over his wife, and parents have God-given authority over their children (and fathers as head of the household have a particular authority over the children). God has given us authority structures in this world, with Himself at the top. He has given civil governments authority over citizens, pastors authority over church members, husbands authority over wives, and parents authority over children. These authority structures are for our good. Someone must rule, and God has assigned this task to men.

The authority structures of the family are *covenantal*, in that they involve the God-ordained relationship of marriage. God has designed men and women differently from one another, and He brings them together in marriage. Both are made in the image of God and thus have equal value and worth (Genesis 1:27), but they do not have equal roles and duties. The Bible does not teach a functional (or mechanical) egalitarianism. A man has covenantal authority over his wife and is to protect and provide for his wife and children. A woman, on the other hand, is to submit to her husband's leadership and care for her children (Titus 2:5).

Christians should therefore affirm patriarchy. You can call it "broad complementarianism" or whatever else you want. The point is that Scripture is clear that God has given men the responsibility to rule in society. Men have authority over their wives, and some particularly gifted men are to serve as pastors of churches and others as political leaders.

Sadly, the modern church has traded the biblical worldview of patriarchy for that of our matriarchal and effeminate culture. The Bible calls for men to rule their households, the church, and society. Men are supposed to protect and provide for their families, which puts their wives in a place of honor. Feminism is rebellion against such God-given authority, and it has resulted in women acting like men and men acting like women. Without godly male rule, we are left with single mothers, fatherless children, promiscuity, cohabitation, abortion, rape, women "pastors," political correctness, and a father-usurping government that has duped people into thinking it will fix all our woes. Let us cast off such foolishness and restore our society to the rule of fathers.

Chapter 5

GENDER ROLES IN THE CREATION ORDER

IT IS GOOD and right to devote an entire chapter (or two) to the creation account on a theological topic, and this is especially the case for gender roles. As the saying goes, all good theology starts in Genesis. And God has much to say to us about man and woman in Genesis 1–3.

One of the reasons it is so important to go back to the creation account is that interpreters today commonly assert that the Bible's teaching on gender roles is "cultural." Thus, Paul's clear teachings are obscured by this appeal to him being a mere product of his environment. This practice provides feminists a way out. For even if they cannot make a convincing textual argument in their favor, they can always dismiss Paul as a "sexist" and reject his teaching as being based on the "oppressive" culture of his day. The "evangelical" feminists will tone down the criticism by wrapping this claim in the language of redemption.

But this will not work if Paul's teaching on men and women is based on the creation account, as creation is not bound to culture or environment. Adam and Eve lived before sin entered the world. And what God says about man and woman before the fall indicates that it is part of His design. If God gave Adam authority over his wife at creation, then this authority cannot be attributed to sin or culture. It is rooted in God's design, and it is good.

The Glory of Man and Woman

Let us begin by looking at the image of God in Genesis 1. At the beginning of creation, God made humans as two different sexes, male and female:

> So God created man in his own image, in the image of God he created him; male and female he created them (Genesis 1:27).

The word "man" [אָדָם, *adam*] is used generically here to refer to humans. In fact, God named mankind "man" [אָדָם] after Adam, not Eve— "When God created man, he made him in the likeness of God. Male and female he created them, and he blessed them and named them Man when they were created" (Genesis 5:1-2). However, we know that "man" in the image and likeness of God includes both men and women because of the words "male and female he created them" in both Genesis 1:27 and 5:2. Both men and women are made in God's image, and since the image of God is tied with rule over creation, this means *both men and women have authority over creation.*

That God created humans to rule over His creation is clear from the context of Genesis 1:26-28 and the double command to "have dominion"—"Let us make man in our image, after our likeness. And let them have dominion . . . And God said to them, 'Be fruitful and multiply and fill the earth and subdue it, and have dominion . . .'" (1:26, 28). The description of man being made in God's image is sandwiched between the two dominion references. Together a man and woman carry out this dominion mandate through marriage and reproduction. This is sometimes known as the Cultural Mandate. Even this command assumes differing gender roles based on the different bodies and reproductive roles of men and women.

God's creation of humanity was the pinnacle of his creative work. At the end of each day of creation, God pronounced it as "good" (Genesis 1:4, 10, 12, 18, 21, 25). However, after the creation of the man, God said it was "not good" that he was alone (2:18). Then after the creation of the woman, God said it was "*very* good" (1:31). Thus, the situation went from "good" to "not good" to "very good." And this state of "very good" resulted from *the creation of woman.*

Woman is the crown of creation. She is a "helper" fit for man (Genesis 2:18), and together men and women marry, have children, and rule over creation. This marital relationship is bound by covenant (Malachi 2:14), and though woman was "taken out of" man, they are joined together in a "one flesh" relationship (Genesis 2:23-24). God intended men and women to be kings and queens, crowning them with "glory and honor" and giving them "dominion" over all of creation (Psalm 8:5-6). As the proverb says, "An excellent wife is the crown of her husband" (Proverbs 12:4).

Thus, we see from creation that both men and women are made in God's image and are part of God's good creation. Men and women share equal worth before God. But they are also different. These differences are most apparent in the physical differences between men and women. But contrary to much modern thought, these physical and biological differences affect a person's *entire being*. Men and women have different bodies, minds, personalities,[1] and dispositions. Another way of saying this is that *men and women have different natures*. And from these differing natures flow differing functions. God has designed men and women differently, and He has designed them to relate to one another differently.

So while the Bible affirms that men and women are equal in worth and value, it explicitly *rejects natural and functional equality*. God has designed men and women to rule over creation together, but this rule consists of different relations and roles in human relationships (marriage, church, and society). As we will see, a husband has authority over his wife, and such authority is tied with tasks assigned by God. What are often called "gender roles" are not mere social expressions but are tasks and duties rooted in nature and creation.

---

1. There is increasing scientific literature establishing the personality differences between men and women. See Scott Barry Kaufman, "Taking Sex Differences in Personality Seriously," *ScientificAmerican.com* (December 12, 2019), https://blogs.scientificamerican.com/beautiful-minds/taking-sex-differences-in-personality-seriously/.

God's Roles for Man at Creation (Genesis 2:15)

Man's primary roles are seen in the following verse from Genesis 2:

> The LORD God took the man and put him in the garden of Eden to work it and keep it (Genesis 2:15).

After Yahweh formed Adam from the ground, He planted a garden in Eden and put Adam in that garden (Genesis 2:7-8). As seen from 2:15, God gave Adam two tasks: (1) *work* the garden; and (2) *keep* the garden. Work and keep. These tasks go hand in hand, but they can also be distinguished. The word for "work" is from the Hebrew עבד (*avad*) and can also mean "serve." The word is later used for religious service to God (e.g. Deuteronomy 4:19), including service at the tabernacle (Numbers 4:23-24, 26).

The man's work in Genesis 2 is connected with the land and food. Genesis 2:5 says there was "no man to work the ground." But when the man was formed, God planted a "garden" and made trees to spring up that were "good for food" (Genesis 2:8-9). After the description of man's task to "work" the ground in 2:15, God spoke to Adam about eating food—"You may surely *eat* of every tree of the garden, but of the tree of the knowledge of good and evil you shall not *eat*, for in the day that you *eat* of it you shall surely die" (2:16-17).

The word for "keep" is from the Hebrew שמר (*shamar*) and can also mean to "guard" (cf. Genesis 4:9; 30:31).[2] "Guard" is probably the better translation in Genesis 2:15 when we consider that there was an intruder in the garden, the serpent (3:1), whom Adam should have destroyed. Further, this word is used by several translations (ESV, NASB, NET) in 3:24 when the cherubim and a flaming sword were placed to "guard"

---

2. Victor P. Hamilton, *The Book of Genesis: Chapters 1–17* (The New International Commentary on the Old Testament; Grand Rapids, MI: Eerdmans), 171: "The basic meaning of this root is 'to exercise great care over,' to the point, if necessary, of guarding . . . The garden is something to be protected more than it is something to be possessed."

the tree of life. Like עבד (*avad*), the word שמר (*shamar*) is often used in a religious context, such as for "keeping" God's covenant and statutes (Genesis 17:9; Leviticus 18:5) and "guarding" the tabernacle (Numbers 1:53; 3:7-8). The word is also used in Aaron's prayer for Yahweh to "bless you and keep you" [וְיִשְׁמְרֶךָ], surely a reference to God's protection of His people (Numbers 6:24).

These two Hebrew words are also used together to describe the role of the priests in the temple (Numbers 3:7-8; 8:26; 18:5-6). The role of the Levites as "guards" is seen throughout the book of Numbers—"And the Levites shall keep guard over the tabernacle of the testimony" (Numbers 1:53). There are significant parallels in the language used for Adam's duty in the garden and the Levites' duty in the tabernacle.[3] Just as God put Adam in the garden to "work/serve" and "keep/guard" it (Genesis 2:15), so the Levites were told to "serve" and "guard" the sanctuary of the tabernacle/temple:

> And Yahweh God took the man and put him in the garden of Eden to serve it and guard it [לְעָבְדָהּ וּלְשָׁמְרָהּ] (Genesis 2:15, author's translation).
>
> And they [the Levites] shall guard [וְשָׁמְרוּ] all the furnishings of the tent of meeting and guard [מִשְׁמֶרֶת] the sons of Israel as they serve [לַעֲבֹד אֶת־עֲבֹדַת] the tabernacle (Numbers 3:8, author's translation).

The similar use of language suggests that the garden of Eden was a temple of God and that Adam had a priestly role. God's presence was in the garden, and like the Levites, Adam was to serve God there and protect

---

3. An excellent example of a Levite guarding God's worship is found in Numbers 25:6-8, where Phinehas (Aaron's grandson) stopped God's plague by spearing an Israelite man and a Midianite woman in the "chamber" (קֻבָּה, *qubbah*). This could refer to part of the family tent or the tabernacle area. The latter is suggested by the context of the tent of meeting and the whole assembly in 25:6. Either way, because of Phinehas' zeal for the worship of Yahweh (recalling the Levites in Exodus 32), God gave him the "covenant of perpetual priesthood" (Numbers 25:13).

His worship from enemies. Adam should have guarded the temple-garden from the intruder serpent, just as the Levites were to guard the tabernacle/temple from idolaters.

Man's Role to Provide Affirmed Post-Fall

Thus we see that God gave man the tasks to *provide* and *protect*. When understood in relation to his wife, Adam was to work the garden to bring forth food to feed his family and guard the garden in order to protect his wife who was there with him. Adam failed in both these areas, as he and his wife ate from the forbidden tree and he failed to prevent the serpent from entering the garden, who in turn deceived Eve into eating from the tree of the knowledge of good and evil (Genesis 3:1-6). One of the most damning details of the account is where it says Adam was "with" Eve when she ate from the forbidden tree (Genesis 3:6). Adam did nothing while the serpent deceived his wife and she took from the forbidden tree. He then followed her in sinning against God by eating the fruit.

Since one of Adam's primary tasks was to work, it should come as no surprise that God punished him *in the area of work*. As part of the judgment for his sin, man will now work by "pain" and "sweat." God said to Adam:

> Because you have listened to the voice of your wife and have eaten of the tree of which I commanded you, "You shall not eat of it," cursed is the ground because of you; *in pain you shall eat of it all the days of your life*; thorns and thistles it shall bring forth for you; and you shall eat the plants of the field. *By the sweat of your face you shall eat bread*, till you return to the ground, for out of it you were taken; for you are dust, and to dust you shall return (Genesis 3:17-19).

Notice two things. First, God does not *curse* man. He only curses the ground (and the serpent; 3:14). God *punishes* Adam and Eve. There is a difference. Second, Adam's work of the land is connected with food. Just as Adam's "work" in Genesis 2:15 is connected with "eating" in 2:16-17, so God connects the two in Adam's judgment. Since Adam sinned in eating, it would now be harder for Adam to eat. Adam's work would be far less pleasant than in the garden. Now he would eat of the ground "in pain" and eat bread "by the sweat" of his face (3:17, 19).

This punishment does not change God's given duty for man to work and provide for his family. Adam's task would continue, though it would be harder in the fallen world. Yahweh also "sent Adam out from the garden of Eden to work the ground from which he was taken" (Genesis 3:23). Banished from the garden, God now sent Adam to work the ground *outside* the garden.

This should be sufficient to establish man's God-given role to provide for his family through work. Though many men are no longer farmers, they still fulfill the role of working to provide food for themselves and their families. Paul urged Christians to work with their hands (1 Thessalonians 4:11), and he said, "If anyone is not willing to work, let him not eat" (2 Thessalonians 3:10). There are other passages in Scripture that speak of a man providing for his family. Though a case law dealing with a second wife, Exodus 21:10 requires the husband to provide food and clothing for his wife—"he shall not diminish her food, her clothing, or her marital rights." Turning to the New Testament, the Apostle Paul says,

> But if anyone does not provide for his relatives, and especially for members of his household, he has denied the faith and is worse than an unbeliever (1 Timothy 5:8).

Paul's reference to "anyone" certainly includes men, but it likely refers to men specifically, as it comes in the context of the role of widows who no longer have husbands to provide for them (1 Timothy 5:3-16). The entire passage is predicated on men providing for their wives, with widows being left in a vulnerable position because they no longer have a husband, particularly in ancient societies. Paul literally speaks of someone providing for "his own, and especially his household" [τῶν ἰδίων καὶ μάλιστα οἰκείων]. (The ESV uses the word "relatives" to clarify "his own.")

So Paul in 1 Timothy 5:8 is saying that someone must provide for his own "household." And who is *head* of that household? That would be the man. Paul is placing this particular responsibility of provision on men. A man is the "head" of his wife (Ephesians 5:23) and has authority over her (Numbers 30:6-8). The language of 1 Timothy 5:8 is similar to that of Paul's requirements for elders and shows he has a man in mind. In his requirements for a pastor/elder, Paul requires a man to "manage his own household well" [τοῦ ἰδίου οἴκου καλῶς προϊστάμενον] (1 Timothy 3:4). While some argue elders could be women here, we know Paul is speaking of only men since he requires an elder to be a "man of one woman" [μιᾶς γυναικὸς ἄνδρα] (1 Timothy 3:2). This is not a gender-neutral way to include women, as Paul later requires a widow to be a "woman of one man" [ἑνὸς ἀνδρὸς γυνή] (1 Timothy 5:9; Titus 1:6). These are not inclusive descriptions but refer to positions reserved exclusively for men (elder) and women (widow). Thus, Paul's requirement that "someone" provide for his family in 1 Timothy 5:8 is particularly aimed at men.

Man's Role to Protect Affirmed Post-Fall

Men are also supposed to *protect* their families. This does not come up as much in Genesis 3 as the role to provide, other than Adam's failure to carry out his Genesis 2:15 task to "guard" the garden from the serpent (3:1-6). However, later Scriptures do speak of a man's task to protect his wife. That a man is "head" of his wife means that he has covenantal authority over her, and that carries with it covenant responsibilities (1 Corinthians 11:3; Ephesians 5:23). A husband is supposed to love his wife "as Christ loved the church and gave himself up for her" (Ephesians 5:25), which means that a husband must be willing to even *die for his wife*. This obligation to protect is why only men served as soldiers throughout the Old Testament. God appointed men, not women, to go to war and fight for

Israel (Numbers 1:2-3; Deuteronomy 22:5; see chapter 11). Men put their lives on the line for their wives and children.

Both roles of a man to protect and provide are also referenced by God in His description as the father of the fatherless and the husband to Israel. Deuteronomy 10:18 says of God, "He executes justice for the fatherless and the widow, and loves the sojourner, giving him food and clothing." This verse speaks of the provision of food and clothing, as well as protection by executing justice. Psalm 68:5 says that God is the "Father of the fatherless and protector of widows." Orphans and widows were vulnerable in the ancient world (and still are today), and God acts like a father and husband to them by providing and protecting. Also, Jeremiah 31:32 speaks of a new covenant, "not like the covenant that I made with their fathers on the day when I took them by the hand to bring them out of the land of Egypt, my covenant that they broke, though I was their husband, declares the LORD." God's provision and protection of Israel as their husband implies these are the proper roles of a man.

These manly roles to protect and provide are wrapped up in man's nature. Men are physically stronger than women (1 Peter 3:7), and they are not hindered from work by pregnancy and nursing (Titus 2:4-5). Biology matters when it comes to gender roles and life tasks. But so does the order of creation, as the Apostle Paul bases the prohibition of women teaching and exercising authority over men in the church on Adam being "formed first" (1 Timothy 2:12-13).

What this comes down to is that God has designed men to lead. A man has authority over his wife, and with that authority comes the responsibilities to love, protect, and provide for her (Ephesians 5:22-33). It is for this reason that Adam was held accountable for Eve's sin. Though both Adam and Eve took from the forbidden tree, God first only called for the man (the "you" in Genesis 3:9 is singular). The standard for a godly man is that he "manage his household well" and keep "his children submissive" (1 Timothy 3:4). All of this is to be done in love, for the good of everyone involved. God gives men a position of authority, and with this comes great responsibility to provide for and protect their family members. Such leadership is to be exercised in whatever other spheres God places a man, including the church and civil government.

God's Roles for Woman at Creation (Genesis 2:18)

Unlike men, God has not given women the primary roles to provide and protect. That is not to say that a woman may not or should not protect her children or bring in any income. However, God has *primarily* given those tasks to men. Man's role in life was defined directly (Genesis 2:15). But to the great annoyance of feminists, God has defined woman's role in relation to man:

> Then the LORD God said, "It is not good that the man should be alone; I will make him a helper fit for him" (Genesis 2:18).

Prior to the creation of man, everything in creation was "good" (Genesis 1:4, 10, 12, 18, 21, 25). But now something is "not good" (2:18). It was not good for man to be by himself, so God made woman as a "helper" [עֵזֶר, *ezer*] for man. She is "fit for him" [כְּנֶגְדּוֹ, *kenegdo*], or literally "according to the opposite of him." The idea is that a woman complements a man. She supplies what a man lacks, and implicitly a man supplies what a woman lacks.

The knee-jerk reaction of feminists is to retort that "helper" [עֵזֶר] cannot mean woman is under man's authority (subordinate) since the word is also used to describe God as "helper" and God is not subordinate to humans. However, the analogy of God's role as a "helper" cannot be imported into woman's role as man's "helper" in Genesis 2:18 just because the word is used for both. Words can be used in different ways, and context is important. The word "helper" is used to refer to God's assistance (Exodus 18:4; Deuteronomy 33:7, 26, 29; Psalm 30:10; 33:20; 115:9-11; 124:8; 146:5), as well as military aid (Isaiah 30:5; Ezekiel 12:14; Hosea 13:9). The one being helped is inadequate on his own and needs assistance (Joshua 1:14; 10:4, 6; 1 Chronicles 12:17, 19, 21, 22). When the Bible speaks of God as man's "helper," it means He chooses to render assistance to humans.[4] But whereas God's helping role is voluntary, woman's is not. She has a duty to help her husband.

Feminists are worried that "helper" in Genesis 2:18 teaches that a woman is of inferior rank to her husband because she is under his authority. However, the main point of this verse is not that woman is under her husband's authority (though she is), but rather that God created woman to aid man. *Woman's very being is wrapped up in her role as a helper.* This is never said of man, though a man obviously helps his wife in other ways. And though God is a "helper" to His people, He is not a being created to help man. God is the creator and ruler of the world, whereas woman was created to help man. She was made for this very purpose.

What this means is that God did not create woman to pursue her own career path. Rather, God created woman to help man, the worker and keeper of the garden. Woman provides something to man that he did not have without her, including companionship and children. Man is inadequate alone. As the Apostle Paul says, "For man was not made from woman, but woman from man. Neither was man created for woman, but woman for man" (1 Corinthians 11:8-9). Man came from the ground and his labor is directed toward the ground. Woman came from the man and her labor is directed toward the man.

Now it should be noted that woman's role is not as explicit in Genesis 2 as it is for man in 2:15. However, it is not hard to see just how Eve was to "help" Adam. She was, of course, a companion for him, making him lonely no more. But her greatest role as helper was to *bear children*. As man and woman come together in marriage as "one flesh" (2:24), the woman, Lord willing, becomes pregnant and produces children. Together a man and woman thus fulfill God's command to "Be fruitful and multiply and fill the earth" (1:28). (Of course, this is a fallen world and some women may not be able to have children. They may want to consider adopting children in need of parents.)

It is for this reason that Adam called his wife Eve [חַוָּה, *hawah*],

---

4. Köstenberger and Köstenberger, *God's Design for Man and Woman*, 36.

"life-giver" in Hebrew, "because she was the mother of all living" (Genesis 3:20). Thus, we see that woman is *a life-giving creature*. Whereas man [אָדָם, *adam*] was named after the ground [אֲדָמָה, *adama*] from which he came, woman is named after her life-giving ability. (Adam actually named her twice, first as "woman" according to her nature in 2:24 and second as Eve according to her ability.) So the very names of the first humans are wrapped up in their roles. Adam was a worker, and Eve was a life-giver.

Woman's Roles Affirmed Post-Fall

When we seek to understand woman's role in relation to her husband, we see that God has given woman the tasks to *bear children* and *care for the home*. Bearing children does not mean just giving birth to children, as they must also be nursed and cared for. Further, a woman should help her husband by caring for the home, a task that becomes more explicit later in Scripture.

Since one of Eve's primary tasks was to bear children, it should come as no surprise that after she sinned by eating the forbidden fruit, God punished her *in the area of childbearing*. Women would still bear children, but it would be in "pain." God said to Eve:

> I will surely multiply your pain in childbearing; in pain you shall bring forth children. Your desire shall be contrary to your husband, but he shall rule over you (Genesis 3:16).

Just as God punished man with "pain" in his primary role to work and provide (Genesis 3:17), so God punished woman with "pain" in her primary role to bear children. Both will "labor" in pain (pun intended). However, this punishment does not change God's given task for woman to bear children. This important role is affirmed throughout Scripture, beginning with Eve bearing children after the fall (4:1-2, 25). Childbearing is called "the way of women" (Genesis 18:11), and it is seen as the central role of women throughout the Bible, from Sarah, Rebekah, and Rachel in Genesis to Elizabeth and Mary in the Gospels. As argued in chapter 2, the Apostle Paul speaks of "childbearing" as the thing most associated with womanhood, and thus godly women will seek to marry and have children (1 Timothy 2:15). Right before God pronounced the woman's pain in childbearing (Genesis 3:16), He foretold that the woman's "offspring" would bruise the head of the serpent (3:15). This connection should not be ignored, as it was through woman's bearing children in pain that the devil-crushing Messiah came. Childbirth is essential to the covenant.

However, a woman's task is not complete simply by birthing children. There is much work to do around the home in order to raise such children and support her husband as he seeks to provide for the family. Caring for the home is part of a woman's role as a helper to her husband. Thus, the Apostle Paul commands older women to train younger women "to love their husbands and children, to be self-controlled, pure, *working at home*, kind, and submissive to their husbands, that the word of God may not be reviled" (Titus 2:4-5). The Greek word for "working at home" [οἰκουργός, *oikourgos*] is a combination of the words for "home" and "work," and it is defined as "pert. to carrying out household responsibilities."[5] There is much work to do at home, and that is where godly women should focus their efforts.[6]

In his instructions for widows, Paul lists both childbearing and household management as tasks for wives—"I would have younger widows marry, bear children, *manage their households*, and give the adversary no occasion for slander" (1 Timothy 5:14). This verb for "manage their households," οἰκοδεσποτεῖν (*oikodespotein*), is similar to the adjective οἰκουργός in Titus 2:5, with both having the same root for home [οἶκος, *oikos*].

But does not Paul elsewhere speak of household management as a man's task? The answer is that there are different Greek words behind the household "management" of men and women. Paul uses the word

---

5. BDAG, 700.
6. Köstenberger and Köstenberger, *God's Design for Man and Woman*, 233: "This emphasizes the domestic sphere of activity as central for the woman. It means that she devotes her energies to running her household and managing her home."

προΐστημι (*proistemi*) for a man's "management" of the home, particularly in the context of elders in the church (1 Thessalonians 5:12; 1 Timothy 3:4-5, 12; 5:17). Whereas προΐστημι means "to exercise a position of leadership, *rule, direct, be at the head (of)*,"[7] the word for woman's management, οἰκοδεσποτέω in 1 Timothy 5:14, is domestic-oriented, meaning to "*manage one's household, keep house.*"[8]

Women and the Home

These passages do not prohibit a woman from working outside the home. However, they do teach that a woman's work is to be *primarily homeward*, which likely will not leave much time for work outside the home, especially as children are born. As anyone who has lived apart from their parents can attest, there is much important work to be done around the house (cooking, washing dishes, cleaning, laundry, etc.), and this drastically increases once a couple has children. This type of homemaking is exemplified in the poem about the "excellent wife" in Proverbs 31. She takes care of the home by making sure her family eats (Proverbs 31:14-16) and is clothed (31:19-24). She even sells merchandise, showing that a homemaker can contribute income to the family (31:18). However, this is not done to the neglect of her other household duties.

These womanly roles to bear children and care for the home are wrapped up in woman's nature. Biologically, women bear children in the womb and nurse children with their breasts—an inconvenient fact for feminists who fight against such nature. But nature cannot be separated from role and function. Men have bodies suited for work, particularly physical labor, and women have bodies suited for raising children. These are not roles to be rejected but differences to be celebrated.

Essentially what this comes down to is that God designed women to be *helpers* to their husbands. The Apostle Paul affirms this when he says that man was *not* "created for woman, but woman for man" (1 Corinthians

---

7. BDAG, 870.
8. Ibid., 695.

11:9). As one under the authority of her husband, a woman is to help him by bearing children and caring for the home. In doing so, a woman complements her husband's role as a leader who protects and provides for his family. Of course, this implies that a woman needs to *be protected* and *provided for*, just as a man needs a helper to bear children and care for the home. A husband is to meet these needs of his wife, love her (Ephesians 5:25), be gentle with her (Colossians 3:19), and live with her in an "understanding way, showing honor to the woman as the weaker vessel" (1 Peter 3:7). A woman is to respond properly to her husband's leadership by showing him "respect" (Ephesians 5:33).

This is not to say women have no authority of their own. Rather, both men and women have authority over creation, with man having preeminence. The woman's function is "to be a help-meet to man in the exercise of his dominion and authority." She provides "companionship in his calling" and thus there is a "community in authority." But the woman still has real authority. She is comparable to what a prime minister is to a king, still holding authority herself, but being under the authority of another.[9]

Creation Transcends Culture

That gender roles are grounded in the creation order means they are not merely cultural. Rather, gender roles transcend culture, as they are rooted in God's design and the differing natural consistencies of men and women. It will not do to appeal to cultural influences in explaining why Paul commands wives to submit to their husbands in Ephesians 5 or why he prohibits women pastors in 1 Timothy 2. In fact, Paul explicitly appeals to creation as the basis for why women cannot teach or hold positions

---

9. R.J. Rushdoony, *The Institutes of Biblical Law*, 164: "the authority of the woman as help-meet is no less real than that of a prime minister to a king; the prime minister is not a slave because he is not king, nor is the woman a slave because she is not a man. The description of a virtuous woman, or a godly wife, in Proverbs 31:10-31 is not of a helpless slave nor of a pretty parasite, but rather of a competent wife, manager, business-woman, and mother—a person of real authority."

of authority over men in the church—"For Adam was formed first, not Eve" (1 Timothy 2:13). Gender roles may be expressed in different ways in different cultures. But all cultures must demand that men—as those having covenantal authority in marriage—protect and provide for their wives. And all cultures must demand that women—as givers of life and helpers to their husbands—bear and raise children. This is what nature teaches, and it is good.

Chapter 6

HIERARCHY AND AUTHORITY IN THE CREATION ORDER

AS OUR EXAMINATION of the creation account has shown thus far, God gave men the roles to provide and protect and women the roles to bear children and aid their husbands. These roles are expanded upon and affirmed throughout Scripture. But the key is that *gender roles are rooted in creation*. God gave these duties *before* the fall. They are part of the ideal, the original design. God made creation good, and therefore these gender roles rooted in creation are good, though the fall introduced strife into the roles of both men and women.

But what about male authority? Is hierarchy part of the creation order, or did it enter the world as a result of sin? This is an important issue, as many egalitarians hold that hierarchy in the marriage relationship was not part of creation but was introduced at the fall in Genesis 3:16. Egalitarians then argue that unity in Christ overcomes male authority and we must return to the creation ideal of non-hierarchical marriage.

Does Creation Teach Hierarchy in Marriage?

We will begin with the common arguments for hierarchy in the creation order, followed by the egalitarian response. Many complementarian works contend that Adam had authority over Eve prior to the fall based on the following points:

1. Adam was created first (Genesis 2:7, 18-23; 1 Timothy 2:13).
2. Eve was created as a helper for Adam (Genesis 2:18; 1 Corinthians 11:9).
3. Adam named Eve (Genesis 2:23; 3:20).
4. God named humanity after Adam (Genesis 5:1-2; cf. 1:26).
5. Adam represented the human race in the garden (Romans 5:12-21; 1 Corinthians 15:22, 45-49).[1]

Thus, there are three arguments based on Adam's relation to Eve and two arguments based on God's declaration of Adam as representative of humanity. In addition to these five points, complementarians argue that prior to God's judgment in Genesis 3:16, God first called Adam to account even though Eve sinned first (Genesis 3:6, 9), showing that God held Adam to be the marital authority responsible for Eve's actions (more on this below). Yet egalitarians dispute these points, arguing that they do not teach hierarchy and male headship at creation. This rejection is essential to the egalitarian position, for if Adam had authority over his wife prior to Genesis 3:16, then that is the creation ideal and not something from the fall to be overcome.

Here we will interact with the arguments of egalitarian Old Testament scholar Richard Davidson because he presents one of the strongest cases for the position that Adam did not have authority over Eve prior to the fall. In his book *Flame of Yahweh: Sexuality in the Old Testament*, Davidson affirms the New Testament's teaching that a husband has authority over his wife, but he argues this hierarchy is rooted in the fall, where God said to Eve, "Your desire shall be for your husband, and he shall rule over you" (Genesis 3:16). According to Davidson, the fall exposed women to subjection to

---

1. Wayne Grudem gives 10 arguments supporting male headship before the fall, but the latter four are related more to his broader argument. Grudem, *Countering the Claims of Evangelical Feminism*, 21–22, 72; Grudem, *Evangelical Feminism and Biblical Truth*, 109.

their husbands. Thus, Davidson can still affirm Paul's teaching that wives should submit to husbands (Ephesians 5:22), but he says this was not part of the original creation. Davidson reasons from this that, despite Paul's commands, husbands and wives should seek the egalitarian ideal (thus placing his position firmly in the egalitarian camp).[2]

In order to make his case for creational egalitarianism, Davidson first responds to arguments for creational hierarchy. Davidson rejects point 4 above that God's naming humanity after Adam in Genesis 5:1-2 teaches hierarchy. Davidson says that the Hebrew word אָדָם (*adam*) "never means 'man' (in the sense or implication of male gender) in Scripture." He continues, "The problem is a modern language translation issue, not an aspect of the Hebrew text. The word *adam* is a generic term meaning 'human person' or 'humanity.' Aside from Gen 1–3, where it refers to the first human person, Adam, this term is never in the whole HB [Hebrew Bible] used to designate a 'man' in the sense of male (as opposed to female). The use of *adam* does not whisper male headship as a creation ordinance."[3]

However, Davidson fails to adequately represent this argument. The point is that the word אָדָם (*adam*) is used for the first man, Adam, in Genesis 1–3, and then God names mankind after him in Genesis 5:1-2. Yes, the Hebrew אָדָם (*adam*) is a generic term for humanity, but Genesis 5:2 says that God created them "male and female" and "named them Man [אָדָם]." And the very next verse uses the word אָדָם to refer to Adam specifically, who "lived 130 years" and "fathered a son in his own likeness, after his image" (Genesis 5:3). In other words, both the first man and the human race share the same name, "man/Adam." This is not the case for woman.

---

2. Richard Davidson, *Flame of Yahweh: Sexuality in the Old Testament* (Peabody, MA: Hendrickson, 2007), 643: "The ultimate ideal for husband-wife relations is still the partnership of equals that is set forth from the beginning in Genesis 2:24: 'they become one flesh' (quoted in Eph 5:31). By citing Genesis 2:24 in the larger context of a call for mutual submission (Eph 5:21), Paul implicitly issues a divine redemptive invitation offering enabling power to return as much as possible to the pre-fall total egalitarianism in the marriage relationship, without denying the validity of the servant leadership principle as it may be needed in a sinful world to preserve unity and harmony in the home."

3. Ibid., 23–24.

This supports the view that God at creation gave men a leadership role over women. This argument is further supported by point 5 above that Adam, not Eve, represented all humans in the garden and all fell in him (Romans 5:12-21). Unfortunately, Davidson never mentions this point.

Davidson focuses his treatment of hierarchy in creation on arguments found in Genesis 2. He summarizes what he considers to be the five arguments for a creation order teaching a "hierarchical ranking of the sexes" in Genesis 2:

1. "Man is created first and woman last" (Genesis 2:7, 22).
2. "Man, not woman, is spoken to by God and does the speaking" (2:16-17, 23).
3. "Woman is formed for the sake of man, to be his 'partner'" (2:18-20).
4. "Woman is created from man's rib" (2:21-22).
5. "The man names the woman" (2:23).[4]

Thus, Davidson adds two additional arguments to the hierarchical arguments cited above, that God spoke to man (point 2) and that woman was created from Adam's rib (point 4). These are weaker arguments for hierarchy in creation, which is why I did not mention them above and why many complementarians also do not make use of them.

After attempting to refute each of the five points he cites, Davidson concludes, "The man and the woman before the fall are presented as fully equal in rank, with no hint of an ontological or functional hierarchy, no leadership/submission relationship between husband and wife."[5] However, while Davidson raises some valid points, his reasoning contains five problems.

First, Davidson's criticism of point 1 (that Adam being created first teaches hierarchy) undermines Paul's reasoning in 1 Timothy 2:13. Davidson says, "[T]he *sequence* of man's and woman's creation has no significance for implications of the society's view of or assumptions regarding

---

4. Ibid., 27.
5. Ibid., 34–35.

hierarchy."[6] However, Davidson's claim is in direct contradiction to the Apostle Paul, who prohibits women from teaching and exercising authority in the church on that basis ("for") that "Adam was formed first, then Eve" (1 Timothy 2:13). Paul thought the creation order had implications for hierarchy, both for marriage and the church at large. (Davidson thinks 1 Timothy 2 only applies to marriage, but the point still stands.)

Second, Davidson's argument against point 2 (that God speaking only to Adam teaches hierarchy) fails to account for Adam's teaching role regarding the prohibition of eating from the tree of the knowledge of good and evil. God spoke the prohibition only to Adam because Eve had not yet been created. Yet we know that Eve was aware of the prohibition, seen in her response to the serpent—"We may eat of the fruit of the trees in the garden, but God said, 'You shall not eat of the fruit of the tree that is in the midst of the garden, neither shall you touch it, lest you die'" (Genesis 3:2-3). We do not know how Eve became aware of this prohibition, whether it was from God directly or from Adam. However, it is likely that Adam taught her the Law (the prohibition), since Adam was given the task to "guard" the garden (2:15) and this was directly followed by God's command not to eat of the forbidden tree (2:16-17). There is no record God ever restated this prohibition. Thus, Adam likely had a teaching role, which implies authority over Eve. Teaching is an authoritative task.

Third, Davidson's argument against points 3 and 4 (that Eve being created for and from Adam teaches hierarchy) undermines Paul's reasoning in 1 Corinthians 11:2-16. Davidson asserts that "ezer kenegdo ['helper fit for him'] in no way implies a male leadership or female submission as part of the creation order" and that "derivation does not imply subordination."[7] Davidson and other egalitarians can dispute this point all they want, but they must still take up the conclusions of the Apostle Paul, who in 1 Corinthians 11:8-9 says that a woman is under male authority because she was made "from man" and "for man." Paul says that "the head of a

---

6. Ibid., 28; quoting Richard Hess, "Equality with and without Innocence: Genesis 1–3," in *Discovering Biblical Equality: Complementarity Without Hierarchy*, 85–86.

7. Ibid., 30.

wife [woman] is her husband [man]" (1 Corinthians 11:3) and she should therefore cover her physical head when praying or prophesying because she is under the authority of a metaphorical head (11:4-6, 10). But a man is not to cover his head because he is not under a woman's authority—"For man was not made from woman, but woman from man. Neither was man created for woman, but woman for man" (11:8-9). Thus, contrary to Davidson, Paul infers male headship and hierarchy from the fact that woman was created "from" and "for" Adam (see chapter 7 for more on this passage).

Fourth, Davidson's argument against point 5 (that Adam's naming of Eve teaches hierarchy) is weak. The case for hierarchy in naming appeals to Adam's naming of the animals in Genesis 2:19, but Davidson claims that Adam did not exercise authority over the animals in naming them but only "classified" them. However, the text says Adam actually *named* all the animals—"whatever the man called every living creature, that was its name" (2:19). It is hard to see how this is not understood as some sense of authority that God delegated to Adam over the animals. When it comes to naming Eve, Davidson says it is "most probable" that Adam did not name the woman before the fall because the designation "woman" [אִשָּׁה, *isha*] occurs in Genesis 2:22 prior to Adam meeting and naming her in 2:23.[8] However, the author of Genesis easily could have used the name that Adam provided in 2:23 to describe this newly formed creature in the previous verse. Davidson grants that Adam named his wife "Eve" in Genesis 3:20, but he says, "[E]ven there it is more probable that he is discerning what she already was by the promise of God, 'mother of all living' (3:20), and not exercising authority over her."[9] This borders on the absurd. Obviously, Adam "discerned" that Eve was the "mother of all living" or "life-giver" (the meaning of the Hebrew "Eve"). But is this not how naming often works? Parents throughout the Bible make discernments about their children (either of their behavior or God's works/words) and then exercise their parental authority by giving the child a name based on

---

8. Ibid., 33.
9. Ibid., 34.

that discernment (e.g. Genesis 25:25-26; 1 Samuel 1:20). Discerning and exercising authority are not mutually exclusive behaviors. Adam's naming of Eve supports the case that he had an authoritative role over her.

Fifth, Davidson fails to consider the argument that Adam's task to "guard" the garden (Genesis 2:15) gave him a protective role over his wife and thus establishes hierarchy. (Many complementarians also fail to make this point.) A protective role is tied with authority, seen throughout Scripture with a parent's authority over children, a husband's authority over his wife, and civil government's authority over citizens. Adam's task to guard his wife carried with it authority over his wife. Eve was never given this task to guard the garden.

Davidson is thus incorrect in concluding that there was no hierarchy before the fall. Adam had authority over Eve as her guardian, protector, and teacher. The Apostle Paul held that male headship and hierarchy are taught from the creation account, both in Adam being formed first and Eve being made "for" and "from" Adam. Further, God named mankind after the man and not the woman (Genesis 1:27; 5:1-2).

Adam's Authority over Eve in the Fall (Genesis 3)

Man's authority is not limited to creation in Genesis 2, but is also taught in the account of the fall in Genesis 3. Davidson thinks this hierarchy does not come until God's judgment of Eve in Genesis 3:16, but his analysis fails to account for God's actions throughout Genesis 3. Adam's authority over Eve is demonstrated in three ways in Genesis 3:

1. God went to Adam first after he and Eve sinned (Genesis 3:9) even though Eve sinned first (3:6).
2. God rebuked Adam for listening to Eve (3:17).
3. God only told Adam he would die (3:19), yet Eve also died.

That God went to Adam first after both Adam and Eve sinned shows that Adam had covenantal authority over and responsibility for Eve. God could have gone to Eve first or both at the same time, yet He went directly to Adam. God's action here cannot be attributed to the supposed introduction of hierarchy in the fall (Genesis 3:16), as this happened *before* that pronouncement and is thus part of God's design at creation.

As for God's rebuke of Adam for listening to Eve in Genesis 3:17 ("Because you have listened to the voice of your wife and have eaten of the tree of which I commanded you . . ."), the implication is that Adam was supposed to lead his wife, not be led by her. Though this rebuke by God comes after 3:16, it is not based in God's pronouncement of judgment there but points back to God's design at creation. Adam was not supposed to "obey" [שָׁמַעְתָּ, *shamata*] Eve but obey God. He was to instruct and guard her, not be instructed by her (and certainly not to sin!).

As for death as judgment, God only told Adam that he would die—"for you are dust, and to dust you shall return" (Genesis 3:19). This verse uses the singular "you" in Hebrew, and nowhere is Eve told that she would die. Even the original prohibition that promised death if Adam ate of the forbidden tree used the singular "you"—"in the day that you eat of it you shall surely die" (2:17). Yet when Eve repeated this to the serpent, she used the plural "you"—"You shall not eat . . . lest you die" (3:3). Assuming Adam taught Eve the prohibition, she certainly understood that eating meant death for her. The point is that in the pronouncement of judgment to Adam and Eve after their sin, God only told Adam he would die—yet Eve also died. This is because Adam represented Eve in the garden as her covenant head. Adam's death meant Eve's death.

This reading of Adam's authority in Genesis 3 is confirmed by the Apostle Paul's teaching that Adam, not Eve, represented humanity in the garden (Romans 5:12-21; 1 Corinthians 15:22). Adam had headship over all of his future posterity, and with his fall came the fall of all humans. Sin and death came into the world "through one man" (Romans 5:12), and "death reigned through that one man" (Romans 5:17). Humans are born sinful and die because of Adam's actions, not Eve's. Further, Paul says that "all" sinned in Adam and "all" were condemned in him (Romans 5:12, 18). This would include Eve. Therefore, Adam represented Eve in the garden as her covenant head.

Yet Davidson says that those who see hierarchy in Genesis 3:1-13 are "reading into the text what does not exist in the chapter, just as they have done in Genesis 1–2."[10] He provides seven reasons from the text as to why God's questioning Adam first (even though Eve sinned first) does not show that Adam had "representative authority" over Eve. However, most of these reasons do not actually explain why God questioned Adam first. In seeking to explain why God questioned Adam first, Davidson appeals to the fact that God only addressed Adam in the singular "you" (and not plural), that Adam only explained his own behavior and not Eve's, that God also summoned the woman to answer for herself, and that in this legal trial God must examine each witness.[11] But none of these points actually explains why God approached Adam first, and none undermines Adam's representative role. God's addressing Adam in the singular does not exclude Adam's accountability for his wife. Adam's explaining his own behavior (and not Eve's) might have been part of his continued abdication of responsibility. And Adam's authority and responsibility for Eve does not exclude Eve's own responsibility and need to answer for herself.

Thus, Davidson really only gives two explanations as to why God approached Adam first in Genesis 3: (1) Man was created first and received the prohibition first; and (2) A chiastic structure of interrogation in 3:9-13 (man-woman-serpent) proceeds in reverse order from that in which the characters are introduced in 3:1-8 (serpent-woman-man).[12] However, while a chiasm may exist in the passage, this does not explain *why* Adam was addressed first. Literary features do not exclude drawing other points from the text. It can be true that God approached Adam first because of his authority *and* that this formed a chiasm to fit with the beginning of the chapter.

Thus, this boils down to Davidson only providing one actual reason for God's approaching Adam first even though Eve sinned first, which is that Adam was created first and received the prohibition first. But recall that Davidson earlier rejected that Adam being formed first has any

---

10. Ibid., 67.
11. Ibid., 66–67.
12. Ibid. There is also repetition of the order of 3:1-8 in 3:14-17 (serpent-woman-man).

implications for hierarchy—"[T]he *sequence* of man's and woman's creation has no significance for implications of the society's view of or assumptions regarding hierarchy."[13] Thus, Davidson wants to have it both ways—he wants to affirm that Adam being created first does not show hierarchy over Eve, but he also wants to affirm that Adam being created first is the reason why God approached him first. But again, this does not really explain why God approached Adam first. What is it about Adam's chronological priority that led God to approach him first? Davidson wants to appeal to the creation order but not acknowledge the obvious, that this means Adam had authority over his wife. Again, Davidson's position is contrary to the Apostle Paul, who cited Adam being created first as the *basis* for not permitting a woman to teach or exercise authority over a man (1 Timothy 2:12-13). Davidson cannot have it both ways. Either Adam's chronological priority in creation means he had authority over Eve or it does not. But if it does not, there is no substantial basis as to why God approached Adam first rather than both Adam and Eve at the same time.

Egalitarian Richard Hess also rejects the argument that God's approaching Adam first implies Adam's covenantal responsibility over Eve. Like Davidson, Hess cites the reverse order of the characters in Genesis 3:1-8 and the point that Adam received the prohibition of eating from the tree first.[14] Davidson and Hess are correct that Adam received the prohibition first, as Eve was not even created at this point (Genesis 2:16-17). But again, this fails to address *why* God gave Adam the prohibition first. Why did God not wait until He created Eve and then give the prohibition to both of them?

Adam's reception of the prohibition first cannot be separated from Adam's being created first. Yet both Davidson and Hess deny that Adam being created first means Adam had authority over Eve in marriage. However, as noted above, we do not know how Eve came to know about God's prohibition of eating from the tree of knowledge of good and evil

---

13. Ibid., 28.
14. Richard Hess, "Equality with and without Innocence: Genesis 1–3," in *Discovering Biblical Equality: Complementarity Without Hierarchy*, 89–90.

(Genesis 3:3), whether Adam taught her or whether God told her directly. If Adam taught Eve the prohibition, this further strengthens the argument that Adam had covenantal authority over her, as he taught her God's Law. This was suggested above, since God gave Adam the task to "guard" the garden and immediately followed this with the prohibition (2:15-17), as well as there being no record of God ever restating the prohibition.

Further, it does not make sense that God would give the prohibition to both Adam and Eve (as it would be Adam's second time receiving the command) or that He would speak to Eve alone now that she and Adam were a married couple. But even if God gave the prohibition to Eve directly, it still leaves God questioning Adam prior to Eve, despite Eve sinning first. In this case, God gave the prohibition to both (and it was even fresher in Eve's mind), but God still questioned Adam first. In Hess' reasoning, God questioned Adam first because He gave Adam the prohibition first. Yet this cannot be separated from God creating Adam first. In the end, *both Davidson and Hess appeal to Adam's chronological priority as the basis for God appearing to him first after the fall, yet they reject Adam's priority as having significance for authority in the marriage relationship* (and male-female relations in general). They refuse to draw the obvious conclusion and thus undermine the teaching of the Apostle Paul (1 Timothy 2:12-14).

Contrary to Davidson and Hess, Adam had authority over Eve at creation. Adam was to guard the garden and his wife, and he was to teach her God's Law to not eat of the forbidden tree (Genesis 2:15-17). Yet Adam sinned in obeying his wife (3:17) instead of guarding and leading her. God thus questioned Adam first (3:9), even though Eve sinned first (3:6). Adam's authority over Eve was tied to his being created prior to Eve, a fact that the Apostle Paul recognized in forbidding women to teach or exercise authority over men (1 Timothy 2:12). Adam's authority is also seen in Eve being made "from" and "for" Adam, which the apostle thought demonstrated male headship (1 Corinthians 11:2-16). The egalitarian reading of Genesis 1–3 runs contrary to the creation account, as well as the Apostle Paul's reading of this passage. To summarize, there are actually 10 arguments supporting Adam's authority over Eve in Genesis 1–3:

1. Adam was created first (Genesis 2:7, 18-23; 1 Timothy 2:13).
2. Adam had a protective role over Eve in the garden (Genesis 2:15).
3. Adam had a teaching role over Eve as the one who taught her God's Law (Genesis 2:16-17; 3:2-3).
4. Eve was created as a helper for Adam (Genesis 2:18; 1 Corinthians 11:9).
5. Adam named Eve (Genesis 2:23; 3:20).
6. God went to Adam first after he and Eve sinned (Genesis 3:9) even though Eve sinned first (3:6).
7. God rebuked Adam for listening to Eve (Genesis 3:17).
8. God only told Adam he would die, yet Eve also died (Genesis 3:19).
9. God named humanity after Adam (Genesis 5:1-2; cf. 1:26).
10. Adam represented the human race in the garden (Romans 5:12-21; 1 Corinthians 15:22, 45-49).

These points are ordered according to their place in Scripture. Points 1–5 are all arguments from Genesis 2, points 6–8 are from Genesis 3, and points 9–10 are from later passages of Scripture but rooted in creation. Together, these 10 arguments form a strong case for hierarchy in the creation order.

Conflict and Rule in Marriage (Genesis 3:16)

Since some egalitarians hold that hierarchy was first introduced in Genesis 3:16 in the fall, we must address this verse. While marital hierarchy was introduced at creation, it is also the case that the fall corrupted this relationship and introduced strife between husband and wife. Sin has corrupted everything, including marriage. But is this marital strife specifically foretold by God in Genesis 3:16? When God pronounced judgment against Eve, He said to her:

> Your desire shall be contrary to your husband, but he shall rule over you (Genesis 3:16).

The difficulty of this verse has led to several interpretations. Assuming hierarchy was part of creation (as argued above), there are three possible views. God's pronouncement in Genesis 3:16 could:

1. *reaffirm* the creation marital hierarchy as a continued blessing;
2. *describe* the perversion of marital roles; or
3. *predict* that the wife will desire to escape the husband's authority but *prescribe* that the husband must exercise godly rule to restrain his wife.[15]

View 1, which sees Genesis 3:16 as a reaffirmation of creational hierarchy, takes the actions of both the husband and wife as positive (the wife is devoted to her husband, and the husband leads her). This fits the context of children in the preceding clause of 3:16 ("I will surely multiply your pain in childbearing; in pain you shall bring forth children") and thus pairs childbirth with the woman's desire/devotion to her husband rather than introducing a second judgment upon the woman. Together this would mean that in spite of woman enduring pain in childbearing, she will still be devoted her husband and have children with him. The challenge for this view is that the context of Genesis 3:16 deals with God's judgment upon Eve, and thus it is hard to understand why the man's "rule" is mentioned here if it is positive. One possibility is that since the woman broke from the authority of her husband in her transgression (3:1-6), God "redirected" her "to the place that suits her in creation."[16] In this case, Genesis 3:16 is "a summons to return to the creation subordination to the man."[17]

View 2, which sees this as a perversion of creational hierarchy, has two possibilities. One option takes the actions of both the husband and the wife as negative (the wife is devoted to usurping her husband's authority, and the husband exercises an abusive authority over her), while the

---

15. See Davidson, *Flame of Yahweh*, 60–65 for a helpful overview and chart of six views of Genesis 3:16, on which the three mentioned here are based. The first three views see hierarchy as part of the creation with the fall violating this hierarchy, while the latter three reject hierarchy at creation.
16. Werner Neuer, *Man and Woman in Christian Perspective*, 80.
17. Ibid.

second option takes the wife's "devotion" as positive but the husband's "rule" as negative (even when the wife is devoted to her husband, he may still abuse authority over her). View 2 is a common historical view, seen in Calvin's words that Eve had "previously been subject to her husband, but that was a liberal and gentle subjection; now, however, she is cast into servitude."[18] The ESV adopts the first option of view 2—"Your desire shall be contrary to your husband, but he shall rule over you." The NET Bible uses stronger words—"You will want to control your husband, but he will dominate you."

View 3 takes the wife's actions as negative and the husband's actions as positive (the wife is devoted to usurping her husband's authority, and the husband "must" exercise godly rule in order to overcome her attempted usurpation). This view relies heavily on the parallel construction of Genesis 4:7. It appears to be a modern view, first advocated by Susan Foh in the 1970s.[19]

Which interpretation of Genesis 3:16 we adopt will not have a significant impact on our understanding of marital hierarchy and gender roles. This is because we have already established that the creation account teaches hierarchy prior to the fall. Regardless of which of the three views is correct, *it is still the case that God put the husband in authority over his wife and that sin has introduced corruption into this relationship*. This is not the case for egalitarians since they deny creational hierarchy and want to ground later biblical male headship in the fall. Egalitarians thus have

---

18. John Calvin, *Commentaries on the Book of Genesis*, vol 1 (trans. John King; Grand Rapids, MI: Eerdmans, 1948), 172: "The second punishment which he exacts is *subjection*. For this form of speech, 'Thy desire shall be unto thy husband,' is of the same force as if he had said that she should not be free and at her own command, but subject to the authority of her husband and dependent upon his will; or as if he had said, 'Thou shalt desire nothing but what thy husband wishes.' As it is declared afterwards, 'Unto thee shall be his desire,' (Genesis 4:7). Thus the woman, who had perversely exceeded her proper bounds, is forced back to her own position. She had, indeed, previously been subject to her husband, but that was a liberal and gentle subjection; now, however, she is cast into servitude."

19. See Susan T. Foh, *Women and the Word of God* (Phillipsburg, NJ: Presbyterian and Reformed Publishing, 1979), 67–69; Susan T. Foh, "What Is the Woman's Desire?" *Westminster Theological Journal* 37 (1975): 376–383.

a strong motivation for adopting a form of view 2, with the particular emphasis that man's "rule" is introduced here as God's judgment upon Eve.

Interpretive Challenges of Genesis 3:16

Let us make mention of the interpretive challenges of this verse, as well as likely conclusions. First, there is the question of the meaning of the rare Hebrew word תְּשׁוּקָה (*teshuqa*), which is usually translated "desire." It is only used two other times in the Old Testament—a chapter later in Genesis 4:7 to describe sin's "desire" for Cain and then in Song of Songs 7:10[20] for apparent sexual desire ("I am my beloved's, and his desire is for me"). However, philologist Andrew Macintosh has recently argued that תְּשׁוּקָה does not mean "desire" but rather "concern, preoccupation, (single-minded) devotion, focus." His argument is based on the word's use in the Hebrew Bible (especially Genesis 4:7), the Dead Sea Scrolls, and comparative philology of Arabic.[21] Macintosh's proposal of "devotion" for תְּשׁוּקָה fits all three passages using the word in the Hebrew Bible—woman's "devotion" will be to her husband (Genesis 3:16), sin's "devotion" was to Cain (Genesis 4:7), and the beloved's "devotion" was to the woman (Song of Songs 7:10).

Second, there is debate over the construction of the Hebrew preposition אֶל (*el*), whether the woman's "devotion" is "to/for" her husband or "against" him. The above 2016 edition of the ESV recognizes this issue and thus footnotes "contrary to" with "Or *shall be toward* (see 4:7)." Interestingly, the above 2016 edition was a change from the 2011 edition that preferred a form of the footnote reading—"Your desire shall be for your husband, and he shall rule over you" (Genesis 3:16). The adversative of the preposition אֶל (*el*) is rare but possible,[22] and examples include Cain

---

20. Song of Songs 7:11 in the Masoretic Text
21. A.A. Macintosh, "The Meaning of Hebrew תשוקה," *Journal of Semitic Studies* 51/2 (Autumn 2016): 365–387.
22. Bruce K. Waltke and M. O'Connor, *An Introduction to Biblical Hebrew Syntax* (Winona Lake, IN: Eisenbrauns, 1990), 193.

rising up "against" Abel [אֶל־הֶבֶל] (Genesis 4:8) and Yahweh's anger burning "against" Israel [אֶל־יִשְׂרָאֵל] (Numbers 32:14). The action in these examples is still "to/toward" the person, but the context shows the action is hostile and thus "against/contrary to" the person. However, if Macintosh is correct that תְּשׁוּקָה means "(single-minded) devotion," it is hard to understand how the curse brought woman such a devotion to undermining her husband's authority. This does not seem true in life, nor does it fit the typical use of devotion. Therefore, it is more likely that תְּשׁוּקָה is used positively of a woman's "devotion" to her husband and that the typical meaning of "to" or "toward" for the preposition אֶל (*el*) is being used.

Third, there is the question whether the word מֹשֵׁל (*mashal*), usually translated "rule," is used positively or negatively in this context. The word emphasizes dominion[23] and is often used in a positive sense (Judges 8:23; 2 Samuel 23:3; Isaiah 40:10; 63:19; Micah 5:2; Zechariah 6:13; 9:10; Proverbs 17:2). However, it could be understood negatively here if the emphasis is on control or domination, especially in the context of God's judgment on Eve.

Fourth, there is the issue of how to translate the imperfect form of the verb מֹשֵׁל ("rule") in the second clause of Genesis 3:16, whether to indicate future certainty ("he will rule"), prescription ("he must rule"),[24] or potential ("he can/may rule").[25] All are possible, as English can express the nature of the imperfect Hebrew verb using a modal (e.g. must, can, may, should). The best meaning must be determined by the context.

---

23. מֹשֵׁל is defined as "rule, govern, have dominance over" in *New International Dictionary of Old Testament Theology & Exegesis*, vol 2 (ed. Willem A. VanGemeren; Grand Rapids, MI: Zondervan; 1997), 1136.

24. The injunctive imperfect (or non-perfective of injunction) "requests or commands that the subject of the verb perform the action of the verb" and is typically translated "must," "shall," "are to," or "will." Ronald J. Williams, *Williams' Hebrew Syntax* (3rd ed.; University of Toronto Press, 2007), 72.

25. The potential imperfect (or non-perfective of capability) "expresses (or denies) the ability to do or be something." Ibid., 70. Similarly, the non-perfective of possibility "denotes the possibility that the subject may perform an action," usually translated "may." Waltke and O'Connor, *An Introduction to Biblical Hebrew Syntax*, 508.

Many commentators appeal to the parallel construction of Genesis 4:7 to shed light on 3:16. After Cain became angry because God did not have regard for his offering, God said to Cain:

> If you do well, will you not be accepted? And if you do not do well, sin is crouching at the door. Its desire is contrary to you, but you must rule over it (Genesis 4:7).

As with Genesis 3:16, the ESV footnotes "contrary to" with "Or *is toward.*" Also like 3:16, the above 2016 edition was a change from the 2011 edition that preferred a form of the footnote reading—"Its desire is for you, but you must rule over it" (Genesis 4:7). This verse uses the same words for "devotion" [תְּשׁוּקָה] and "rule" [מׁשל] as in Genesis 3:16. Literally, this says, "And to you [is] its devotion, and you shall/must/can/may rule over it." Presumably, the "it" is "sin," the closest antecedent. However, the word "sin" [חַטָּאת, *chattat*] here is feminine and "it" is masculine, which is why the King James translated this as "unto thee shall be *his* desire, and thou shalt rule over *him.*" In this case, "his" and "him" could refer to Abel,[26] who was last mentioned in Genesis 4:4 but is part of the context

---

26. L. Michael Morales, "Crouching Demon, Hidden Lamb: Resurrecting an Exegetical Fossil in Genesis 4.7," *Bible Translator* 63:4 (2012): 185–191. Morales follows much of the argument of Joaquim Azevedo, "At the Door of Paradise: A Contextual Interpretation of Gen 4:7," *Biblische Notizen* 100 (1999): 45–59. Morales proposes the following translation of Genesis 4:7, where "his desire" and "him" refer to Abel—"If you do well will not [your countenance] be lifted? If you do not do well, at the door a sin offering is lying down. Now to you will be his desire but you must rule over him." Morales argues that חַטָּאת (*chattat*) should be translated as "sin offering" rather than the more common "sin." While the verb רֹבֵץ (*rovets*, "lying down") is masculine, it can refer to the feminine חַטָּאת (*chattat*) because this was actually a *male* animal used for a sin offering (cf. Exodus 29:14; Leviticus 4:21, 23-24). Morales also argues that the "door" [פֶּתַח, *petach*] refers to the entrance to the garden of Eden (Genesis 3:24), a connection also seen where the Israelites brought their offerings to the "door/entrance" [פֶּתַח, *petach*] of the temple (Leviticus 1:3; 3:2; 4:4, 14). Morales takes "his" [תְּשׁוּקָתוֹ, "his desire"] and "him" [תִּמְשָׁל־בּוֹ, "rule over him"] to refer back to Abel in Genesis 4:4, while recognizing the difficulty in the antecedent being so far away. Yet Morales says

of God's address to Cain. However, the immediate context of "devotion" is *sin* crouching at the door, and it makes little sense that Abel's devotion is to or against Cain. A better understanding is that the masculine "his" and "him" refer to sin portrayed as the serpent who lies at Cain's door and is "devoted" to him,[27] followed by God telling Cain that he has the ability to "rule" over sin. Though the serpent is not mentioned in 4:7, the prior chapter provides the background of the serpent, and the language of "resting/crouching" is beastly imagery (Genesis 49:9). Thus, sin is resting at Cain's door like the serpent in the garden (Genesis 3:1).

Seeing these two parallel verses together is helpful. The following are the different possible ways of reading the text, along with the Hebrew:

And to/against your husband [will be] your devotion,
and he will/must/may rule over you (Genesis 3:16).

וְאֶל־אִישֵׁךְ֙ תְּשׁ֣וּקָתֵ֔ךְ וְה֖וּא יִמְשָׁל־בָּֽךְ

And to/against you [is] its/his devotion,
and you shall/must/may rule over it/him (Genesis 4:7).

וְאֵלֶ֙יךָ֙ תְּשׁ֣וּקָת֔וֹ וְאַתָּ֖ה תִּמְשָׁל־בּֽוֹ

Though not determinative, the proximity between Genesis 3:16 and 4:7, along with the parallel constructions, supports the case that they have a similar meaning. The ESV, NASB, and NET translations all adopt the future certainty of the verb משל (*mashal*) in 3:16 ("he shall/will rule") but prescription in 4:7 ("you must rule"). Thus, they interpret the same

---

this fits the context and is less problematic than the traditional translation where "his" and "him" refer to the feminine חַטָּאת (*chattat*).

27. Macintosh, "The Meaning of Hebrew תשוקה," *Journal of Semitic Studies*: 372. Macintosh cites R.P. Gordon in support that the serpent "rests" at the door rather than "crouches" before attack (Genesis 49:9). R.P. Gordon, "'Couch' or 'Crouch'? Genesis 4:7 and the Temptation of Cain," in *On Stone and Scroll: Essays in Honour of G.I. Davies* (eds. J.K. Aitken, K.J. Dell, and B.A. Mastin; Berlin/Boston: De Gruyter, 2011), 195–209.

grammatical constructions differently. View 3 of Genesis 3:16 argues that both passages should be understood consistently and that 3:16 should also be translated prescriptively ("must"), as in 4:7.

However, as seen above, Genesis 4:7 also has its difficulties, and its meaning may not parallel 3:16 as closely as it appears. Further, while the prescriptive understanding in 4:7 is possible, so is the potential "can/may." In this case, God told Cain that sin's devotion was to him, but Cain had the *ability* to rule over it. This potential translation also works in Genesis 3:16—even though the woman's devotion would be to her husband, he had the ability to abuse authority over her. This would lead to the following translations:

And your devotion will be to your husband,
yet he may rule over you (Genesis 3:16).

And its devotion is to you,
yet you may rule over it (Genesis 4:7).

This translation adopts view 2 that Genesis 3:16 *describes* a perversion of the marital relationship, but it places the negative emphasis on the role of the man. It could also be translated as, "Even though you are devoted to your husband, he may abuse authority over you." This translation of Genesis 3:16 has several advantages: (1) It adopts the better translation "devotion" for תְּשׁוּקָה (*teshuqa*) instead of "desire;" (2) It uses the typical meaning ("to/toward") of the preposition אֶל (*el*) rather than the rare adversative ("against/contrary to"); (3) It fits the context of God pronouncing judgment on the woman in Genesis 3 (unlike view 1), though it is not judgment on the man (that comes in the following section in 3:17-19); and (4) It maintains the parallel construction of both 3:16 and 4:7 (though not the "must" of view 3).

The Corruption of Man's Authority

Thus, Genesis 3:16 is not a prediction that husbands "will" abuse authority over their wives (as that is not always the case), nor is it a prescription that a husband "must" overcome some negative usurpation on the part of the wife (as the wife's "devotion" is not negative). Rather, God pronounced the potential for a husband to abuse his authority over his wife as a result of the fall—even when she is devoted to her husband. Similarly, Genesis 4:7 is not a prediction that Cain would overcome sin (for he did not), nor is it a prescription that he "must" overcome it. Rather, God told Cain that he had the ability to overcome sin. Cain could have conquered sin, but he instead gave in and became a murderer (Genesis 4:8).

Regardless of how we understand Genesis 3:16, the point still stands that the fall introduced frustration into the marriage relationship. (This is true even if view 1 is adopted.) It was not that a husband's authority and a wife's submission were introduced as a result of the fall (as some egalitarians claim happened in Genesis 3:16), but rather that this hierarchical relationship was part of the created order and was now *frustrated* by the fall. Like all things, a husband's authority and a wife's submission are subject to corruption because of sin. Yet hierarchy between the sexes comes from the creation order, not the fall. It is not something to be overcome but something to be embraced as God's good design.

Chapter 7

MASCULINE AUTHORITY STARTS IN THE HOME

AS WESTERN SOCIETY collapses around us, there is plenty of blame to go around. Government is oppressive, the church is weak, and the schools are failing. But at the end of the day, all of this starts in the home. The family is the cornerstone of civilization. When the family is weakened, everything else starts to fall apart. And part of the reason the family has become so weak is because society has abandoned God's design of male headship.

Male Headship in the Home (the Household Codes)

Strong homes build strong churches and a strong society. So it is no surprise that God's Word has plenty to say on the subject of the home, much of which centers around male authority. Let us begin by looking at the apostolic teaching that a husband has authority over his wife. The Apostle Paul says:

> [22] Wives, submit to your own husbands, as to the Lord. [23] For the husband is the head of the wife even as Christ is the head of the church, his body, and is himself its Savior. [24] Now as the church

submits to Christ, so also wives should submit in everything to their husbands (Ephesians 5:22-24).

This passage is followed by the high command for husbands to love their wives as Christ loved the church (Ephesians 5:25-27). The husband is to imitate the Lord Jesus Christ. For now, however, our focus is the husband's authority. God has placed the husband as the "head" [κεφαλὴ, *kephale*] of his wife, in the same way that Christ is the "head" of the church (5:23). For this reason, wives are to "submit" [ὑποτάσσεται, *hupotassetai*] to their husbands, in the same way that the church submits to Christ (5:24). Paul elsewhere says:

> [18] Wives, submit to your husbands, as is fitting in the Lord.
> [19] Husbands, love your wives, and do not be harsh with them (Colossians 3:18-19).

Again, wives are commanded to "submit" [ὑποτάσσεσθε] to their husbands, a practice "fitting" for women who belong to Christ ("in the Lord"). And husbands are to "love" their wives and be gentle with them. Similarly, in his letter to Titus, Paul instructs older women to train younger women to "love their husbands and children, to be self-controlled, pure, working at home, kind, and submissive [ὑποτασσομένας] to their own husbands, that the word of God may not be reviled" (Titus 2:4-5). Both Colossians 3:18-19 and Titus 2:4-5 mention a wife's submission without making mention of the husband being "head." The Apostle Peter also instructs wives to submit to their husbands:

> [1] Likewise, wives, be subject to your own husbands, so that even if some do not obey the word, they may be won without a word by the conduct of their wives, [2] when they see your respectful and pure conduct. [3] Do not let your adorning be external—the braiding of hair and the putting on of gold jewelry, or the clothing you wear— [4] but let your adorning be the hidden person of the heart

with the imperishable beauty of a gentle and quiet spirit, which in God's sight is very precious. ⁵ For this is how the holy women who hoped in God used to adorn themselves, by submitting to their own husbands, ⁶ as Sarah obeyed Abraham, calling him lord. And you are her children, if you do good and do not fear anything that is frightening. ⁷ Likewise, husbands, live with your wives in an understanding way, showing honor to the woman as the weaker vessel, since they are heirs with you of the grace of life, so that your prayers may not be hindered (1 Peter 3:1-7).

Similar to Paul, Peter says wives should "be subject" [ὑποτασσόμεναι] to their husbands (1 Peter 3:1). Peter appeals to "holy women" of the Old Testament, who adorned themselves with the "beauty of a gentle and quiet spirit" (1 Peter 3:4-5). He specifically appeals to Sarah, who "obeyed" [ὑπήκουσεν, *hupekousen*] Abraham and called him "lord" [κύριον, *kurion*] (3:6). Peter is citing Genesis 18:12, where Sarah referred to Abraham as "my lord" [אֲדֹנִי, *adoni*]. Of course, Sarah did not use the word "lord" in the same way as it is used as a title for God. She used it as a respectful title of authority for her husband. But it acknowledged his authority nonetheless. Thus, Peter speaks of a man's authority apart from describing the man as "head" as Paul did in Ephesians 5:22-24. Instead Peter describes the husband as "lord" over the wife (1 Peter 3:6).

Like Paul, Peter also places high requirements upon husbands—"Likewise, husbands, live with your wives in an understanding way, showing honor to the woman as the weaker vessel, since they are heirs with you of the grace of life, so that your prayers may not be hindered" (1 Peter 3:7). While women are to submit to husbands, husbands are to "honor" their wives and live with them in an understanding way. God may not listen to prayers from men who dishonor their wives—"so that your prayers may not be hindered." Yet even this requirement for husbands invokes controversy, as Peter's basis for honoring wives is that woman is a "weaker vessel" [ἀσθενεστέρῳ σκεύει, *asthenestero skeuei*]. Peter does not elaborate on this phrase, though it surely involves comparative physical weakness and from the context may convey comparative emotional weakness.

Male Headship and Authority (1 Corinthians 11:2-16)

Though more difficult to interpret, 1 Corinthians 11 is also relevant to the issue of a man's authority in marriage. This is the same Paul who wrote the above household codes on male headship in the home:

> [2] Now I commend you because you remember me in everything and maintain the traditions even as I delivered them to you. [3] But I want you to understand that the head of every man is Christ, the head of a wife [woman] is her husband [man], and the head of Christ is God. [4] Every man who prays or prophesies with his head covered dishonors his head, [5] but every wife [woman] who prays or prophesies with her head uncovered dishonors her head, since it is the same as if her head were shaven. [6] For if a wife [woman] will not cover her head, then she should cut her hair short. But since it is disgraceful for a wife [woman] to cut off her hair or shave her head, let her cover her head. [7] For a man ought not to cover his head, since he is the image and glory of God, but woman is the glory of man. [8] For man was not made from woman, but woman from man. [9] Neither was man created for woman, but woman for man. [10] That is why a wife [woman] ought to have a symbol of authority on her head, because of the angels. [11] Nevertheless, in the Lord woman is not independent of man nor man of woman; [12] for as woman was made from man, so man is now born of woman. And all things are from God. [13] Judge for yourselves: is it proper for a wife [woman] to pray to God with her head uncovered? [14] Does not nature itself teach you that if a man wears long hair it is a disgrace for him, [15] but if a woman has long hair, it is her glory? For her hair is given to her for a covering. [16] If anyone is inclined to be contentious, we have no such practice, nor do the churches of God (1 Corinthians 11:2-16).

This passage is sometimes ignored because of the difficulty of its teaching on head coverings. However, it is important because, similar to

Ephesians 5, Paul also mentions male headship—"the head of every man is Christ, the head of a wife [woman] is her husband [man], and the head of Christ is God" (1 Corinthians 11:3). Paul uses the word "head" [κεφαλὴ] three times to describe three different authorities—Christ is the head of every man, man is the head of woman, and God is the head of Christ.[1]

It should be noted that the ESV obscures things by translating the second clause of 1 Corinthians 11:3 as "wife" and "husband" rather than "man" and "woman" (hence my bracketing of "man" and "woman" above). While ἀνήρ (*aner*) can mean either "man" or "husband," the ESV is inconsistent, seen in its translation of ἀνήρ in the first clause of 11:3 as "man" but then as "husband" in the second clause. The ESV also translates γυνή (*gune*) as "wife" instead of "woman" in 11:5, 6, 10, and 13. The ESV translators are interpreting this passage as a reference to husbands and wives, but there is nothing in the context of 1 Corinthians 11 that necessitates that Paul is speaking of the husband-wife relationship. Contrary to the ESV, other translations such as the NASB, KJV, and NET translate these terms as "man" and "woman" consistently throughout. The reason this matters is that the ESV translation of "wife" throughout implies that *unmarried* women are free to uncover their heads. However, an unmarried woman is still under the covenantal authority of a man prior to marriage, namely her father (Numbers 30:3-5).

Paul uses male headship as the basis for his instructions on head coverings, using the word "head" both literally and metaphorically throughout. A man who prays or prophesies with his physical head *covered* dishonors his metaphorical head—Christ (1 Corinthians 11:4), while every woman who prays or prophesies with her physical head *uncovered* dishonors her metaphorical head—man (11:5). For our purposes, it is unnecessary to determine exactly what the head coverings were, whether a hat/veil, long hair, or hair done up.[2]

---

1. Advocates of the eternal functional subordination of the Son (ESS) appeal to this passage, but this refers to God the Father being head over the *incarnate* Son of God, which is apparent from the title "Christ" (meaning "anointed one").

2. There is vast disagreement among commentators as to the identity of "head coverings" in 1 Corinthians 11. Some argue that the covering was a hat or

More relevant here is that Paul explains *why* women should cover their heads—"For a man ought not to cover his head, since he is the image and glory of God, but woman is the glory of man" (1 Corinthians 11:7). While this may sound like Paul denies that women are made in God's image, he never says such. In fact, he later says that "we have borne the image of the earthly man" in reference to Adam (1 Corinthians 15:49), implying that all humans, including women, are made in God's image. This is consistent with Genesis 1:26-28, which teaches that both men and women are made in God's image and together are to have "dominion" over the earth.³ The generic word "man" [אָדָם, *adam*] surely means "mankind" here because of the use of the plural verb ("let them have dominion") and the elaboration in Genesis 1:27 that "male and female he created them."

What then does Paul mean in 1 Corinthians 11:7 that man "is the image and glory of God, but woman is the glory of man"? Paul could be saying that Adam was made *directly* in God's image from the dust (Genesis 2:7), while Eve was indirectly made in God's image as she was made from Adam's rib (Genesis 2:22). This appeal to creation is seen in Paul's following explanation as to how woman is the glory of man—"For man was not made from woman, but woman from man. Neither was man created for woman, but woman for man" (1 Corinthians 11:8-9). Alternatively,

---

veil. Others argue it was hair done up and that long hair worn down suggested promiscuity in Roman culture. However, Paul concludes by saying that nature teaches that a man should have shorter hair and a woman should have longer hair (11:14-15). This supports taking the head covering as a woman's long hair (though they can accent this natural covering with a hat or veil).

3. Contra Hodge, who says, "The only sense in which the man, in distinction from the woman, is the image of God, is that he represents the authority of God. He is invested with dominion . . . So far, therefore, as the image of God consists in knowledge, righteousness and holiness, Eve as truly, and as much as Adam, bore the likeness of her Maker. But in the dominion with which man was invested over the earth, Adam was the representative of God." He goes on to say that woman "is not designed to reflect the glory of God as a ruler." Charles Hodge, *An Exposition of the First Epistle to the Corinthians* (1857–1859; repr., Carlisle, PA: Banner of Truth, 1974), 210.

Paul could mean that only man images God in the sense of authority relationships.[4]

It is worth noting that Paul does not say that man is the "image" and "likeness" of God (Genesis 1:26), but rather that man is the "image" and "glory" [δόξα, *doxa*] of God. The emphasis in 1 Corinthians 11:7 is on *glory*, not the image—man "is the image and glory of God, but woman is the glory of man." Thus, Paul emphasizes the differences in that woman was made to glorify man, to bring him honor as the one in authority over her. James Hurley appeals to the use of "glory" for the sun, moon, and stars in 1 Corinthians 15:40-41, meaning that "the glory of a thing . . . points to or manifests its dignity, honour or station." Thus, "a woman would be the 'glory' of her husband as she stands in a proper relation to him, thereby manifesting his station."[5] Man is the glory of God (1 Corinthians 11:7), woman is the glory of man (11:7), and long hair is the glory of woman (11:15). Thus, a man is to have his head uncovered in order to honor God (11:7, 14), and a woman is to have her head covered in order to honor man (11:5, 10).

Paul concludes, "That is why a wife [woman] ought to have a symbol of authority on her head, because of the angels" (1 Corinthians 11:10). The reference to angels is uncertain.[6] It should be noted that the word "symbol" is not found in the Greek. Paul simply says a woman should "have authority on her head" [ἐξουσίαν ἔχειν ἐπὶ τῆς κεφαλῆς]. Paul's

---

4. James B. Hurley, *Man and Woman in Biblical Perspective* (Grand Rapids, MI: Zondervan, 1981), 173: "The woman is not called to image God or Christ *in the relation which she sustains to her husband.* She images instead the response of the church to God and Christ by willing, loving self-subjection (Eph. 5:22-23). In *this particular sense* of authority relationships, the main topic of 1 Corinthians 11, it is absolutely appropriate to say that the man images God and that the woman does not."

5. Ibid., 174.

6. "Angels" [ἀγγέλους] usually refers to spirit beings, though it sometimes means "messengers." The most probable explanation is that angels are present when Christians worship God. Paul could be referring to the sons of God in Genesis 6:1-4 taking wives for themselves, meaning women should cover their heads to avoid attracting angels. Or Paul could mean women should cover their heads so as to avoid offending the angels.

entire argument is that a woman should have the proper sign of authority on her head (a head covering) in certain settings because she is directly under the authority of a man[7] (either her husband or her father if she is single; cf. Numbers 30), while a man should have his head uncovered because he is directly under the authority of Christ. (Of course, a woman is still under Christ's authority, but she is also under the authority of a man.) Though there are challenges in interpreting this passage, the key takeaway for our purposes is that Paul plainly speaks of man having authority over woman.

Objection 1—κεφαλή Does Not Mean "Authority" but "Source"

The above passages establish that men have authority in the home. Yet egalitarians raise several arguments seeking to show that these passages do not actually teach male headship and authority. The first argument against male authority in marriage is that κεφαλή (*kephale*) does not mean "head" but "source" or "origin" and therefore a husband does not have authority over his wife.

In his commentary on 1 Corinthians 11, egalitarian Gordon Fee takes

---

7. Some egalitarians have followed M.D. Hooker's argument that "authority" [ἐξουσίαν] never has a passive meaning and thus in 1 Corinthians 11:10 refers to a woman's authority over herself (supporting her right to prophesy), not a man's authority over her. Thomas Schreiner ably critiques Hooker's argument in "Head Coverings, Prophecies, and the Trinity: 1 Corinthians 11:2-16," in *Recovering Biblical Manhood and Womanhood*, 134–136. In short, there are not many examples of "authority" being used symbolically as in 11:10, so the parallel argument is not decisive. The entire passage makes the point that woman is under the authority of man and therefore it does not make sense that Paul would then assert in 11:10 that a woman has her own authority. Thiselton notes that the patristic commentators "saw no problem in understanding ἐξουσία in an active sense as metonymy for *a sign of power over*." Anthony C. Thiselton, *The First Epistle to the Corinthians* (New International Greek Testament Commentary; Grand Rapids: Eerdmans, 2000), 838.

κεφαλή as "source," especially "source of life" or "origin."[8] He says that "Paul's concern is not hierarchical (who has authority over whom), but relational (the unique relationships that are predicated on one's being the source of the other's existence). Indeed, he says nothing about man's authority."[9] Fee concludes that God is the "head" of Christ (11:3) in the sense that "God is the source of Christ."[10]

In response to this, it should be noted that the word κεφαλή literally refers to a person's head, such as when Jesus speaks of the "hairs of your head" [κεφαλῆς] (Matthew 10:30). Thus, the debate is over what Paul means when he uses κεφαλή metaphorically to describe the relationship of man to woman, as in 1 Corinthians 11:3 and Ephesians 5:23. In addition to 1 Corinthians 11:3, the word κεφαλή is used five other times in Paul's letters as a metaphor to describe *Jesus' relationship to the church*:

> And he put all things under his feet and gave him as head [κεφαλὴν] over all things to the church (Ephesians 1:22).

> Rather, speaking the truth in love, we are to grow up in every way into him who is the head [κεφαλή], into Christ (Ephesians 4:15).

> For the husband is the head [κεφαλή] of the wife even as Christ is the head [κεφαλή] of the church, his body, and is himself its Savior (Ephesians 5:23).

> And he is the head [κεφαλή] of the body, the church. He is the beginning, the firstborn from the dead, that in everything he might be preeminent (Colossians 1:18).

> and you have been filled in him, who is the head [κεφαλή] of all rule and authority (Colossians 2:10).

---

8. Gordon Fee, *The First Epistle to the Corinthians* (New International Commentary on the New Testament; Grand Rapids, MI: Eerdmans, 2014), 555.
9. Ibid., 556.
10. Ibid., 557.

Paul's use of κεφαλὴ as a metaphor for Christ should shed light on his use as a metaphor for husbands, especially since Paul compares the two in Ephesians 5:23. The husband is the "head" of the wife just as Christ is "head" of the church. The meaning of "authority" for κεφαλὴ fits in all of these passages because of the context of Christ ruling over the cosmos (Ephesians 1:22; Colossians 2:10) and ruling over His people (Ephesians 4:15; 5:23; Colossians 1:18). While "source" could make some sense in Colossians 1:18 because of the word "beginning," it does not make sense of the other passages. Ephesians 1:20-22 speaks of Christ sitting at the Father's right hand "above all rule and authority" and the Father giving Christ to the church as "head over all things." Colossians 2:10 says that Christ "is the head of all rule and authority." These passages all convey authority.

This is why the revered Greek lexicon BDAG places all of the above uses of κεφαλὴ, including 1 Corinthians 11:3 and Ephesians 5:23, under the definition of "a being of high status, *head*." It says, "in the case of living beings, to denote superior rank," and then it cites Jephthah as "head" as having the symbol of father in Judges 11:11 [LXX] (see also Judges 10:18; 11:8, 9; 2 Samuel 22:44 [LXX]).[11] Wayne Grudem has written extensively in defense of κεφαλὴ as "authority" in the New Testament on the basis that this is a common usage in both biblical and extra-biblical literature and that there are "no *unambiguous* examples before or during the time of the New Testament" where κεφαλὴ means "source."[12]

Furthermore, the context of "submission" in Ephesians 5:22-33 and other parallel passages should shed light on Paul's use of κεφαλὴ in both Ephesians 5:23 and 1 Corinthians 11:3. Paul commands wives to "submit" to husbands in Ephesians 5:22, Colossians 3:18, and Titus 2:5. And Peter commands wives to "submit" to husbands in 1 Peter 3:1, 5. All of these passages imply the man has authority over his wife, as only the wife is told to submit. Peter even uses the word "lord" to describe Abraham's

---

11. BDAG, 542.

12. Wayne Grudem, "The meaning of *Kephale* ('Head'): A Response to Recent Studies," in *Recovering Biblical Manhood and Womanhood*, 468; see also Wayne Grudem, "The Meaning of κεφαλὴ ('Head'): An Evaluation of New Evidence, Real and Alleged," *Journal of the Evangelical Theological Society* 44 (2001): 26–65.

relationship to Sarah (1 Peter 3:6). The context of these passages dealing with husband-wife relationships requires the meaning of "authority" for κεφαλὴ. "Source" does not adequately account for Paul's requirement that wives "submit" to their husbands.

While 1 Corinthians 11:2-16 does not tie a wife's "submission" with the husband as "head" as explicitly as Ephesians 5:22-24 does, the context still speaks of a woman having "authority" on her head, based on woman's purpose—"Neither was man created for woman, but woman for man. That is why a wife [woman] ought to have a symbol of authority on her head" (1 Corinthians 11:9-10). The issue in 1 Corinthians 11 is how a man's authority as "head" of woman "should be reflected in worship."[13] Woman was made for man and is to have a symbol of authority on her head to signify man's authority over her. Thus, man is the "head" of woman. Similarly, God is the "head" of Christ in that the Father has authority over the incarnate Christ (1 Corinthians 11:3).

Therefore, κεφαλὴ should be understood as a metaphor in these passages for "authority." However, even if the word did mean "source," this would still convey authority, as God is our ultimate source and therefore has authority over us. Egalitarians can dispute the meaning of κεφαλὴ all they want, but at the end of the day, wives are still told to "submit" to their husbands, as the church "submits" to Christ (Ephesians 5:24). People submit to those in authority over them. Just as Jesus holds authority over the church, so husbands hold authority over their wives.

Some scholars who reject "source" for κεφαλὴ still adopt the meaning of "prominence" or "preeminence" instead of "authority."[14] However, while this translation is better than "source," it is still lacking. Christ does not just have "prominence" over the church or "prominence" over

---

13. Paul Gardner, *1 Corinthians* (Zondervan Exegetical Commentary on the New Testament; Grand Rapids, MI: Zondervan, 2018), 484. Gardner adopts the view advocated here that κεφαλὴ means "authority."

14. Andrew Perriman, *Speaking of Women: Interpreting Paul* (Leicester: Apollos, 1998), 13–33; David E. Garland, *1 Corinthians* (Baker Exegetical Commentary on the New Testament; Grand Rapids: MI: Baker Academic, 2003), 516; Thiselton, *The First Epistle to the Corinthians*, 812–822.

all things. Rather, Christ as "head" has *authority* and *rules* over both the church and the cosmos (Ephesians 1:20-22; Colossians 2:10). In the same way, wives are told to "submit" to their husbands, implying that the husband as "head" has some sort of authority over her (Ephesians 5:24). As two advocates of the translation of "prominence" have said, "Even if by 'head' Paul means 'more prominent/preeminent partner' or (less likely) 'one through whom the other exists,' his language and the flow of the argument seem to reflect an assumed hierarchy through which glory and shame flow upward from those with lower status to those above them. In this context the word almost certainly refers to one with authority over the other."[15]

Objection 2—Paul Commands "Mutual Submission"

The second argument against male authority in marriage is that Paul commands "mutual submission" in Ephesians 5:21. When Paul says "submitting to one another" [Ὑποτασσόμενοι ἀλλήλοις], this means that husbands also have to submit to their wives. Egalitarian Philip Payne claims that the dependence of the command for wives to "submit" in Ephesians 5:22 on the verb in 5:21 (the Greek is an ellipsis) "shows that Paul expects husbands to submit to their wives, too."[16]

However, the argument for "mutual submission" entirely ignores the context of this phrase. In Ephesians 5:18, Paul commands Christians to be filled with the Holy Spirit. This main verb "be filled" [πληροῦσθε] is then modified by three sets of participles that show what it looks like to be filled with God's Spirit: (1) "addressing" [λαλοῦντες] one another in song and "singing" [ᾄδοντες] and "making melody" [ψάλλοντες], (2) "giving thanks" [εὐχαριστοῦντες] to God, and (3) "submitting" [Ὑποτασσόμενοι] to one another (Ephesians 5:19-21). Paul only elaborates on the third and

---

15. Roy E. Ciampa and Brian S. Rosner, *The First Letter to the Corinthians* (The Pillar New Testament Commentary; Grand Rapids, MI: Eerdmans, 2010), 509.
16. Philip B. Payne, *Man and Woman, One in Christ: An Exegetical and Theological Study of Paul's Letters* (Grand Rapids, MI: Zondervan, 2009), 277.

final participle. He thus shows exactly what he means by "submitting to one another," as this is immediately followed by the command "Wives, submit to your own husbands, as to the Lord" (Ephesians 5:22). In Greek, the word "submit" does not exist in 5:22. It is an ellipsis that assumes the prior verb. Paul literally says, "Wives . . . to your own husbands, as to the Lord." But the implied verb is obvious. It is "submit" from the prior verse (5:21). Paul does the same thing in 5:24, literally saying, "But as the church submits to Christ, thus also wives . . . to husbands in everything." The entire point is that a wife is to submit to her husband, with Christ's authority over the church serving as the analogy for a husband's authority over his wife.

Yet Paul does not stop there. He expands upon "submitting to one another" (Ephesians 5:21), not only by commanding wives to submit to husbands (5:22), but also commanding children to "obey" [ὑπακούετε] parents (6:1) and slaves to "obey" [ὑπακούετε] masters (6:5). Therefore, by "submitting to one another" (5:21), Paul means "submitting to those in authority over you." Husbands have authority over wives, parents have authority over children, and masters have authority over slaves. This does not mean women are in subjection to everyone else, as they have authority over their children. And men too are under authority and subjection—to God, elders, and civil government (Exodus 20:12; Romans 13:1; Hebrews 13:17). When Paul says "submitting to one another" in Ephesians 5:21, he does *not* mean "everyone should submit to everyone else." This would be absurd, as submission assumes authority, and we cannot all have authority over everyone else. The word for "submit" is ὑποτάσσω (*hupotasso*), which BDAG defines as "*become subject*" and "*subject oneself, be subjected or subordinated, obey.*"[17] We submit to civil government because it has authority over us (Romans 13:1), and we submit to God because He has authority over us (James 4:7). We are not to submit to those who do not have authority over us.

Some egalitarians argue that "one another" (ἀλλήλων, *allelon*) is always

---

17. BDAG, 1042.

reciprocal.[18] However, there are examples in the New Testament where the word *cannot* mean everyone is doing the same thing to one another at the same time. For example, Revelation 6:4 says, "so that people should slay one another" [ἀλλήλους], and this cannot mean everyone kills each other at the same time. Rather, it means that some people kill other people. (See also Matthew 24:10; Luke 2:15; 12:1; 24:32; 1 Corinthians 11:33; Galatians 6:2.) When it comes to Ephesians 5, the context *demands* this limited understanding of ἀλλήλων. It is ridiculous to conclude that Paul wanted husbands to submit to wives, masters to obey slaves, and parents to obey children. Mutual submission would render his commands to these groups meaningless.

If Paul intended for husbands to submit to wives, as egalitarians claim, why did he not just say so? This appeal to "mutual submission" will not work in other passages such as Colossians 3:18-19[19] and 1 Peter 3:1—"Wives, submit to your husbands, as is fitting in the Lord" and "wives, be subject to your own husbands"—neither of which say anything about "mutual submission." The same is true for Titus 2:4-5—"Older women are to train younger women to love their husbands and children, to be self-controlled, pure, working at home, kind, and submissive [ὑποτασσομένας] to their own husbands, that the word of God may not be reviled." Those under authority should submit to those in authority over them. This is part of what it means to "be filled with the Spirit" (Ephesians 5:18). And those who refuse to submit to their God-ordained authorities are resisting the Spirit of God.

---

18. Payne, *Man and Woman, One in Christ*, 280.

19. Contra Keener, *Paul, Women & Wives*, 134, who claims that "Paul sometimes summarized only one side of this mutual submission formula, as in Colossians 3:18 . . . But argues for mutual submission when he explains his position more fully." Again, if Paul intended mutual submission, he could have easily commanded husbands to submit to wives just as clearly as he commanded wives to submit to husbands. Yet neither he nor Peter ever said such a thing. Moreover, Keener has it exactly backwards—Paul's words "submitting to one another" in Ephesians 5:21 do not "explain his position [on submission] more fully," but rather Paul's commands for wives, slaves, and children to obey in 5:22–6:9 explain more fully what he meant by "submitting to one another" in 5:21.

Objection 3—Paul's Hermeneutic Moves Us Beyond the Submission Based on Greco-Roman Cultural Structures

The third argument against male authority in marriage is that Paul was working within Greco-Roman boundaries (of marriage, children, and slavery), and now that things have changed, we cannot adhere to his teaching strictly today. Paul's own hermeneutic moves us beyond patriarchy and a wife's submission, just as it moved us toward the abolition of slavery.

This is a more sophisticated argument than merely challenging the meaning of "head" as authority or appealing to "mutual submission," and it therefore takes more space to understand and refute. This argument admits that Paul commanded wives to submit to husbands, but it seeks to overcome this command by tying it to the culture of Paul's day. It is no wonder this argument is adopted by many egalitarian scholars, such as I. Howard Marshall, Gordon Fee, and William Webb.[20]

We will focus first on I. Howard Marshall's chapter in *Discovering Biblical Equality*, which argues there is a parallel between patriarchal marriage and slavery. According to Marshall, Paul was working within his cultural boundaries—"What Paul is doing is to indicate the way wives should be submissive within a society where such submission was expected, just as he can also tell slaves how they are to be obedient in the slave-master relationship."[21] However, things have now changed, and Christian theologians today "recognize that slavery is not an acceptable form of relationship" based on "larger biblical considerations" that all humans being

---

20. William Webb argues for a "redemptive-movement hermeneutic," which means that we are to follow the direction of God's ethics and move beyond the New Testament. See William J. Webb, *Slaves, Women and Homosexuals* (Downers Grove, IL: InterVarsity Press, 2001); William J. Webb, "A Redemptive-Movement Hermeneutic: The Slavery Analogy," in *Discovering Biblical Equality*, 382–400. For responses to Webb, see Wayne Grudem, "Shall We Move Beyond the New Testament to a Better Ethic?" *Journal of the Evangelical Theological Society* 47/2 (2004): 299–346; also published in Grudem, *Evangelical Feminism and Biblical Truth* (Sisters, OR: Multnomah, 2004), 600–645; Benjamin Reaoch, *Women, Slaves, and the Gender Debate* (Phillipsburg, NJ: P&R Publishing, 2012).

21. I. Howard Marshall, "Mutual Love and Submission in Marriage: Colossians 3:18-19 and Ephesians 5:21-33," in *Discovering Biblical Equality*, 199.

are made in God's image.[22] Marshall claims that this is something the Bible authors did not understand—"The recognition that slavery is incompatible with Christian faith goes beyond the explicit teaching of Scripture while being fully scriptural: we now recognize (as the biblical writers were not yet able to do) that slavery is inconsistent with the biblical understanding of humanity in creation and redemption."[23]

The same goes for marriage, as "expectations" for marriage in the Western world have changed—"Many husbands and wives see one another as equal partners, and one-sided subordination of the wife to the husband is seen as inappropriate and is not demanded."[24] Thus, "the *structure* of marriage is no longer to be understood in patriarchal terms."[25] Because of this cultural change, Marshall concludes, "We must go beyond the letter of Scripture when the trajectory of scriptural teaching takes us further than what Scripture explicitly says and requires us to recognize that some culturally specific scriptural teachings and commands are no longer mandatory."[26]

On what Scriptural basis should Christians go beyond Paul's commands regarding patriarchal marriage? Marshall argues this is based on the Bible's teaching of "mutual submission," appealing to Ephesians 5:21 and Paul's instruction in Galatians 5:13 for Christians to "serve one another" through love. Thus, Marshall does not deny that a wife should submit to her husband. (He even admits "head" means more than "source.")[27] Marshall simply adds that *a husband should also submit to his wife*—"For what is being done is not to deny that wives should submit to their husbands as to the Lord but to add that husbands must also submit to their wives as to the Lord."[28]

Marshall appeals to Paul's own principle that a husband should "love" his wife, an improvement on Greco-Roman patriarchy that Marshall calls

---

22. Ibid., 189.
23. Ibid., 201.
24. Ibid., 193.
25. Ibid., 203.
26. Ibid., 201–202.
27. Ibid., 198.
28. Ibid., 204.

"love-patriarchy." Similarly, Paul's principles put us today in a position to move past patriarchal marriage entirely, just as we moved past slavery. Marshall says, "From patriarchalism we have moved to love-patriarchalism, and the road is open to mutual love between brothers and sisters in Christ. This final step was not taken by Paul, any more than he took the step from accepting slavery to recognizing that his own teaching contained the seeds of its inevitable abolition."[29] As Marshall explains, "Christian love by the husband requires him also to respect and submit to his wife. This insight could not be expected to develop immediately, and the New Testament writers should not be faulted for not spelling this out explicitly. The implications of Ephesians 5:21 and other passages noted above must be allowed to have their proper force."[30]

Similar to Marshall, Gordon Fee argues we should move past patriarchy based on Scriptural principles, such as the teaching of Galatians 3:28 that "there is no male and female" in Christ. Fee says that Paul's "new creation theology" of Galatians 3:28 "sounds the death knell to the old order, even though its structures remained in the surrounding culture."[31] He continues, "[E]ven though our text does not explicitly mention roles and structures, its new creation theological setting calls these into question in a most profound way."[32] Fee says this new order "radically" alters the husband-wife relationship, and, "To conclude otherwise forces one logically into the position of justifying slavery as a God-ordained structure for the present age, since the two household codes (Eph 5:21–6:9; Col 3:18–4:1) assume both realities in the same structure: the Greco-Roman household of the privileged. Those who advocate the continuation of male authority today have failed to address this problem adequately."[33]

I have quoted this argument by Marshall and Fee at length to show exactly what these egalitarian theologians are saying, which is that *Paul*

---

29. Ibid., 194.
30. Ibid., 202–203.
31. Gordon D. Fee, "Male and Female in the New Creation," in *Discovering Biblical Equality*, 184.
32. Ibid., 185.
33. Ibid., 184.

put in place principles to overcome his own culturally-limited teaching of male headship in marriage. How should we respond to this?

First and foremost, the fundamental flaw with this argument is that it ignores the basis of Paul's teaching on male headship, as *Paul bases the husband's headship and the wife's submission on the model of Christ and the church*, not Greco-Roman culture. Paul says, "the husband is the head of the wife as Christ is the head of the church" (Ephesians 5:23). And "as the church submits to Christ, so also wives should submit in everything to their husbands" (5:24). The husband is to love his wife "as Christ loved the church and gave himself up for her" (5:25). Thus, the husband is to imitate Christ. The entire marriage relationship points to "Christ and the church" (5:32). Would Marshall and Fee have Christ submit to the church? Of course not. Christ has authority over the church, and the church must submit to Christ. Similarly, God has placed the husband in authority over his wife, and the wife must submit to her husband.

Such role distinctions are not in contradiction to the teachings of Paul elsewhere, such as Galatians 3:28, Galatians 5:13, and Ephesians 5:21. We already addressed Ephesians 5:21, showing that Paul did not command "mutual submission" but meant that everyone should submit to those in particular authority over them. Paul did not command parents to obey children, masters to obey slaves, or husbands to submit to wives. As for Galatians 5:13 and Paul's command to "through love serve one another," this is perfectly consistent with hierarchical marriage. In fact, Paul commanded husbands to "love" their wives in the context of the husband having headship in marriage (Ephesians 5:25). Part of headship means leading and loving the wife to the greatest extent possible, serving her just as Jesus served and even died for the church (Matthew 20:28). Yet the hierarchical structure remains—the church is to submit to Jesus and wives are to submit to husbands.

Galatians 3:28 is no different. It does *nothing* to undermine gender roles, in the same way that it did not turn a Greek into a Jew ("neither Jew nor Greek") nor make a slave a free man ("neither slave nor free"). Roles and distinctions still exist in society as part of the created order. Let us quote the broader passage to make this clear:

> ²⁵ But now that faith has come, we are no longer under a guardian, ²⁶ for in Christ Jesus you are all sons of God, through faith. ²⁷ For as many of you as were baptized into Christ have put on Christ. ²⁸ There is neither Jew nor Greek, there is neither slave nor free, there is no male and female, for you are all one in Christ Jesus. ²⁹ And if you are Christ's, then you are Abraham's offspring, heirs according to promise (Galatians 3:25-29).

The prior context of Galatians 3:28 deals with the place of the Gentiles in the church. Paul recounts his rebuke of Peter for seeking to require the Gentiles to live like Jews by being circumcised (Galatians 2:14). Then Paul makes clear that justification is "through faith," not by "works of the law" (2:16), and those who have "faith" in Christ are "sons of Abraham (3:7). Thus, Galatians 3:28 is within the context of Jew-Gentile relations, and Paul uses "Greek" to refer to Gentiles, as he does elsewhere (Romans 1:16; 2:9-10; 10:12; Galatians 2:3; Colossians 3:11). Paul in Galatians 3:28 is making the point that *there is unity among Jews and Gentiles through faith in Christ.* In the same way, there is unity in faith among slaves and freemen, as well as men and women. Paul is explaining the implications of unity in Christ.³⁴ Faith in Christ brings unity that transcends slavery and sex distinctions, as all Christians are "sons of God, through faith" and "Abraham's offspring, heirs according to promise" (Galatians 3:26, 29). Yet a slave must still obey his master, and a wife must still submit to her husband. That anyone would conclude from Galatians 3:28 that a woman can be a pastor or that a man must submit to his wife is truly astonishing. It is exegesis of the worst order and is not worthy of the term "scholarship."

Finally, it should be noted that there is a difference between slavery and marriage. Egalitarians who make this comparison echo their feminist

---

34. Contra Philip Payne, who claims the above interpretation of Galatians 3:28 makes this verse "redundant" with 3:26. Payne goes so far as to claim that Galatians 3:28 "explicitly affirms, without any qualification, that these divisions do not exist in the body of Christ." Payne, *Man and Woman, One in Christ*, 79–80. If this were the case, one wonders how Paul could then command wives to submit to their husbands and slaves to obey their masters (Ephesians 5:22; 6:5).

forerunners who decried the marriage relationship as "slavery" for the woman. The fact is that the Bible assumes slavery as part of the ancient world. God allowed for slavery both in the Old and New Testaments, but He also regulated it. The Mosaic law placed restrictions upon Israelite slave practices, and the Apostle Paul required Christian masters to treat their slaves well (Ephesians 6:9; Colossians 4:1). Yet the Bible never requires slavery, and it does not base it on God's design at creation as it does with marriage.[35] Thus, Marshall is correct to say Paul was working within the Greco-Roman structure when giving instructions for slaves and masters, but the same cannot be said of marriage. Marriage and male headship are based in creation and on Christ's headship over His church.

We should make note of the parent-child relationship since Marshall also appeals to changes in this relationship as the basis for overthrowing male headship in marriage. Marshall claims the circumstances of children have changed—"in the ancient world this subordination continued to a more advanced age than would be natural for us," and "the father as patriarch had a much greater authority . . . A modern son or daughter can claim independence of parents in a way that is not contemplated in Paul's commandment, understood in its contemporary social setting."[36] Of course, it may be that such modern "independence" is not a biblical practice. However, Paul's instructions in Ephesians 6 likely concern younger children. Marshall dismisses this explanation, but he ignores two points of evidence. First, Paul commands children to "obey" in Ephesians 6:1 (instead of the Fifth Commandment's requirement of "honor," which binds even adults). Second, Paul's instruction to fathers in Ephesians 6:4

---

35. Keener says appealing to marriage as God-ordained at creation merely begs the question, as the real issue is whether a wife's *submission* is God-ordained at creation. Keener, *Paul, Women & Wives*, 208. Typical of egalitarians, Keener thinks a wife's subordination is only rooted in the fall of Genesis 3:16, but we have spent an entire chapter showing otherwise (chapter 6). Moreover, Paul bases God's design for male headship in marriage on the relationship between Christ and the church (Ephesians 5:31-32).

36. Marshall, "Mutual Love and Submission in Marriage," in *Discovering Biblical Equality*, 188.

concerns *raising* children ("bring them up in the discipline and instruction of the Lord"). Thus, Paul is speaking to younger children in Ephesians 6.

The chief problem with Marshall's argument is that the parent-child relationship is also based in creation, as parents have authority over their children. Parental hierarchy is not based in Greco-Roman culture but on God's design for the family structure. Thus, God commands children to obey their parents as part of His moral law, the Fifth Commandment (Exodus 20:12; Deuteronomy 5:16; Ephesians 6:2). Regardless, Marshall still affirms the biblical principle that children must obey parents, and the parent-child relationship therefore does not serve his argument in overturning male headship in marriage.

The fact is that hierarchy in marriage and parenting are both based on God's design for the family, and these authority structures have nowhere been overturned. Rather, they have been reaffirmed in Christ. The commands for slavery no longer apply where slavery has been abolished. But where there are marriages and children—which is every society—wives must submit to their husbands and children must obey their parents.

The Old Testament Basis of Male Headship (Numbers 30)

While discussions of male headship often focus on the New Testament, we should not ignore the Old Testament background. Male headship is there from the beginning. We have already looked at Adam's role at creation. However, there is a very important passage on male headship tucked away at the end of the book of Numbers. It concerns women and the vows they make, but it has much to say about women and authority.

In this passage, Moses declares to the heads of Israel's tribes, "This is what the LORD has commanded" (Numbers 30:1). Moses begins by stating that a man is bound by his oath—"If a man vows a vow to the Lord, or swears an oath to bind himself by a pledge, he shall not break his word. He shall do according to all that proceeds out of his mouth" (30:2). Moses then gives instructions for single women who make vows:

> ³ If a woman vows a vow to the Lord and binds herself by a pledge, while within her father's house in her youth, ⁴ and her father hears of her vow and of her pledge by which she has bound herself and says nothing to her, then all her vows shall stand, and every pledge by which she has bound herself shall stand. ⁵ But if her father opposes her on the day that he hears of it, no vow of hers, no pledge by which she has bound herself shall stand. And the Lord will forgive her, because her father opposed her (Numbers 30:3-5).

This concerns a woman who resides "within her father's house in her youth," which in Hebrew culture would have been every woman prior to marriage. Though the word "authority" is not used, such a woman is clearly under her father's authority. The woman's father can nullify her vow if he "opposes her on the day that he hears of it" (Numbers 30:5). This is similar to how a father can nullify a marriage covenant made through sexual intercourse between his unmarried daughter and an unmarried man (Deuteronomy 22:28-29). The passage also gives instructions for a married woman who makes a vow:

> ⁶ If she marries a husband, while under her vows or any thoughtless utterance of her lips by which she has bound herself, ⁷ and her husband hears of it and says nothing to her on the day that he hears, then her vows shall stand, and her pledges by which she has bound herself shall stand. ⁸ But if, on the day that her husband comes to hear of it, he opposes her, then he makes void her vow that was on her, and the thoughtless utterance of her lips by which she bound herself. And the Lord will forgive her (Numbers 30:6-8).

Instead of her father having the right to nullify her vow, her husband now has that right. The married woman is no longer under her father's authority but her husband's authority. A father's authority over his daughter is transferred to her husband when she marries. Thus, a woman is either under the authority of her father or under the authority of her husband.

The man in authority over her can make her vow "null and void" (Numbers 30:12). The only exception to this is a widow or divorcee—"But any vow of a widow or of a divorced woman, anything by which she has bound herself, shall stand against her" (30:9). A married woman who has lost her covenant authority through death or divorce is now independent. But this is not a good thing, as she is left unprotected and unprovided for. In the ancient world, this was a dangerous position, and thus remarriage was strongly encouraged.

Therefore, we see that male headship is based in the Old Testament Scriptures. Egalitarians can argue all they want against the meaning of "head" as authority in the New Testament, but their efforts are futile. The whole Bible teaches that a man has covenantal authority in marriage. Women have always been under authority, either that of their fathers or their husbands. Paul taught the same principles found in the Hebrew Bible.

Man Has Covenantal Authority in Marriage

The key principle in all the passages we have examined is that *men have covenantal authority over their wives*. This authority comes from God. Of course, authority brings responsibility. Men have a responsibility to protect their wives and provide for their physical and spiritual well-being. Many today give lip service to male authority and verbally acknowledge that a man is head of his wife. Yet when asked what this means, they often resort to defining headship as egalitarian practice with the man having a mere tie-breaking vote. This is not biblical authority but a "complementarianism" of the softest fabric.

Authority means authority. No one would say God's authority only entails a tie-breaking authority over our requests or that parents' authority involves children having a near-equal say to parents. Authority means one party has power over and leads the other party. A husband is to lead his wife. And this is not just a "servant leadership," though a husband certainly should serve his wife. Godly leaders serve those under their authority, just as Jesus came to serve those under His authority (Matthew 20:25-28). A husband should listen to his wife and love her and honor her. But it should be clear that a man and his wife are not equal in this sense. There is only one covenant head.

Marriage creates a new family unit. Husband and wife are no longer two individuals but one flesh (Genesis 2:24; Matthew 19:5). Marriage creates a household, an οἶκος (*oikos*). Contrary to modern individualism, it is the household that is the basic unit in society. We still function as individuals and are responsible for our actions, but we are not mere individuals. We all come from two parents, and most of us marry and form new families at some point. This is the household. And its significance is demonstrated in that God has laid out household instructions throughout His Word.

Man Is the Spiritual Leader of the Family

What does covenantal authority entail? First, covenantal authority means *a man must lead his wife and children spiritually*. It all starts with the Christian faith. Husbands have a responsibility to lead their wives towards Christ. This means the husband is to make sure the couple is praying, reading Scripture, attending church, and worshiping God with their whole lives. If the wife is struggling spiritually, the husband has an obligation to help her and seek her spiritual good. Her spiritual well-being is his responsibility.

Men must also lead in training their children in the faith. God has commanded parents to teach God's Word to their children—"these words that I command you today shall be on your heart. You shall teach them diligently to your children, and shall talk of them when you sit in your house, and when you walk by the way, and when you lie down, and when you rise" (Deuteronomy 6:6-7). Paul echoes this when he writes, "Fathers, do not provoke your children to anger, but bring them up in the discipline and instruction of the Lord" (Ephesians 6:4). Notice the instruction is specifically to "fathers" [οἱ πατέρες, *hoi pateres*].[37] Though children

---

37. While οἱ πατέρες can refer to "parents" in general, as in Hebrews 11:23, the context here indicates Paul is addressing "fathers" in particular (as translated by the ESV, KJV, NASB, and NET). As O'Brien notes, there is a change in wording

are to obey both "parents," honoring both father and mother (the Fifth Commandment), fathers have a special responsibility to raise children in the Christian faith (Ephesians 6:1-4).

One of the purposes of marriage is to produce "godly offspring," or more literally, a "godly seed" (Malachi 2:15). Children are made "holy"—set apart and sanctified—by having just one Christian parent (1 Corinthians 7:14). Thus, this is a great obligation given to parents to raise their children to love and worship and obey Jesus Christ. And this obligation ultimately rests with fathers.

The Covenant Head Protects and Provides

Second, covenantal authority means *a man must provide for and protect his wife and children*. As seen from our study of Genesis 2–3, God gave man the task of working the ground to bring forth food. While we are not all farmers today, all men have the duty to provide for their families (see chapter 5). And just as Adam was to "guard" the garden (Genesis 2:15), so men are to protect the household. This includes physical protection. A man must protect his wife and children from harm, and he should use force if necessary. It is entirely reasonable for a man to keep a firearm in his home for protection from intruders. There is a proper time to carry and use a weapon (Luke 22:36). However, a man should also make decisions so as to keep his family out of dangerous situations. Examples include not

---

to οἱ πατέρες in Ephesians 6:4 from τοῖς γονεῦσιν ("parents") in 6:1, and "in both Graeco-Roman and Jewish writings, fathers were responsible for the education of their children." Peter T. O'Brien, *The Letter to the Ephesians* (The Pillar New Testament Commentary; Grand Rapids, MI: Eerdmans, 1999), 445. Two additional points can be made. First, Paul uses the word παιδείᾳ ("instruction") in Ephesians 6:4, which is a word used four times in the context of a father's obligation to "discipline" his son (Hebrews 12:5, 7, 8, 11). Second, Paul distinguishes between "father" and "mother" [τὸν πατέρα σου καὶ τὴν μητέρα] in Ephesians 6:2, using the singular πατέρα and then the plural πατέρες two verses later in 6:4. If Paul wanted to speak specifically to fathers, οἱ πατέρες were the words to use.

letting one's wife walk alone in a dangerous area of town, as well as keeping one's children out of physically (and spiritually) dangerous school settings.

A man must also protect his children from their own sin and unruliness. Children need teaching and discipline, and Hebrews 12 implies fathers have a special role in disciplining children. The author of Hebrews compares the discipline of earthly fathers to that of our heavenly Father:

> God is treating you as sons. *For what son is there whom his father does not discipline?* If you are left without discipline, in which all have participated, then you are illegitimate children and not sons. Besides this, we have had earthly *fathers who disciplined us* and we respected them. Shall we not much more be subject to the Father of spirits and live? For they disciplined us for a short time as it seemed best to them, but he disciplines us for our good, that we may share his holiness. For the moment all discipline seems painful rather than pleasant, but later it yields the peaceful fruit of righteousness to those who have been trained by it (Hebrews 12:7-11).

When fathers do not discipline their children, those children suffer. They do not develop good character and habits in life, and they often become lawless and disrespectful adults. But the godly father disciplines his children for their own good. Such discipline "yields the peaceful fruit of righteousness to those who have been trained by it" (Hebrews 12:11).

The man must also protect his marriage, both internally and externally. Internally, the man must seek to build and maintain a strong marriage. He must love his wife and honor her (Ephesians 5:25; 1 Peter 3:7). Externally, the man must keep outsiders out of his marriage, particularly the marriage bed—"Let marriage be held in honor among all, and let the marriage bed be undefiled, for God will judge the sexually immoral and adulterous" (Hebrews 13:4). Adultery is commonplace today because men do not properly guard themselves and their wives. Like all marital responsibilities, sexual faithfulness starts with the husband. A man should seek regular relations with his wife—"because of the temptation to sexual immorality, each man should have his own wife and each woman her own husband. The husband should give to his wife her conjugal rights, and likewise the wife to her husband" (1 Corinthians 7:2-3). Husband and wife have authority over the other spouse's body, and they should not deprive one another (7:4). Regular sexual relations protect against the work of Satan to destroy the marriage (7:5). Regular relations renew the "one flesh" marriage covenant (Genesis 2:24) and keep husband and wife sexually content.

Contrary to the lies of our culture, a real man—a godly man—is faithful to his wife. Promiscuity is not manly but a corruption of true masculinity, where men seek to "conquer" women but do not want to produce children with them and provide for them. Today, this also takes the form of pictures of fake women and internet whores. Such behavior is not masculine but breeds impotency. Real men are potent, seeking to produce children with one woman and raise them to be godly men and women.

God's will is that a godly man "abstain from sexual immorality" and "control his own body in holiness and honor" (1 Thessalonians 4:3-4).[38] Men who stray are those who are dissatisfied. Thus, a man should avoid adultery by rejoicing in the wife God has given him—"Drink water from your own cistern, flowing water from your own well . . . Let your fountain be blessed, and rejoice in the wife of your youth, a lovely deer, a graceful doe. Let her breasts fill you at all times with delight; be intoxicated always in her love. Why should you be intoxicated, my son, with a forbidden woman and embrace the bosom of an adulteress?" (Proverbs 5:15, 18-20).

The Beauty of Male Headship

As go the men, so go the women and children. God has made men and women to be different, and this is for the good of everyone. Gender roles

---

38. The literal Greek is "possess/acquire his own vessel" [τὸ ἑαυτοῦ σκεῦος κτᾶσθαι]. "Vessel" could refer to a man's "wife" (as in 1 Peter 3:7), as in a man should "acquire his own wife in holiness and honor." Or "vessel" could refer to a man's "body" (or be a euphemism for the male sexual organ), as in "possess his own body in holiness and honor." It is possible Paul intentionally left this ambiguous.

are to be embraced as a blessing to both husband and wife. God has put the man in authority over his wife. He does not say the man should "be" the head, but rather that he "is" the head. A husband has an authority of office. But he must also exercise that authority in a way that gains the respect of his wife and children. There is such a thing as a bad head of household.

Headship means responsibility. God has given men the special responsibility to lead their families. They hold a position of covenantal authority, and this means men must spiritually lead, provide for, and protect their wives and children. Yet feminists would put this responsibility on both husband and wife as mere individuals, rejecting the man's authority as covenant head. In doing so, they put a burden on women that they are not supposed to bear. And for women who still have children, they now carry the double burden of bearing children and providing for their families. Feminists want to democratize the family, but this will not work. Two parties cannot both have an equal vote. There must be a head, and that head is the man.

We live in a society that tears down male headship and thus tears down the family and civilization. Strong societies are built on strong families, and strong families are built on godly male headship. When a husband provides for his family, he frees up his wife to raise and nurse children and care for the home. And when a wife cares for the home and children, she frees up her husband to work and be creative. Scripture shows a better way than feminism. Male headship is a good thing, a beautiful thing. This is God's design. It is not oppressive or overbearing. Male headship properly exercised is for the good of everyone.

Chapter 8

PASTORS AND ELDERS MUST BE MEN
(1 TIMOTHY 2 & 3)

ALL THE SPIRITUAL leaders of old were men. This was by God's design, as He created men to hold authority. It was also the case that *leaders had to fight*. Abraham, Moses, Joshua, and David were all warriors. And the Levites were God's warrior-priests who guarded the tabernacle/temple (Exodus 32:27-29; Numbers 1:53). Church leaders today also have to fight, though it is a spiritual war—"We wrestle not against flesh and blood, but against the rulers, against the authorities, against the cosmic powers over this present darkness, against the spiritual forces of evil in the heavenly places" (Ephesians 6:12).

Both men and women are in this war together, but they do not share the same roles. When it comes to the church, God has only called men to lead. Thus, the Apostle Paul uses combat language to describe the role of the pastor, telling his disciple Timothy to "wage the good warfare" (1 Timothy 1:18), "fight the good fight of the faith" (1 Timothy 6:12), and "share in suffering as a good soldier of Christ Jesus" (2 Timothy 2:3). Pastors are warrior-shepherds who guard the flock of Christ. And such a role is only to be taken up by men. The pastorate is a call to arms.

God's Call, Not Ours

There is a sense in which a church "calls" a minister, by choosing a candidate and voting to confirm him. This is known as the external call. But first must come the internal call, God's inward working on a man's heart that leads him to the ministry. Many people claim to have this inward call, but it must be tested by God's Word.

God has laid down requirements for pastors and elders, and one of those requirements is that the person is a man. God only calls men to serve in the office of elder. (We will assume the view that a pastor is an elder, so we will use the word "elder" in this chapter to include pastors.[1]) It

---

1. This is known as the two-office view of church leadership, which holds that there are two offices (elder and deacon) with two orders of elder (teaching elder/pastor/minister and ruling elder). This view is based on the following points: (1) There are only two offices mentioned in the New Testament, "overseer" [ἐπίσκοπος] and "deacon" [διάκονος] (Philippians 1:1; 1 Timothy 3:1, 8); (2) The words for "elder" [πρεσβύτερος], "overseer" [ἐπίσκοπος], and "pastor" [ποιμήν] are used interchangeably (Acts 20:17, 28; Titus 1:5-7; 1 Peter 5:1-2); and (3) 1 Timothy 5:17 speaks of "elders" [πρεσβύτεροι] both "ruling" and "preaching and teaching" (just as the "overseers" [ἐπίσκοποι] both rule and teach in 3:2, 5), and this implies that only some elders "labor in preaching and teaching." This two-office view was defended by the Southern Presbyterians, including James Henley Thornwell and Robert Lewis Dabney. Based on this two-office view, the requirements in 1 Timothy 3 and Titus 1 apply to both orders of elders. Thus, throughout this chapter we refer to the one office of "elder." However, if one adopts the three-office view that the pastor/minister is a separate office from elder (a common view of the Reformation, with Calvin and the Westminster divines also holding to the fourth office of doctor of the church), the arguments in this chapter still apply, except for those based on 1 Timothy 3 and Titus 1 (as the three-office view limits these passages to the office of pastor/minister). The three-office view holds that the New Testament elder corresponds to the Old Testament elder and that the New Testament pastor/minister corresponds to the priest and Levite, the teachers of the Old Testament. The three-office view roots the role of ruling elder in Romans 12:7-8 [προϊστάμενος, "the one who leads"] and 1 Corinthians 12:28 [κυβερνήσεις, "administrating"], holding that while the priests and Levites shared the task of ruling with elders (Deuteronomy 17:8-13; 21:5; 1 Chronicles 23:3-4), their primary task was teaching the Word. Thus, while the three-office view can apply all the arguments in this chapter to the office of pastor, it is more dependent on the Old Testament example in arguing that only men can

does not matter how heartfelt a person's story is of God's internal call if it is contrary to God's written Word. It is Scripture that must be used to measure all internal claims. Thus, when examining whether women may be elders, we must look at what God's Word says about the issue.

We will begin by showing that Paul requires elders to be men in 1 Timothy 3 and Titus 1. Then we will show that 1 Timothy 2 prohibits women from teaching or exercising authority over men in church. In the next chapter, we will show that 1 Corinthians 14 prohibits women from speaking publicly in church. These interpretations lead to the following conclusions: (1) Women may not serve as elders; and (2) Women may not teach theology to men or exercise authority over them, but rather they should refrain from speaking publicly in church. We will conclude this topic by arguing that the pastoral tasks of preaching and ruling are masculine tasks. All of this is in continuity with the Old Testament practice of male-only teachers and rulers (priests and elders).

Elders Must Be Men (1 Timothy 3:1-7; Titus 1:5-9)

The Apostle Paul gives explicit requirements for an "overseer" (elder) in 1 Timothy 3 and Titus 1:

> [1] The saying is trustworthy: If anyone aspires to the office of overseer, he desires a noble task. [2] Therefore an overseer must be above reproach, the husband of one wife, sober-minded, self-controlled, respectable, hospitable, able to teach, [3] not a drunkard, not violent but gentle, not quarrelsome, not a lover of money. [4] He must manage his own household well, with all dignity keeping his children submissive, [5] for if someone does not know how to manage

---

be elders. For more on this debate, see the Knight–Rayburn exchange: George W. Knight III, "Two Offices (Elders/Bishops and Deacons) and Two Orders of Elders (Preaching/Teaching Elders and Ruling Elders): A New Testament Study," *Presbyterion* 11 (Spring 1985): 1–12; Robert S. Rayburn, "Ministers, Elders, and Deacons," *Presbyterion* 12 (Fall 1986): 105–114.

his own household, how will he care for God's church? ⁶ He must not be a recent convert, or he may become puffed up with conceit and fall into the condemnation of the devil. ⁷ Moreover, he must be well thought of by outsiders, so that he may not fall into disgrace, into a snare of the devil (1 Timothy 3:1-7).

⁵ This is why I left you in Crete, so that you might put what remained into order, and appoint elders in every town as I directed you— ⁶ if anyone is above reproach, the husband of one wife, and his children are believers and not open to the charge of debauchery or insubordination. ⁷ For an overseer, as God's steward, must be above reproach. He must not be arrogant or quick-tempered or a drunkard or violent or greedy for gain, ⁸ but hospitable, a lover of good, self-controlled, upright, holy, and disciplined. ⁹ He must hold firm to the trustworthy word as taught, so that he may be able to give instruction in sound doctrine and also to rebuke those who contradict it (Titus 1:5-9).

Egalitarians argue that the Greek word for "overseer" [ἐπίσκοπος, *episkopos*] can include both men and women. They are correct in pointing out that ἐπίσκοπος is a masculine word and that the masculine would be used if Paul meant to include both men and women. However, context must determine whether ἐπίσκοπος includes women, and the context provides several reasons for concluding that Paul only meant for men to be considered for the office of elder.

First, *Paul requires an elder to be a "man"* [ἄνδρα, *andra*]. This is part of Paul's phrase that an elder must be "the husband of one wife," or literally "the man of one woman" [μιᾶς γυναικὸς ἄνδρα] (1 Timothy 3:2; Titus 1:6). While the exact meaning of the phrase is debated, it seems both to prohibit polygamy and to require sexual fidelity. Egalitarians argue that a woman who is only married to one man meets this requirement. However, Paul uses the exact opposite phrase—"wife of one husband" [ἑνὸς ἀνδρὸς γυνή]—for the requirement for enrolling widows in the church in 1 Timothy 5:9. No one argues that Paul was enrolling male widowers in 1 Timothy 5, as he requires the person to be a "woman" and he uses feminine nouns throughout the passage (5:10-16). This was clearly a position for widows, who needed to be taken care of by the church because of the challenges of the ancient world for women without husbands or male family.

There is a parallel between 1 Timothy 3:2 and 1 Timothy 5:9. Either Paul meant to include both men and women in the office of elder *and* men and women in the enrollment of widows/widowers, or Paul meant to limit the office of elder to men and the enrollment of widows to women. If the former, one would expect Paul to use the masculine for both positions ("man of one woman"), including in 1 Timothy 5. But he did not do so. Instead Paul uses "woman of one man" in 1 Timothy 5:9 to limit enrollment of widows to women. In the same way, he uses "man of one woman" in 1 Timothy 3:2 to limit the office of elder to men.[2]

Second, *Paul requires an elder to be able to teach God's Word, which is a task reserved for men.* Paul says an elder must be "able to teach" and "able to give instruction in sound doctrine" (1 Timothy 3:2; Titus 1:9; cf. Ephesians 4:11; 1 Timothy 5:17), and teaching is a task that he limits to men in 1 Timothy 2:12. This point is connected with the interpretation of 1 Timothy 2 (see below). We will add here that only the *male* Levites had a teaching role in Israel (Deuteronomy 21:5; 33:10; 2 Chronicles 17:7-9; 35:3; Nehemiah 8:7-9; Malachi 2:4-7). Along with guarding the worship of Yahweh, one of the reasons the Levites were scattered throughout Israel was probably so they could instruct the Israelites in God's Word. Teaching God's Word has always been a manly task.

Third, *Paul connects the role of elder to that of the man as head of the household.* Paul says an elder must "manage his own household well" and keep "his children submissive." This leads him to ask—"if someone does not know how to manage his own household, how will he care for God's church?" (1 Timothy 3:4-5). Thus Paul connects household management with the management of God's house, the church. The role of keeping

---

2. This point is conveniently ignored by egalitarian treatments of this passage, such as Payne, *Man and Woman, One in Christ*, 445–459.

children "submissive" is a task given particularly to men, as "fathers" are to "discipline" their children (Hebrews 12:7-11) and bring them up in the Lord's "discipline" (Ephesians 6:4). The verb used for elders in 1 Timothy 3:4 is προΐστημι (*proistemi*), which means "to exercise a position of leadership, *rule, direct, be at the head (of)*"[3] (also used in 1 Thessalonians 5:12; 1 Timothy 3:12; 5:17). This sort of ruling management is associated with man as the head of the household, not woman.[4] And if a woman is not the ruler of her house, how can she rule God's house?

Thus, a woman cannot lead the church as an elder because a woman is not even the head of her own household (1 Corinthians 11:2-16; Ephesians 5:22-33; Colossians 3:18; Titus 2:3-5; 1 Peter 3:1-6). The church is an extension of the family, the family of believers. The family also serves as a model for the church. Thus, *the principles of the family, including male headship, extend out to the church*. A woman serving as an elder would result in a woman exercising authority over male heads of other families and even her own husband.

Paul could have used language that included women in his description of elders if that is what he intended. In fact, Paul did distinguish "women" from the male deacons in 1 Timothy 3:11, using the word "likewise," just as he used "likewise" to distinguish deacons from elders in 3:8. While some argue that this means the women were also deaconesses, it more likely means women (or deacons' wives) had some role alongside the deacons in their service, which was not the case with elders.[5] The point is that Paul speaks of women as a separate group from the deacons (1 Timothy

---

3. BDAG, 870.

4. Philip H. Towner, *The Letters to Timothy and Titus* (The New International Commentary on the New Testament; Grand Rapids, MI: Eerdmans, 2006), 256: "[T]his is the verb used to describe the father's responsibility within the household," citing Philo's *On Sobriety* as an example.

5. There is disagreement over whether women can serve as deaconesses, even among those who firmly hold that only men can serve as elders. This is in part because of Paul's reference to Γυναῖκας ("women/wives") in 1 Timothy 3:11 amidst his requirements for deacons (1 Timothy 3:8-13). This debate is related but not essential to the argument in this chapter. For more detail, see the argument against deaconesses in chapter 4, pages 91–95.

3:8-13) and thus only speaks of men deacons in 3:8-10, 12-13. Since there are similar requirements for elders and deacons ("husband of one wife," "managing their household well"), this further supports the case that Paul only refers to men in his discussion of elders (3:1-7).

Considering the patriarchal culture of Israel, one would have expected Paul to be *clear and unambiguous* in overturning male rule—if that is what he wanted to do. If Paul intended to include women as candidates for elder, as egalitarians claim, then he did a very poor job. Of course, that is not what Paul did, as he did not intend for women to be elders but carried on the Old Testament practice of male rule in the church. Elders are shepherds and overseers of the flock, and they hold an office reserved for men.

Women Are Not to Teach or Exercise Authority Over Men (1 Timothy 2:8-15)

Next we come to one of the most important and thus controversial passages on the subject of men in church leadership. This passage comes right before Paul's requirements for elders in 1 Timothy 3, which we just discussed. It is helpful to see the full context and Paul's reasoning:

> [8] I desire then that in every place the men should pray, lifting holy hands without anger or quarreling; [9] likewise also that women should adorn themselves in respectable apparel, with modesty and self-control, not with braided hair and gold or pearls or costly attire, [10] but with what is proper for women who profess godliness—with good works. [11] Let a woman learn quietly with all submissiveness. [12] I do not permit a woman to teach or to exercise authority over a man; rather, she is to remain quiet. [13] For Adam was formed first, then Eve; [14] and Adam was not deceived, but the woman was deceived and became a transgressor. [15] Yet she will be saved through childbearing—if they continue in faith and love and holiness, with self-control (1 Timothy 2:8-15).

We will argue that Paul in this passage prohibits women both from teaching Scripture and theology to men and from exercising authority over them (1 Timothy 2:12). This prohibition is not specific to culture or the circumstances at Ephesus, since Paul roots this in the creation order—man was created first (and thus was given authority over woman), and woman was deceived, not man (and thus woman is not fit to teach man) (2:13-14). Rather, women are to remain silent in the context of theological instruction, with a spirit of submission (2:11-12). They are to carry out their God-given role as women, exemplified in childbearing, rather than carry out the tasks given to men. The faith that leads to salvation will produce obedience to God's design for men and women (2:15).

The context of these instructions in 1 Timothy 2:8-15 is not explicit, but there are two reasons to think Paul is describing the *public church assembly*. First, Paul only desires that the "men" pray (1 Timothy 2:8) and makes no mention of women praying,[6] though women would surely be encouraged to pray in private settings. Second, teaching and exercising authority over men in the church (2:12) would primarily take place in publicly assembled worship. Therefore, Paul likely gives instructions here for the public church assembly, though the principles are not necessarily restricted to this context.

After instructing men to pray and women to dress modestly (1 Timothy 2:8-10), Paul commands women to "learn quietly with all submissiveness" (2:11). Then he says, "I do not permit a woman to teach or to exercise authority over a man; rather, she is to remain quiet" (2:12). Paul gives this command in the first person singular, "I do not permit"

---

6. Some argue that the verb "I want" [Βούλομαι] and the infinitive "to pray" [προσεύχεσθαι] should also be included in the instructions for women in 1 Timothy 2:9, thus yielding, "Likewise I desire that women pray in respectable apparel." However, 2:9 already has its own infinitive "to adorn" [κοσμεῖν], which parallels the infinitive "to pray" for men in 2:8. Further, the entire context of 2:8-15 concerns women's behavior without mentioning prayer. The majority of English translations follow this reading. See James Greenbury, "The Contribution of 1 Timothy 2:8-15 and 1 Corinthians 11:5 to the Discussion Concerning Women Speaking in Church," *Presbyterion* 44/2 (Fall 2018): 56–60.

[ἐπιτρέπω, *epitrepo*], which carries the authority of Christ's apostle.[7] Paul prohibits women from two tasks: (1) teaching [διδάσκειν, *didaskein*], and (2) exercising authority [αὐθεντεῖν, *authentein*] over men. The first verb, διδάσκειν, is the common word for "teaching" in the New Testament and Septuagint.

The second verb, αὐθεντεῖν, is used only here in the New Testament (known as a *hapax legomenon*). BDAG defines it as "to assume a stance of independent authority, *give orders to, dictate to*."[8] This word has been the source of controversy because of its rarity. Many egalitarians have argued that the verb αὐθεντέω (*authenteo*) has a pejorative meaning ("domineer") or ingressive meaning ("assume authority"),[9] either of which would support their claim that Paul was not giving a universal prohibition against women teaching or exercising authority over men (since this would still allow women to exercise *proper* authority). However, Al Wolters has established that the pejorative and ingressive meanings are "very unlikely" and that "αὐθεντέω in general is used overwhelmingly in a positive or neutral sense." This is in part based on the fact that the word "often occurs in Christian contexts with God or Jesus Christ as its subject."[10] Contextually,

---

7. Payne has argued that ἐπιτρέπω is a temporary prohibition based on the fact that other uses in the New Testament involve the permission of a temporary action. However, this is because the action involved is often brief, such as saying farewell (Luke 9:61). None of the other 16 uses of ἐπιτρέπω in the New Testament is a first-person verb, and only one other involves a negation—the parallel passage in 1 Corinthians 14:34, which uses οὐ ("not"). Moreover, Paul bases his prohibition on the creation order ("for Adam was formed first, then Eve"), not some present situation. Thus, Payne's claim that Paul "did not give 1 Tim 2:12's restrictions on women in the Ephesian church any universalizing qualifier" is plainly wrong. Payne, *Man and Woman, One in Christ*, 320–321.

8. BDAG, 150.

9. Payne, *Man and Woman, One in Christ*, 385. Payne argues for the meaning "assume authority."

10. Al Wolters, "The Meaning of Αὐθεντέω," in *Women in the Church: An Interpretation & Application of 1 Timothy 2:9-15* (eds. Andreas J. Köstenberger and Thomas R. Schreiner; 3rd ed.; Wheaton, IL: Crossway, 2016), 113: "my basic thesis in this chapter is that αὐθεντέω in 1 Timothy 2:12 is very unlikely to have either a pejorative or an ingressive meaning. A number of converging lines

it also does not make sense that Paul would prohibit only women from the negative behavior of "domineering." If the meaning were negative, we would expect Paul to prohibit both men and women from engaging in such activity. Therefore, αὐθεντεῖν in 1 Timothy 2:12 should be understood as "to exercise authority."

Some argue that these two verbs, διδάσκειν and αὐθεντεῖν, form a hendiadys referring to one function, "a single internally cohering idea."[11] In this case, these two verbs would combine to refer to an "authoritative teaching."[12] There are three reasons this should be rejected and instead should be translated "teach or exercise authority." First, the word in between the two verbs, οὐδὲ (*oude*), is a negative coordinating conjunction that means "nor" or "or." While it can join "'two closely related items,' it does not usually join together words that restate the same thing or that are mutually interpreting."[13] Second, Paul separates the two verbs rather than keep them next to each other, placing "teach" at the front of the sentence and the phrase "I do not permit a woman" between the two verbs [διδάσκειν δὲ γυναικὶ οὐκ ἐπιτρέπω οὐδὲ αὐθεντεῖν ἀνδρός].[14]

---

of evidence have confirmed this thesis: cognates, immediate context, ancient versions, patristic commentary, and the broad usage of the verb elsewhere."

11. Payne, *Man and Woman, One in Christ*, 341.

12. Ibid., 358. Combined with his definition of "assume authority" for αὐθεντεῖν, Payne argues these two verbs together mean "to take for herself authority to teach a man without authorization from the church." Ibid., 393.

13. Douglas J. Moo, "What Does It Mean Not to Teach or Have Authority Over Men? 1 Timothy 2:11-15," in *Recovering Biblical Manhood and Womanhood*, 187. Moo is quoting the phrase "two closely related items" from Philip B. Payne, "The Interpretation of I Timothy 2:11-15: A Surrejoinder," 104 (an unpublished paper).

14. Payne points to the similar construction of 1 Timothy 6:16, which speaks of God, "whom no one has ever seen or can see" [ὃν εἶδεν οὐδεὶς ἀνθρώπων οὐδὲ ἰδεῖν δύναται]. He says, "οὐδὲ immediately precedes an infinitive, and in both verses the verbs οὐδὲ joins are about as far removed from each other in their clauses as possible. Thus, the distance between the two infinitives in 1 Tim 2:12 does not militate against its οὐδὲ forming a single internally cohering idea." Payne, *Man and Woman, One in Christ*, 347. There are two problems with appealing to this passage. First, there is no main verb between the infinitives in 1 Timothy 6:16 as there is in 1 Timothy 2:12. The only words between are "no one" [οὐδεὶς

Third, Paul distinguishes between the tasks of teaching and ruling later in the letter in 1 Timothy 5:17. Though he uses a different word for "rule" [προεστῶτες], this still supports the distinction between two related tasks of teaching and ruling.

Paul is thus prohibiting two different tasks, even if they are related. As Andreas Köstenberger says, there is "a difference between a single idea that *encompasses* two elements joined by οὐδὲ . . . and a single idea that *combines* two elements joined by οὐδὲ."[15] In other words, the verbs can be related but not merged. Köstenberger also argues that οὐδὲ joins two activities that are both viewed positively or negatively.[16] Thus, the egalitarian attempt to define αὐθεντεῖν negatively ("assume authority") and then combine it with the positive διδάσκειν does not work. Consistency would require egalitarians to also take διδάσκειν negatively, but most egalitarians (including Philip Payne) do not do this because of its overwhelmingly positive meaning. Furthermore, even if these verbs were to form one concept, this activity is still contrasted [ἀλλ᾽, "but/rather"] with "quietness/silence" [ἡσυχία]. This contrast does not leave room for the egalitarian argument that Paul permits women to teach men in some capacity as long as it does not undermine proper church authority.

It is important to note the object of the verbs in 1 Timothy 2:12—"a man." Women are not permitted "to teach or exercise authority *over a man*." The genitive noun "man" [ἀνδρός] certainly modifies "exercise authority" [αὐθεντεῖν] because the noun immediately follows the verb. Some argue that "man" does not modify "teach" [διδάσκειν] because this verb is placed at the very front of the verse and because this verb is normally followed by a noun in the accusative (e.g. Romans 2:21) or dative form

---

ἀνθρώπων]. Second, the two infinitives [εἶδεν . . . ἰδεῖν] in 1 Timothy 6:16 are not as unified as Payne claims, and thus they do not support Payne's unified reading of the infinitives in 1 Timothy 2:12. Payne argues the infinitives combine to form one action in 1 Timothy 2:12 ("to assume authoritative teaching"), but the infinitives in 1 Timothy 6:16 are related actions that are *still distinct* ("no one has ever seen or can see").

15. Andreas Köstenberger, "A Complex Sentence: The Syntax of 1 Timothy 2:12," in *Women in the Church* (3rd ed.), 147.

16. Ibid., 146.

(e.g. Revelation 2:14), not the genitive as is the case here with ἀνδρός. However, as Moo points out, the word order is not decisive because of the flexibility of Greek word order, and when two verbs take the same object, the object takes "the case demanded by the nearer verb."[17]

If "man" does not modify διδάσκειν, then Paul's prohibition on women teaching in 1 Timothy 2:12 could be even broader than just over men. However, elsewhere Paul says that women do have some teaching role, as he commands older women "to teach what is good" [καλοδιδασκάλους] to younger women, which at least includes biblical principles of Christian behavior (Titus 2:3-5). Thus, it is likely that "man" is the object of "teach" in 1 Timothy 2:12. Paul is not prohibiting women from teaching and exercising authority in their proper sphere, such as in relation to children or over other women, but he is prohibiting women from teaching the Bible and theology to men or exercising authority over them.

Paul follows his prohibition with the adversative ἀλλ' (*all*, "but" or "rather"), contrasting this with the prior clause. Thus, there is a both a negative command (women are not permitted to teach or exercise authority) and a contrasting positive command (women are to remain quiet/silent). This requirement that women be "quiet" (or more likely "silent") rules out the common egalitarian objection that Paul only prohibits an "authoritative teaching" and that women can teach men in a different way (e.g. under the authority of the senior pastor) or setting (e.g. at a campus ministry meeting). In the context of Christian teaching, women are not to teach but instead are to remain silent/quiet.

Should this be understood as "quiet" or "silent"? The word ἡσυχία (*hesuchia*) can refer to a "quiet demeanor" (e.g. 2 Thessalonians 3:12) or "silence" (e.g. Acts 22:2). The meaning of "quiet demeanor" is often favored by commentators today because of its use earlier in 1 Timothy 2:2. However, there are good reasons to adopt the meaning "silence" for ἡσυχία

---

17. Moo, "What Does It Mean Not to Teach or Have Authority Over Men? 1 Timothy 2:11-15," in *Recovering Biblical Manhood and Womanhood*, 497 (endnote 16). On the case issue, Moo cites Herbert Weir Smyth, *Greek Grammar* (Cambridge, MA: Harvard University Press, 1920), 1634.

in 2:11-12. (The word is used in both 2:11 and 2:12.) First, when ἡσυχίᾳ refers to a "quiet demeanor" in other passages, it does not involve speaking (Luke 23:56; 1 Thessalonians 4:11; 2 Thessalonians 3:12; 1 Timothy 2:2; 1 Peter 3:4). Contrast that with Paul's words in 2:11-12 that are in the context of speaking. Second, when ἡσυχίᾳ involves speaking in other passages, as it does here, it means "silence" (Luke 14:4; Acts 21:14; 22:2). Third, Paul addresses the manner in which women are to "learn," which is "with all submissiveness" (1 Timothy 2:11), suggesting the stronger meaning of "silent." Fourth, Paul's command for women to be in ἡσυχίᾳ is strongly contrasted [ἀλλ'] with his prohibition of teaching and exercising authority, also supporting the stronger meaning "silent." "Silence" is in fact the meaning that BDAG assigns to ἡσυχίᾳ here,[18] and it was Calvin's interpretation.[19] Therefore, Paul not only prohibits women from teaching or exercising authority over a man, but he also requires the opposite—that women be "silent" in the public church assembly.

The Basis of Paul's Prohibition (1 Timothy 2:13-14)

What is the basis for Paul's command in 1 Timothy 2:12? In the verses that follow, Paul bases his prohibition on two aspects of the creation account—"For Adam was formed first, then Eve; and Adam was not deceived, but the woman was deceived and became a transgressor" (1 Timothy 2:13-14). Thus, Paul gives two explanations for why he prohibits women from teaching or exercising authority over men: (1) the creation order, as Adam was created first before Eve (Genesis 2:7, 22), and (2) Eve's deception by the serpent, as Adam "was not deceived" (Genesis 3:6, 12).

Some egalitarians argue that "for" [γὰρ] in 1 Timothy 2:13 is explanatory rather than illative (giving a reason), meaning Adam being formed first and Eve being deceived serves as an *illustration* of what happens when

---

18. BDAG, 440.
19. John Calvin, *Commentaries on the Epistles to Timothy, Titus, and Philemon*, 67: "for *quietness* means silence, that they may not take upon them to speak in public."

women falsely teach men.[20] However, this makes little sense. The fact that Adam was created before Eve cannot be understood as an illustration or example of what happens when women falsely teach men. Further, it is fitting that reasons would follow a prohibition. In fact, when Paul gives a command followed by γάρ elsewhere in the Pastoral Epistles, he states the reasons for the command (1 Timothy 4:7-8, 16; 5:4, 11, 15, 18; 2 Timothy 1:6-7; 2:7, 16; 3:5-6; 4:3, 5-6, 9-10, 11, 15; Titus 3:1-3, 9, 12).[21] Thus, Paul commands women not to teach or exercise authority over men because that is not how God has designed men and women at creation.

By citing the creation of Adam and Eve and their sin, Paul appeals to the entire creation account in Genesis 1–3. Paul's choice of Greek words clearly alludes to the Septuagint translation of Genesis 2 and 3. He uses the same word for Adam being "formed" [πλάσσω, *plasso*] in 1 Timothy 2:13 that is used for Adam in Genesis 2:7, 7, 15, 19 [LXX]. Paul then uses the same word for Eve being "deceived" [ἀπατάω, *apatao*] in 1 Timothy 2:14 (cf. 2 Corinthians 11:3) that is used in Genesis 3:13 [LXX]—"The woman said, 'The serpent *deceived* me, and I ate.'"

As for Adam being formed first (1 Timothy 2:13), George Knight says, "With this brief statement on the order of creation Paul appeals to the whole of the creation narrative, as is indicated by his fuller treatment in 1 Cor. 11:8-9." This "whole account" includes the woman being man's "helper" (Genesis 2:18) and the significance of the man naming the woman (Genesis 2:23). Knight concludes, "So it is not mere chronology ('first . . . then . . .') that Paul appeals to here but what is entailed in this

---

20. Payne, *Man and Woman, One in Christ*, 399–415. Payne goes so far as to say, "If Paul's restriction in 2:12 is rooted in creation and verses 13-14 imply a principle of creation, what is that principle? Paul gives us no explanation here of what significance he draws from Adam being formed first." Ibid., 402. Of course, Paul did explain the significance of Adam being formed first, which is that women are not to "teach or exercise authority over men" (1 Timothy 2:12). It is quite clear that Paul takes the order of creation to mean that men and women should relate to each other differently, which includes women not holding leadership over men in the church.

21. Schreiner, "An Interpretation of 1 Timothy 2:9-15," in *Women in the Church* (3rd ed.), 200.

chronology."²² Thus, Paul's appeal to Adam being formed first is an appeal to the hierarchy of rank and Adam's authority over Eve.

Many refer to Adam's chronological priority here as "primogeniture" (the special rights that came along with firstborn status), but Knight rightly recognizes that Paul is appealing to a similar but different Old Testament concept.²³ However, the Old Testament practice of primogeniture at least shows that chronological priority had some significance (and still does in some cultures).

That being said, Paul does appeal to two specific facts of creation in 1 Timothy 2:13-14, and it is very possible these correspond to the two tasks prohibited for women. Teaching may correspond to Adam's being formed first (as he had an obligation to teach God's Law to the woman created after him), and exercising authority may correspond to Eve's deception (as she usurped Adam's authority over her). Alternatively, it may be that exercising authority corresponds to Adam's being formed first (as he carried authority over his wife) and teaching corresponds to Eve's deception (as she was more prone to deception).

It is significant that Paul roots his prohibition in creation, as the prohibition is not something to be overcome through redemption in Christ.²⁴ Adam was formed prior to Eve, and this fact has implications for men and women for whom Christ is restoring the natural order. Paul's prohibition on women teaching and exercising authority over men is rooted in God's original design, where Adam held authority over Eve in the garden. Adam had the obligation to teach God's Law to Eve and to protect her, as she was made after him and for him. The order of creation expresses God's differing design for men and women.

---

22. George W. Knight III, *The Pastoral Epistles: A Commentary on the Greek Text* (The New International Greek Testament Commentary; Grand Rapids, MI: Eerdmans, 1992), 143.

23. Ibid.

24. Douglas Moo, "What Does It Mean Not to Teach or Have Authority Over Men?" in *Recovering Biblical Manhood and Womanhood*, 190: "For by rooting these prohibitions in the circumstances of creation rather than in the circumstances of the fall, Paul shows that he does not consider these restrictions to be the product of the curse and presumably, therefore, to be phased out by redemption."

The Significance of Eve's Deception (1 Timothy 2:14)

Paul also mentions Eve's deception as part of the basis for his prohibition, specifically saying that "Adam was not deceived, but the woman was deceived and became a transgressor" (1 Timothy 2:14). What does he mean by this? There are two possibilities.[25]

The first option is that Eve by her womanly nature was more prone to deception than man. Eve's deception exemplifies the differing natures and inclinations of men and women, and thus women are prohibited from teaching and exercising authority over men. As Neuer explains, woman has a "greater susceptibility to temptation" that "makes her less suited to the office of teacher than a man."[26] This was the most common historical interpretation. Yet Thomas Schreiner notes that this view "is usually dismissed out of hand today because it is so shocking to modern sensibilities."[27] Schreiner himself rejects this interpretation "since it implies that women are ontologically and intellectually inferior."[28] However, Schreiner's conclusion is questionable, as it assumes that men and women cannot have different strengths and weaknesses. Peter calls woman the "weaker vessel" (1 Peter 3:7), yet that does not mean she is less valuable than man, nor does it mean she has no comparative strengths. It is possible women are

---

25. Calvin adds a third interpretation, holding that "women are made subordinate on account of Eve's transgression," a punishment that is rooted in Genesis 3:16. According to Calvin, Adam also sinned, but Eve was the "source" of the fall and "more at fault than man," and thus "Eve's trespass had to be punished in every woman" (similar to how "God punished the whole human race for Adam's sin"). Apart from the fall, women would still have been "subordinate" to men, but now it is a harsher rule that can feel like "bondage." John Calvin, *Sermons on 1 Timothy* (trans. Robert White; Carlisle, PA: Banner of Truth, 2018), 266–267, 269–270, 273. I do not find Calvin's interpretation persuasive since it strays from Paul's focus on Adam's lack of deception. Further, Paul makes no mention of God's punishment in Genesis 3:16.

26. Neuer, *Man and Woman in Christian Perspective*, 120.

27. Schreiner, "An Interpretation of 1 Timothy 2:9-15," in *Women in the Church* (3rd ed.), 214.

28. Ibid.

more prone to deception as part of their emotional wiring, which does not mean women are less intelligent than men—just different.

Daniel Doriani argues that this position "proves too much," since if "women lack discernment, they should not be permitted to teach other women or children either."[29] This critique also fails, as Paul would only mean that women should not teach *men* because women are more prone to deception when compared to men. Women are not more prone to deception than children or other women, and thus women can teach these groups. Interestingly, Doriani still ends up holding a variation of this position, which is that God shaped male and female minds, proclivities, and even bodies differently so as to "reflect his decree."[30] He says that women are not intellectually inferior and do not have "less capacity than men," but women "have different inclinations," and "God created women with an orientation toward relationships more than analysis."[31] In this case, Paul would mean that women are less inclined towards doctrine than men, and thus women are less suited for teaching men.

George Knight adds the insightful point that *God designed woman to follow*. He asks, "Why did the serpent approach her, not Adam? We may deduce that the serpent was aware that she was more susceptible to his deception. Why so? Because she had been created to be a helper to another and to submit to him. God had made her willing to follow. What was, and still is, her virtue and strength, the serpent utilized and twisted to harm her."[32] Thus, woman is more susceptible to deception because God designed her to follow, not lead. What is her great strength can also be exposed as her great weakness. And since women are more susceptible to deception than men, they are not to teach or exercise authority over men.

---

29. Daniel Doriani, "A History of the Interpretation of 1 Timothy 2," in *Women in the Church* (1st ed.), 258–259.
30. Ibid., 263.
31. Ibid.
32. George W. Knight III, "The Role of Women in the Church," in *Confessing our Hope: Essays Celebrating the Life and Ministry of Morton H. Smith* (eds. Joseph A. Pipa, Jr. and C.N. Willborn; Taylors, SC: Southern Presbyterian Press, 2004), 198.

The second option for interpreting 1 Timothy 2:14 is that Eve's deception serves as an example of what happens when male authority is subverted. Eve usurped Adam's leadership role and was subsequently deceived, whereas it should have been Adam who dealt with the serpent. Eve's deception was thus tied with her exercising improper authority over Adam, the very thing Paul was instructing women not to do,[33] and her deception highlights Adam's failure to exercise his authority and guard her from the serpent. This second interpretation seeks to explain Paul's concern to prohibit women from teaching *men* in particular, as it focuses on role reversal rather than woman's flaws.[34]

However, there are problems with this second view. First, Paul explicitly mentions Eve's deception, not role reversal. Second, this view does not account for Paul's emphasis on Adam's *lack* of deception—"*and Adam was not deceived*, but the woman was deceived and became a transgressor" (1 Timothy 2:14). Women are not to teach or exercise authority over men because Adam was not deceived but Eve was. Nothing in the text speaks of Adam's failure to lead, and at best this is implied. Third, this view weakens Paul's prohibition by removing the basis of ontological differences between men and women. Douglas Moo advocates this view, taking Paul to mean that if the women of Ephesus seek the roles given to men in the church, "they will make the same mistake Eve made and bring similar disaster on themselves and the church."[35] Yet it is unclear why "disaster" would come about by women teaching men if Paul's prohibition is not rooted in God's

---

33. Moo, "What Does It Mean Not to Teach or Have Authority Over Men? 1 Timothy 2:11-15," in *Recovering Biblical Manhood and Womanhood*, 190: "More likely, then, verse 14, in conjunction with verse 13, is intended to remind the women at Ephesus that Eve was deceived by the serpent in the Garden (Genesis 3:13) precisely in taking the initiative over the man whom God had given to be with her and to take care for her. In the same way, if the women at the church at Ephesus proclaim their independence from the men of the church, refusing to learn 'in quietness and full submission' (verse 11), seeking roles that have been given to men in the church (verse 12), they will make the same mistake Eve made and bring similar disaster on themselves and the church."
34. Ibid.
35. Ibid.

differing design of men and women. If women are as capable of teaching and exercising authority as men, then what causes a problem? The first view explains that disaster would come about because women are less fit for teaching and exercising authority.

Thus, the first view makes better sense of Paul's reference to Eve's deception, that women are more prone to deception than men due to their differing natures and proclivities, including that God designed women to follow, not lead. This does not rule out the point of the second view that Eve's deception involved a role reversal,[36] but it does not take this to be Paul's main point. In this case, Paul in 1 Timothy 2:13-14 prohibits women from teaching and exercising authority over men based on two principles: (1) Man, who was formed first, is higher in rank and authority; and (2) Woman, who is more prone to deception, is less suited for these tasks.

Is 1 Timothy 2:8-15 Limited to the Public Church Assembly?

This still leaves an important question—what kind of teaching and exercising of authority does Paul have in mind? Can a woman ever teach or exercise authority over a man? As mentioned above, Paul probably has the public church assembly in mind when giving these instructions because he only desires "men" to pray (1 Timothy 2:8) and because teaching primarily takes place in the public church assembly. However, the principles of Paul's instructions should not be limited to the public church assembly. Men should still pray and women should still dress modestly and practice good works (2:8-10) outside of the public assembly. Furthermore, the exercising of authority (2:12), assumed to be the task of elders, is a function that is carried on outside of the public gathering of Christians. In the following chapter, Paul says, "I am writing these things to you so that, if I delay, you

---

36. Knight, "The Role of Women in the Church," in *Confessing our Hope*, 198: "She fell into this sin by reversing the leadership roles which God had ordained for them. She acted as their head, while Adam in turn was not fulfilling his role, but perversely followed her lead."

may know how one ought to behave *in the household of God*" (1 Timothy 3:14-15). Therefore, the application of 1 Timothy 2:8-15 should not be limited to a church worship service but applies to all Christian settings.

However, Paul does not seem to have in mind every form of teaching and every form of authority. The verb διδάσκω (*didasko*) is a very common word in the New Testament for authoritative doctrinal instruction,[37] and the New Testament ties its practice to those who have the "gift" of teaching (1 Corinthians 12:28-30; Ephesians 4:11). It is unlikely that Paul means to prohibit a woman from teaching a literature course to men at the local university. Therefore, if we understand that 1 Timothy 2:12 applies to the church at large and that it includes teaching the Bible and theology, then we must conclude that women are never to teach or exercise authority over men in a Christian setting. Thus, Paul's words would prohibit women from teaching theology to men in Sunday school and small groups, as well as in seminaries, Bible colleges, and high schools.

Women still can and should teach the Bible, but in a limited capacity. Women can teach women and children because they are not adult men. In fact, Paul elsewhere *commands* older women to "teach" and "train" younger women (Titus 2:3-5). Yet Paul also has specific teaching in mind, as "older women" are to "teach what is good, and so train the young women to love their husbands and children, to be self-controlled, pure, working at home, kind, and submissive to their own husbands." Older women are to teach the younger women to be good wives and mothers. Paul did not instruct Timothy to teach these things to the younger women, but instead he was to teach the older women who would then instruct the younger women. Thus, about half of the women in the church (older women) have the duty of instructing the other half of the women (younger women) in Christian living. In this way, Christians "teach and admonish one another," according their proper spheres (Colossians 3:16).

There is even an example of a woman and her husband (Priscilla and Aquila) taking a man (Apollos) aside and instructing him in the faith (Acts

---

37. See the discussion in chapter 10 of John Dickson's argument that διδάσκω only refers to the apostolic doctrine passed down.

18:24-26). However, we should not draw too much from this example (as many egalitarians do), since we do not know the extent of the role Priscilla played. And we should not infer much from the fact that Priscilla is listed before her husband. The passage is also descriptive and not prescriptive. At most this teaches that a woman with her husband can instruct a man in the gospel in a private setting. Earlier in Acts, when the Council of Jerusalem wanted to send people along to explain (and thus teach) their letter to the churches at Antioch, Syria, and Cilicia regarding the requirements for Gentiles, they chose "men" [ἄνδρας] (Acts 15:22, 25). They chose Judas and Silas—both prophets—who would tell the "same things [as the letter] by word of mouth" (Acts 15:27, 32). Though there were prophetesses, when the task involved teaching, the church specifically looked to appoint men, not women.

Objection 1—1 Timothy 2:12 Is Limited by Culture and Context

There are two primary objections to this interpretation of 1 Timothy 2:8-15. The first and most common objection is that this is a culturally-based or context-specific prohibition that no longer applies. This objection usually involves the argument that Paul was dealing with a specific false teaching taking place in Ephesus (1 Timothy 1:3), such as the worship of the pagan goddess Artemis.[38] However, the nature of the false teaching in Ephesus is not entirely clear. We know that the false teaching forbade marriage, which Paul says was the "teaching of demons" (1 Timothy 4:1-3), and we know that Paul commands younger widows to marry and have children, stating that some had "strayed after Satan" (1 Timothy 5:14-15). The implication of these passages is that the false teaching was encouraging women to abandon married life and children. This fits with Paul's exhortation for women to bear children in 2:15—"Yet she will be saved through childbearing" (see chapter 2 for the meaning of this verse).

---

38. Linda L. Belleville, "Teaching and Usurping Authority: 1 Timothy 2:11-15," in *Discovering Biblical Equality*, 219.

Egalitarians sometimes claim that Paul's prohibition in 1 Timothy 2:12 is based on women in Ephesus being less educated.[39] However, this explanation is problematic, for Paul not only fails to mention any lack of female education, but he instead cites the moral problem of deception. Paul does not appeal to Eve's lack of education (for she was aware of God's prohibition), but he emphasizes that she was "deceived" and became a "transgressor" (1 Timothy 2:14).

Other egalitarians suggest that false teachers in Ephesus were targeting women. But the question then becomes—why did Paul only prohibit women from teaching and exercising authority, and why only over men? This egalitarian reasoning assumes that *all* women in Ephesus were deceived by false teaching (implying women are more easily deceived), or, alternatively, that only *some* women were deceived but Paul still restricted *all* women (and no men) from teaching and exercising authority over men (which does not make sense apart from an ontological basis). Some egalitarians suggest that the false teachers in Ephesus were women and that is why Paul prohibits women from teaching and exercising authority. But the only false teachers in Ephesus named in Paul's writings were *men*, namely Hymenaeus, Alexander, and Philetus (1 Timothy 1:19-20; 2 Timothy 2:17-18).

In the end, the specifics of the false teaching really do not matter for our purposes. This is because *Paul grounds his prohibition of women teaching and exercising authority over men in the creation order, not culture or circumstance*—"For Adam was formed first, then Eve; and Adam was not deceived, but the woman was deceived and became a transgressor" (1 Timothy 2:13-14). In other words, this prohibition *transcends culture* because it is based on the natural order.

Some egalitarian interpreters do not think that Adam being created prior to Eve should have any implications, citing that the animals were created prior to Adam. However, there are major differences between humans and animals. Unlike the animals, humans were made in God's image and were explicitly given dominion over the animals (Genesis 1:26, 28). That

---

39. Keener, *Paul, Women & Wives*, 120; Westfall, *Paul and Gender*, 306–307.

the animals were made prior to their human rulers is irrelevant. However, chronological priority does matter when dealing with two humans, a man and a woman both made by God in His image to rule over creation. God could have made Adam and Eve at the exact same time, but He did not do so. Most importantly, *the Apostle Paul thought Adam's chronological priority meant something*.

Such critics often charge that the Bible's teaching of male leadership in the church is a product of ancient custom and the prevalent sexism at the time. However, this is false. Woman priestesses were common within paganism in the ancient world, and Christianity was actually acting *counter-culturally* by prohibiting woman pastors and elders. The church went against the trend of the day, and in order to do so it grounded this prohibition in the creation order.

Some egalitarians argue that we cannot draw too much from Paul's basis in the creation account in 1 Timothy 2:12 because in 1 Corinthians 11:2-16 Paul also bases the requirement for women's head coverings on creation and even most complementarians do not practice that today. In other words, the argument is that complementarians are inconsistent in their treatment of 1 Timothy 2 and 1 Corinthians 11. There are two responses to this charge. First, it is possible that the practice of head coverings should be continued in our own day. If the head covering in 1 Corinthians 11 refers to long hair, this is in many ways already implemented. If the head covering refers to hair done up or a hat, maybe this should be practiced today. For the sake of consistency, it would be better to err on the side of applying both practices (covering heads and prohibiting women from teaching and exercising authority over men) rather than disobey God's commands.

However, there is a second response to this charge of inconsistency, which is that Paul never says in 1 Corinthians 11 that *creation* requires women to wear head coverings. Rather, when discussing creation and woman being created "for" man, Paul says that "nature" teaches that long hair is a woman's "glory"—"For her hair is given to her for a covering" (1 Corinthians 11:14-15). Thus, even if Paul is speaking about the custom of women wearing a hat or veil, it is based on the creation principle that

God gave women long hair as a head covering. *The creation principle is women wearing longer hair than men, while women covering their heads was a custom.* Thus, we should still follow the creation principle in 1 Corinthians 11 that women should wear longer hair than men. In the same way, we should follow the creation principle of man's authority from 1 Timothy 2. Yet there is nothing contextually limited about Paul's prohibition in 1 Timothy 2:12. As Moo says, "In these cases, while the principle always remains in effect, the specific form of behavior will not . . . the difference between this [1 Corinthians 11:2-16] and 1 Timothy 2:12-13 is simply this: in 1 Timothy 2:12-13, the principle cannot be separated from the form of behavior. In other words, for a woman to teach a man or to have authority over a man is, by definition, to void the principle for which Paul quotes the creation account."[40]

Objection 2—1 Timothy 2:12 Applies Only to Husbands/Wives, Not Men/Women

The second objection to our interpretation is that Paul only prohibits a "wife" from teaching and exercising authority over her "husband" (and not all men). This is a possible translation of ἀνήρ (*aner*) and γυνή (*gune*), and context determines whether to translate these terms as man/woman or husband/wife. This argument is often put forth by scholars who affirm that Paul teaches male headship in the home but think women may be elders, such as Richard Davidson[41] and Gordon Hugenberger.[42] Davidson puts forth seven arguments as to why 1 Timothy 2 only prohibits a "wife"

---

40. Douglas Moo, "What Does It Mean Not to Teach or Have Authority Over Men? 1 Timothy 2:11-15," in *Recovering Biblical Manhood and Womanhood*, 191.

41. Davidson, *Flame of Yahweh*, 645: "A number of scholars have argued cogently and convincingly that *gyne* and *aner* in these verses should be translated 'wife' and 'husband' respectively, not simply 'woman' and 'man,'" of which he includes Hugenberger.

42. Gordon P. Hugenberger, "Women in Church Office: Hermeneutics or Exegesis? A Survey of Approaches to 1 Tim 2:8-15," *Journal of the Evangelical Theological Society* 35 (1992): 341–360.

from teaching or having authority over her "husband" and does not refer to men and women in general:

1. "[E]verywhere else in the Pauline writings, and indeed throughout the whole NT, where *gyne* and *aner* are found paired in close proximity, the reference is consistently to wife and husband, not women and men in general."
2. "[T]he movement from the plural in vv. 8-10 to the singular in vv. 11-12 seems to highlight the focus upon the wife and her husband especially in the latter verses."
3. "[T]he reference to the married couple Adam and Eve in vv. 13-14 seems to provide a marital context to the passage."
4. "[T]he reference to childbirth in v. 15 and the shift back to the plural 'they' (probably referring to both husband and wife as parents of the child or perhaps broadening again to speak of wives in general as in vv. 9-10) certainly provide a marital context."
5. "[T]he reference to submission (*hypostasso*) in a setting of man-woman relationships elsewhere in Paul always concerns the submission of the wife to her husband."
6. "[S]trong parallels with 1 Cor 14:34-36 (a passage dealing with husbands and wives, as noted above) point to a similar context of husband-wife relationships in 1 Tim 2. In particular, E. E. Ellis has noted striking verbal and conceptual similarities between the two passages: 'to allow or permit' (*epitrepo*), 'silence' (*sigao, hesychia*), 'submission' (*hypotasso, hypotage*), 'learn' (*manthano*), and the allusion to Gen 2–3."
7. "[T]he most determinative line of evidence supporting the husband-wife context of 1 Tim 2:8-15 is found in the extensive verbal, conceptual, and structural parallels between this passage and the household code of 1 Pet 3 . . . Hugenberger . . . highlights the detailed verbal correspondences, including the rare NT terms for 'adornment' (*kosmios/kosmeo/kosmos*), 'quiet' (*hesychia*), and 'braided' hair (cognate terms *plegma, emploke*), appearing only here in the NT. Both passages have the same structural flow of

logic and thought, moving from a discussion of wifely submission to the specific counsel on her proper adornment and then to an OT paradigm for proper marital relationships (Adam-Eve, Abraham-Sarah). The only significant difference in order is that Paul puts the additional counsel to husbands first (1 Tim 2:8) whereas Peter puts it last (1 Pet 3:7)."[43]

In response, it should first be noted that such a translation ("I do not permit a wife to teach or have authority over her husband") does not conclusively help one's case for women elders, as this still admits that a woman cannot teach or exercise authority over her own husband. The logic of this argument does not make sense. How can a woman who cannot teach or exercise authority over her husband then teach and exercise authority over other men? Moreover, an elder's spouse is presumably part of the congregation, and *the presence of a woman's husband in the congregation would alone bar her from pastoring or even preaching a sermon.*

That being said, this translation of "husband" and "wife" is mistaken. Yes, there are several correct observations made here by Davidson—ἀνήρ and γυνή are often paired in the context of marriage (point 1); Paul cites the married couple Adam and Eve (point 3); submission is often tied with marriage (point 5); there are similarities with 1 Corinthians 14:34-36 (point 6); and there are similarities with 1 Peter 3:1-7 (point 7). (I think points 2 and 4 are rather weak.) However, *there are things that set 1 Timothy 2 apart from other passages on husbands and wives.* Here are several reasons why 1 Timothy 2 is not limited to husbands and wives.

First, Paul in 1 Timothy 2 gives instructions that cannot be limited to married couples. All men should pray, and all women should dress modestly and practice good works (2:8-10). While most men and women were married in the ancient world, there were still widows/widowers and young people who had not yet married. Paul would never have limited his instructions for prayer and modesty to married persons. Thus, the immediate context of the prohibition in 1 Timothy 2:12 is dealing with

---

43. Davidson, *Flame of Yahweh*, 645–647.

men and women, not husbands and wives. Even egalitarian Linda Belleville recognizes this point and dismisses the argument that 1 Timothy 2:12 is limited to husbands and wives—"context determines usage, and 'husband' and 'wife' do not fit. 'I want the men everywhere to pray' (1 Tim 2:8) and 'I also want women . . .' (1 Tim 2:9-10) simply cannot be limited to husbands and wives. Nor can the verses that follow be read that way. Paul does refer to Adam and Eve in 1 Tim 2:13-14; but it is to Adam and Eve as the prototypical male and female, not as a married couple ('formed first,' 'deceived and became a sinner')."[44]

Second, 1 Peter 3 and 1 Corinthians 14:34-35 use different language that makes it clear that married couples are in mind, unlike in 1 Timothy 2. In particular, Peter uses the word ἴδιος (*idios*, "own") in 1 Peter 3:1 to refer to wives' "own husbands" [τοῖς ἰδίοις ἀνδράσιν]. Paul also uses ἴδιος in 1 Corinthians 14:35 to refer to "their husbands" [τοὺς ἰδίους ἄνδρας] (though it is unlikely that the command in 14:34 is limited to married women). Contrast this with 1 Timothy 2, where Paul does not use the word ἴδιος or even the word αὐτός (*autos*) for possession (e.g. τὴν γυναῖκα αὐτοῦ, "his wife" in Matthew 1:24; Ephesians 5:31). Thus, unlike 1 Timothy 2, the context of marriage is made explicit in 1 Peter 3:1 and 1 Corinthians 14:35.

Third, basing male-female relations on Adam and Eve at creation does not require the context of marriage. Paul in 1 Timothy 2 does not appeal to the one-flesh relationship of marriage but to man being made first and woman being deceived. He appeals to them as the prototypical man and woman, which has implications for men and women beyond the marriage relationship.

Therefore, the differences with other passages and the broad instructions for both sexes support the understanding that Paul in 1 Timothy 2:8-15 refers to men and women, not husbands and wives. Paul is prohibiting women from both teaching theology to men and exercising authority over men, and this supports the practice of limiting the office of elder to

---

44. Linda L. Belleville, "Teaching and Usurping Authority: 1 Timothy 2:11-15," in *Discovering Biblical Equality*, 219.

men. Yet, as stated above, even if this passage is about husbands and wives, it still prohibits a wife from teaching and exercising authority over her husband, and she could therefore not be an elder in his church.

Evading God's Command

Like a good defense lawyer, egalitarians love to throw darts at 1 Timothy 2, hoping one of them will stick. As egalitarian R.T. France asserted, "We have to admit that we know too little about the circumstances of the letter, and that there are too many obscure or ambiguous features to the argument, to allow any exegesis to claim to have uttered the last word."[45] Like much of the egalitarian literature, this smacks of the serpent's words in the garden—"Did God actually say?" (Genesis 3:1). This egalitarian evasion will not do. In the end, questioning and debating every aspect of this passage does not obfuscate its plain meaning—a woman is not to teach or exercise authority over a man. And the reason is that man was formed first and the woman was deceived.

---

45. R.T. France, *Women in the Church's Ministry: A Test-Case for Biblical Hermeneutics* (Eugene, OR: Wipf & Stock, 1995), 69–70.

Chapter 9

WOMEN SHOULD KEEP SILENT IN CHURCH
(1 CORINTHIANS 14:34-35)

EVEN MORE CONTROVERSIAL than 1 Timothy 2 are Paul's words found at the end of 1 Corinthians 14:

> [33b] As in all the churches of the saints, [34] the women should keep silent in the churches. For they are not permitted to speak, but should be in submission, as the Law also says. [35] If there is anything they desire to learn, let them ask their husbands at home. For it is shameful for a woman to speak in church (1 Corinthians 14:33b-35).[1]

At face value, Paul sounds like he is prohibiting women from speaking publicly in the assembled church. However, interpreters are quick to point out that this is at odds with his earlier words about women praying and prophesying in church:

> but every wife who prays or prophesies with her head uncovered dishonors her head, since it is the same as if her head were shaven (1 Corinthians 11:5).

---

1. While the latter part of 1 Corinthians 14:33 could be taken with the rest of that verse, most commentators agree that it makes better sense with 14:34-35.

What are we to make of this apparent contradiction? Many liberal-critical scholars and egalitarians now argue that Paul's words in 1 Corinthians 14:34-35 are a scribal interpolation (more on this below). However, assuming these passages are Paul's actual words and they are consistent, there are two options: (1) Paul prohibits women from *all public speech* in worship in 1 Corinthians 14:34-35, and he does not sanction public speaking by women in worship in 11:5; or (2) Paul prohibits women from *some public speech* in worship in 1 Corinthians 14:34-35, and he permits women to pray and prophesy publicly in worship in 11:5.

The latter option, which we may call the particular-speech solution, is widely accepted today. Commentators take the position that Paul uses the verb σιγάω (*sigao*, "remain silent") in 1 Corinthians 14:34-35 to prohibit only a particular form of speech by women in public worship, either tongues, teaching[2] (as in 1 Timothy 2:12), evaluating/weighing prophecy, or asking disruptive questions[3] (sometimes taken in relation to weighing prophecy[4]).

---

2. George Knight, "The Role of Women in the Church," in *Confessing our Hope*, 192–193: "In the case of the women, Paul says that God's order forbids them to speak, i.e., to teach the public assembly, because that would violate how God has ordered in his Law that men and women should relate to one another in the realm of teaching in the public assembly."

3. Craig S. Keener, "Learning in the Assemblies: 1 Corinthians 14:34-35," in *Discovering Biblical Equality*, 161–171. Keener's view is that Paul only prohibited disruptive questions from new learners, most of whom were women. He thinks this was a cultural issue of Paul's day and thus this passage does not prohibit women from speaking in church today. Keener relies heavily on extrabiblical sources regarding women asking questions in the ancient world and thus ignores key aspects of the passage. His interpretation fails for several reasons. First, Paul addresses women in general, not the broader category of "new learners." Second, if Paul simply wanted to prohibit women from asking questions, it does not make sense why he made such a broad prohibition on women's speech ("keep silent . . . not permitted to speak . . . for it is shameful for a woman to speak"). This prohibition is not limited to asking questions. Third, the claim that Paul was only addressing a specific situation of women asking questions in his day does not adequately account for his appeal to "the Law" (likely the creation account as a whole), his requirement of a general "submission" by women, or this being a rule "in all the churches of the saints" (1 Corinthians 14:33-35). Contrary to Keener, Paul gives a general rule and appeals to the very differences of men and women rooted in nature.

4. Anthony Thiselton, *The First Epistle to the Corinthians*, 1158: "the speaking

The most common form of the particular-speech solution is the weighing of prophecy view, that Paul only prohibits women from weighing/evaluating prophecies. Kevin DeYoung summarizes this view of 1 Corinthians 14—"Instead of forbidding women from speaking altogether, he prohibits them from weighing prophecy. Thus, verses 26-28 regulate prophetic speech; verses 30-35 regulate the weighing and sifting of prophetic speech; and verse 29 is the transition verse that joins the two sets of regulative instructions."[5]

However, there are four reasons to reject this weighing of prophecy view of 1 Corinthians 14:34-35. (Since this is now the predominant view, we will focus our critique on it, but the arguments put forth supporting the prohibition of women speaking publicly in church will also rule out the other forms of the particular-speech solution.) First, the weighing of prophecy view was not the historic interpretation of the church. Second, there are serious exegetical problems with the weighing of prophecy view. Third, the historic interpretations provide a better way of reconciling Paul's words in 1 Corinthians 11:5 with the prohibition of women speaking publicly in worship in 14:34-35. Fourth, the weighing of prophecy view does not adequately explain the clear words of 1 Corinthians 14:34-35, which is recognized by commentators who argue this is an interpolation or that these were the words of the Corinthians to which Paul was quoting and responding. We will expand upon these arguments below, concluding that Paul prohibits women from public speech in worship in 1 Corinthians 14:34-35 and that 11:5 only refers to women praying and prophesying in non-public settings.

---

in question denotes the activity of sifting or weighing the words of prophets, especially by asking probing questions about the prophet's theology or even the prophet's lifestyle in public.

5. Kevin DeYoung, *Freedom and Boundaries: A Pastoral Primer on the Role of Women in the Church* (Enumclaw, WA: Pleasant Word, 2006), 71. See also Kevin DeYoung, *Men and Women in the Church: A Short, Biblical, Practical Introduction* (Wheaton, IL: Crossway, 2021), 59–62.

Historic Interpretations of 1 Corinthians 11:5 and 14:34-35

In contrast to the modern interpretation that 1 Corinthians 14:34-35 only prohibits a particular form of speech, the church throughout history understood the passage to prohibit women from speaking publicly in the assembled church. Women are permitted to participate in congregational singing, but they are not to address or speak in front of the public assembly. There are three solutions that theologians throughout history have held as a way of reconciling 1 Corinthians 11:5 and 14:34-35:[6]

1. *The public/private worship solution* holds that 1 Corinthians 11:5 mentions women praying and prophesying in private worship or semi-private gatherings and 1 Corinthians 14:34-35 prohibits women from speaking in the publicly assembled church.
2. *The delayed-condemnation solution* holds that Paul mentions the practice of women publicly praying and prophesying in 1 Corinthians 11:5 for the sake of argument and waits until 1 Corinthians 14:34-35 to condemn it.
3. *The extraordinary-situations solution* holds that Paul lays down a general rule in 1 Corinthians 14:34-35 that women should not speak publicly in worship but mentions the exceptional cases of women publicly praying and prophesying in 1 Corinthians 11:5.

The public/private worship solution was held by Origen[7] (185–254),

---

6. For a helpful explanation of these views, see William Castro, "1 Corinthians 14:34: Did God Really Say…?" *Reformation21.org*, http://www.reformation21.org/blog/2019/06/1-corinthians-1432-did-god-rea.php; J. Carl Laney, "Gender Based Boundaries for Gathered Congregations: An Interpretive History of 1 Corinthians 14:34-35," *The Journal for Biblical Manhood and Womanhood* 7/1 (Spring 2002): 4–13.

7. Origen, "Fragments on 1 Corinthians," cited in Roger Gryson, *The Ministry of Women in the Early Church* (trans. Jean Laporte and Mary Louise Hall; Collegeville, MN: Liturgical Press, 1976), 28: "If the daughters of Philip prophesied, at least they did not speak in the assemblies; for we do not find this fact in evidence in the Acts of the Apostles. Much less in the Old Testament. It is said that Deborah was a prophetess . . . There is no evidence that Deborah delivered speeches to the people, as did Jeremias and Isaias. Huldah, who was a prophetess, did not

B.B. Warfield[8] (1851–1921), and Gordon Clark[9] (1902–1985). The delayed-condemnation solution was held by R.L. Dabney[10] (1820–1898). John Calvin[11] (1509–1564) and Charles Hodge[12] (1797–1878) appealed

---

speak to the people, but only to a man, who consulted her at home. The gospel itself mentions a prophetess Anna . . . but she did not speak publicly. Even if it is granted to a woman to show the sign of prophecy, she is nevertheless not permitted to speak in an assembly. When Mary [Miriam] the prophetess spoke, she was leading a choir of women . . . For [as Paul declares] 'I am not giving permission for a woman to teach,' and even less 'to tell a man what to do.'"

8. B.B. Warfield, "Paul on Women Speaking in Church," *The Presbyterian* (October 30, 1919).

9. Gordon H. Clark, "The Ordination of Women," *The Trinity Review* (January/February 1981): 6.

10. R.L. Dabney, "The Public Preaching of Women," in *Discussions*, vol 2 (1891; repr., Harrisonburg, VA: Sprinkle Publications, 1982), 98: "The apostle is about to prepare the way for his categorical exclusion of women from public discourse. He does so by alluding to the intrusion which had probably begun, along with many other disorders in the Corinthian churches, and by pointing to its obvious unnaturalness."

11. John Calvin, *Commentary on the Epistles of Paul the Apostle to the Corinthians*, vol 1, 356. Commenting on 1 Corinthians 11:5, Calvin says, "It may seem, however, to be superfluous for Paul to forbid the woman to prophesy with her head uncovered, while elsewhere he wholly prohibits women from speaking in the Church (1 Timothy 2:12). It would not, therefore, be allowable for them to prophesy even with a covering upon their head, and hence it follows that it is to no purpose that he argues here as to a covering. It may be replied, that the Apostle, by here condemning the one, does not commend the other. For when he reproves them for prophesying with their head uncovered, he at the same time does not give them permission to prophesy in some other way, but rather delays his condemnation of that vice to another passage, namely in chapter 14. In this reply there is nothing amiss, though at the same time it might suit sufficiently well to say, that the Apostle requires women to show their modesty—not merely in a place in which the whole Church is assembled, but also in any more dignified assembly, either of matrons or of men, such as are sometimes convened in private houses."

12. Charles Hodge, *An Exposition of the First Epistle to the Corinthians*, 208–209, 305. Hodge takes the delayed-condemnation solution in his comment on 1 Corinthians 11:5: "It was Paul's manner to attend to one thing at a time. He is here speaking of the propriety of women speaking in public unveiled, and therefore he says nothing about the propriety of their speaking in public in itself. When that subject comes up, he addresses his judgement in the clearest terms, 14, 34. In here disapproving of the one, says Calvin, he does not approve of the

to both the public/private worship and delayed-condemnation solutions. The extraordinary-situations solution was held by Martin Luther[13] (1483–1546). In their 1914 commentary on 1 Corinthians, Archibald Robertson (1853–1931) and Alfred Plummer (1841–1926) consider the extraordinary-situations solution but also suggest 11:5 is hypothetical.[14] The few modern interpreters who advocate one of these historic views include John MacArthur[15] and Werner Neuer,[16] both of whom advocate the public/private worship solution.

Contrast this with the weighing of prophecy view, which seems to have first been introduced in 1962 by W.C. Klein[17] and then followed by the

---

other." However, Hodge seems to adopt the public/private worship solution in his comment on 14:34: "The apostle himself seems to take for granted, in 11, 5, that women might receive and exercise the gift of prophecy. It is therefore only the public exercise of the gift that is prohibited."

13. Martin Luther, "The Misuse of the Mass," in *Luther's Works*, vol 36 (ed. Helmut Lehmann; Fortress Press, 1959), 151–152: "Paul forbids women to preach in the congregation where men are who are able to speak . . . Order, decency, and honor require, therefore, that women keep silence when the men speak; if, however, there is no man to preach, then it would be necessary that women preach."

14. Archibald Robertson and Alfred Plummer, *A Critical and Exegetical Commentary on the First Epistle of St Paul to the Corinthians* (The International Critical Commentary; 2nd ed.; New York: Charles Scribner's Sons, 1914), 324–325: "We are not sure whether St Paul contemplated the *possibility* of women prophesying in exceptional cases. What is said in xi. 5 may be hypothetical."

15. John MacArthur, *Divine Design: God's Complementary Roles for Men and Women* (Colorado Springs, CO: David C Cook, 2011), 48: "Because 1 Corinthians 11:5 mentions women praying and prophesying, some believe Paul acknowledged the right of women to teach, preach, and lead in the public assembly of the church . . . But Paul did not establish the setting at the official service of worship in the church. It is likely he was referring to praying or prophesying in places other than the church gathering."

16. Neuer, *Man and Woman in Christian Perspective*, 117–118: "1 Corinthians 14:34-5 therefore expresses a total ban on women speaking in church worship. This does not contradict 1 Corinthians 11, where Paul is dealing with women praying and prophesying in small house groups, whereas in 1 Corinthians 14 he speaks explicitly of the whole church being gathered for worship."

17. W.C. Klein, "The Church and Its Prophets," *Anglican Theological Review* 44:1 (1962).

female minister Margaret E. Thrall in 1965.[18] This view was promoted by James Hurley in a 1973 article[19] and then his 1981 book *Man and Woman in Biblical Perspective*,[20] and then followed by Wayne Grudem[21] and D.A. Carson.[22] It is now the predominant view of complementarians and even some egalitarians, such as Anthony Thiselton in his commentary on 1 Corinthians.[23] Considering Grudem's voluminous writings defending complementarianism and Carson's influential essay in *Recovering Biblical Manhood and Womanhood*, as well as the moderate nature of this interpretation, it is no surprise that this has become the dominant view of 1 Corinthians 14:34-35.[24]

Novelty does not make the weighing of prophecy view incorrect, but the departure from theologians of prior centuries does suggest that modern cultural changes might have played a role in encouraging a more palatable interpretation—especially when we note that this weighing of prophecy view was promoted in a commentary by a woman "pastor." It is obvious that many in the church feel pressured to limit the offense of the Bible, and a prohibition on women speaking publicly in church is one of the more offensive teachings. There is a push in many complementarian churches to involve women in as much of the worship service as possible, such as having women publicly read Scripture and publicly lead prayer.

---

18. M.E. Thrall, *I and II Corinthians* (Cambridge, England: Cambridge University Press, 1965).

19. James B. Hurley, "Did Paul Require Veils or the Silence of Women?" *Westminster Theological Journal* (1973): 216–218.

20. James B. Hurley, *Man and Woman in Biblical Perspective* (Grand Rapids, MI: Zondervan; 1981), 185–94.

21. Wayne Grudem, *The Gift of Prophecy in 1 Corinthians* (Washington: University Press of America, 1982), 245–255.

22. D.A. Carson, "'Silent in the Churches': On the Role of Women in 1 Corinthians 14:33b-36," in *Recovering Biblical Manhood and Womanhood*, 140–153.

23. Thiselton, *The First Epistle to the Corinthians*, 1146–1161.

24. See also Paul Gardner, *1 Corinthians* (Zondervan Exegetical Commentary on the New Testament; Grand Rapids, MI: Zondervan, 2018), 628–637; David E. Garland, *1 Corinthians* (Baker Exegetical Commentary on the New Testament; Grand Rapids, MI: Baker, 2003), 664–673.

There is also a push to allow women to preach sermons on the basis that it is exhortation/prophecy and not teaching (see chapter 10). The historic reading of 1 Corinthians 14:34-35 rules out such practices, and that may very well be why so many have abandoned it today.

Problems with the Weighing of Prophecy View of 1 Corinthians 14:34-35

Apart from its novelty, there are several exegetical and theological problems with the weighing of prophecy view of 1 Corinthians 14:34-35.[25] First, Paul forbids women from "speaking" [λαλέω, *laleo*] with no qualifier to restrict the word (14:34), meaning his prohibited speech is broader than just weighing prophecy. Paul could easily have just prohibited women from "weighing" [διακρίνω, *diakrino*] prophecy if that is what he meant. Moreover, when Paul used λαλέω ("speak") with reference to tongues, he added the qualifier γλώσσῃ (*glosse*, "in a tongue") in 1 Corinthians 14:2, 4, 5, 6, 13, 18, 23, and 27. Yet he does no such thing here. Instead, Paul makes his broad prohibition even clearer by adding that women should be "silent" [σιγάω, *sigao*].[26] Most modern commentators tend to interpret 14:34-35 through 11:5 and through the preceding verses of 14:1-33. Yet the actual words of 14:34-35 must be our starting point. And Paul's words are quite clear—women are not to "speak" but are to be "silent" and "in submission," for "it is shameful for a woman to speak in church" (14:34-35).

Second, the weighing of prophecy view does not fit the flow of the passage. The last mention of "weighing" prophesy is made in 1 Corinthians 14:29, yet this view expects us to equate Paul's prohibition of "speaking" in 14:34 with "weighing" prophecy in 14:29, five verses earlier. But if

---

25. These arguments against the weighing of prophecy view are partly based on those found in the excellent article by James Greenbury, "1 Corinthians 14:34-35: Evaluation of Prophecy Revisited," *Journal of the Evangelical Theological Society* 51 (2008): 721–731.

26. BDAG, 922: "to be silent . . . *say nothing, keep still, keep silent.*" This word is also used in 1 Corinthians 14:28 and 14:30.

we follow the immediate context, it would make more sense to link the speech that Paul forbids in 14:34 with the closer antecedent of "prophesying" itself in 14:31, not "weighing" prophecy. Some put forth the argument that 1 Corinthians 14:37 is still concerned with spiritual gifts, including prophecy, and therefore 14:34-35 must also deal with prophecy since it is sandwiched between sections on prophecy.[27] This argument correctly points out that our interpretation must fit the whole context of 1 Corinthians 14. However, 14:36-40 is concerned with *more than merely weighing prophecy*. Paul in these verses speaks of both tongues and prophecy, and he is concerned with order in worship—"If anyone thinks that he is a prophet, or spiritual . . . So, my brothers, earnestly desire to prophesy, and do not forbid speaking in tongues. But all things should be done decently and in order" (14:37, 39-40). Paul is concerned with both prophecy and tongues in this section, and thus Paul's preceding requirement for women to be "silent" in 14:34-35 concerns *at least* prophecy and tongues (and not just weighing prophecy). But there is no indication Paul limits his prohibition on women's speech to only prophecy and tongues. Rather, he uses his discussion of the spiritual gifts as an occasion to clarify the rule that women are to be "silent" in the public assembly ("in church").

The third problem with the weighing of prophecy view is that the words "if there is anything they desire to learn" (1 Corinthians 14:35) do not fit the context of weighing prophecy. These words do not support the conclusion that women were seeking to weigh prophecy in Corinth, but rather that they did not *understand* what was said and thus publicly asked questions of the elders. As James Greenbury says, "Certainly, questions could form a part of an evaluation process, but the view under consideration does not postulate that women were simply asking questions about prophecies, but providing assessments of them."[28] Paul made clear that instead of speaking "in church" and asking questions, women were to be "silent" and ask their husbands "at home" (14:35).

---

27. See Richard B. Gaffin's response to James W. Scott, *New Horizons* 17/3 (March 1996), https://www.opc.org/nh.html?article_id=447.

28. Greenbury, "1 Corinthians 14:34-35: Evaluation of Prophecy Revisited," *JETS* 51 (2008): 726.

Fourth, there is no indication that "weighing" prophecies was audible. Paul says, "Let two or three prophets speak, and let the others weigh what is said" (1 Corinthians 14:29). The word for "weigh," διακρίνω (*diakrino*), means "to differentiate by separating."[29] It can be used for audible speaking (e.g. Acts 11:2), but it can also be used for silent evaluation (e.g. 1 Corinthians 11:31). So what does it mean here? It is likely silent evaluation, as Paul does not mention "weighing" prophecy in his earlier list of forms of public speaking—"a hymn, a lesson, a revelation, a tongue, or an interpretation" (1 Corinthians 14:26). The "interpretation" of a tongue is mentioned, yet there is no mention of "weighing" prophecy. Greenbury contends, "Surely if he [Paul] was so concerned about this form of utterance that he was about to forbid women from taking part in it, he would have included it as one of the modes of church speaking in verse 26."[30]

There is also no mention of the number of people that are supposed to weigh the prophecy. Both for speaking tongues and prophecy, Paul says only two or three may speak (1 Corinthians 14:27, 29). He then says one person can interpret tongues ("let someone interpret," 14:27), but for prophecy he says, "let the others [οἱ ἄλλοι] weigh what is said" (14:29). This could refer to other prophets weighing prophecy, but it is unlikely that Paul would exclude other church leaders, such as apostles and elders, from weighing prophecies. There are also no instructions for weighing prophecy. Therefore, Paul likely means that the *entire church* is to weigh prophecy, and this makes it more likely that this is a *silent* weighing. A silent weighing of prophecy would rule out the view that Paul only prohibits women from weighing prophecy in 1 Corinthians 14:34-35.

Fifth, the weighing of prophecy view holds the untenable position that prophesying is less authoritative than the weighing of prophecy. From this, advocates reason that women are permitted to prophesy but not weigh prophecy. This position rests on the fact that the authority in prophecy is entirely from the Spirit. However, this distinction between prophecy and

---

29. BDAG, 231.
30. Greenbury, "1 Corinthians 14:34-35: Evaluation of Prophecy Revisited," *JETS* 51 (2008): 727.

weighing prophecy is inconsistent, for as Forbes argues, "If a wife's authority in prophecy is not her own, but the Spirit's, and that is why she may prophesy, then her husband's authority in prophecy is not his own either, and so having his prophecy evaluated by his wife is not an overturning of his authority."[31] In other words, if the authority in prophecy is merely from the Spirit, it does not make sense that a woman cannot weigh the prophecy of a man. Yet that is exactly what the weighing of prophecy view holds.

In order to downplay the authority of prophecy in the church, some advocates of this view, such as Grudem and Carson, argue that New Testament prophecy is less authoritative than Old Testament prophecy.[32] However, this division between OT and NT prophecy does not fit the record for several reasons:

1. The New Testament authors use the same Greek word for "prophet" [προφήτης] that is used in the Septuagint to translate the Hebrew [נָבִיא, *navi*]. This presumes continuity of prophecy, unless there is evidence to the contrary.
2. The New Testament prophets held a high position in the church and were even listed ahead of teachers (1 Corinthians 12:28; Ephesians 2:20; 3:5).[33] This sounds more akin to Old Testament prophecy than a "spontaneous" word that may contain errors.
3. Old Testament prophecy was also to be evaluated in Israel (Deuteronomy 13:1-5; 18:20-22), similar to the call to test or evaluate prophecy in the New Testament (1 Corinthians 14:29; 1 Thessalonians 5:20-21).

---

31. Christopher Forbes, *Prophecy and Inspired Speech in Early Christianity and its Hellenistic Environment* (Peabody, MA: Hendrickson, 1997), 273.

32. Grudem, *Systematic Theology*, 1049–1061; Carson, "'Silent in the Churches,'" in *Recovering Biblical Manhood and Womanhood*, 153.

33. Grudem argues that Ephesians 2:20 should be understood as the church being built on the foundation of "apostle-prophets" rather than "apostles and prophets." He argues that this is a "limited group" that does not include all who had the gift of prophecy. Wayne Grudem, *Systematic Theology*, 1051–1052. However, Ephesians 4:11 distinguishes apostles and prophets.

4. Old Testament prophecy is connected with New Testament prophecy in Acts 2:17-21, as Peter applies the prophecy of Joel 2:28-32 to the events that took place in Acts 2:1-13.
5. The New Testament prophet Agabus said, "Thus says the Holy Spirit" (Acts 21:11), echoing the Old Testament prophet's "Thus says the LORD."[34]

Grudem asserts that apostles are the New Testament counterpart to the Old Testament prophets and thus New Testament prophets must be

---

34. Grudem argues that Acts 21:10-11 actually supports his view because Agabus erred in his prophecy. Agabus said, "This is how the Jews at Jerusalem will bind the man who owns this belt and deliver him into the hands of the Gentiles." Grudem says this was erroneous because "the Romans, not the Jews, bound Paul (v. 33; also 22:29)" and the Jews "tried to kill him and he had to be rescued by force (v. 32)." Grudem, *Systematic Theology*, 1052–1054. However, assuming Agabus is a genuine prophet of the Lord, this leaves Grudem attributing a false prophecy to the Holy Spirit ("Thus says the Holy Spirit"). Grudem argues against the following two solutions to this problem: (1) The prophecy was fulfilled in Acts 28:17 when Paul said, "I was delivered as a prisoner from Jerusalem into the hands of the Romans;" or (2) The prophecy was fulfilled in that the Jews were indirectly responsible for Paul being handed over to the Gentiles. In support of the first solution, there are definite parallels in the language between Acts 21:11 and 28:17, with both speaking of Paul being "bound" as a "prisoner" [δήσουσιν, δέσμιος] in/from Jerusalem and "delivered" [παραδώσουσιν, παρεδόθην] "into the hands of the" Gentiles/Romans. Paul's words almost certainly echo Agabus' prophecy. See Sinclair Ferguson, *The Holy Spirit* (Downers Grove, IL: InterVarsity Press, 1996), 218–220. The second solution takes the Jews in Acts 21:11 to refer to the Jewish religious leaders who pressured the Romans to arrest Paul. In the immediate context of Paul's arrival to Jerusalem in Acts 21:17, Jews from Asia stirred up the people who laid hands on him and seized Paul, and then the Roman tribune soldiers arrested him and bound him with chains (21:27, 30, 33). Thus, though the Jews sought to kill Paul, they indirectly delivered him to the Romans. Therefore, it is Grudem who errs (not Agabus) by demanding that prophecy be understood too literally, contrary to the nature of prophecy throughout the Old Testament. As Bock says, "The reference to Jewish involvement in the binding here is 'causative' in force: the Jews will not physically bind Paul but will be responsible for his being arrested . . . The prophecy is accurate in this sense and is not to be pressed too literally." Darrell L. Bock, *Acts* (Baker Exegetical Commentary on the New Testament; Grand Rapids, MI: Baker, 2007), 638.

something different.[35] However, this fails to recognize that there is something new about the coming of Jesus and His appointment of apostles. Jesus is a new Israel and the 12 apostles correspond to the 12 tribes of Israel in the Old Testament. The apostles are prophets, but they are more than that—they are men who witnessed the resurrection and were appointed by Jesus to proclaim the gospel to the nations. Thus, the apostles hold a unique New Testament office, and they do not replace the prophets of the Old Testament.

Therefore, New Testament prophecy is a continuation of the revelatory and authoritative prophecy of the Old Testament. What this means for our purposes is that New Testament prophecy is an authoritative act, more authoritative than weighing/evaluating the prophecy. Yet the weighing of prophecy view permits a woman to prophesy but not participate in what is actually a less authoritative act of weighing prophecy. A better explanation is that women prophetesses, like all women, were not permitted to publicly speak in church. Rather, they were to prophesy in private and not in public worship, just like the prophetesses of old. In addition to the lack of clarity of 1 Corinthians 11:5, the above problems with the weighing of prophecy view of 1 Corinthians 14:34-35 may explain why no one took this view for 1900 years.

The Absolute Prohibition of Women Speaking Publicly in Church

The historic interpretations provide a better way of reconciling Paul's words in 1 Corinthians 11:5 with the prohibition of women speaking publicly in worship in 14:34-35 than the modern problematic weighing of prophecy view. We saw three historic options above: (1) the public/private worship solution, (2) the delayed-condemnation solution, and (3) the extraordinary-situations solution. All three are possible, but Paul's words seem too absolute to accommodate the extraordinary-situations solution. The delayed-condemnation solution could be the case if Paul thought

---

35. Grudem, *Systematic Theology*, 1050.

condemning women prophesying in public worship would distract from his argument about head coverings in 1 Corinthians 11:5. However, the public/private worship solution seems best, and here we will follow B.B. Warfield as our guide.

When seeking to solve the apparent contradiction between 1 Corinthians 11:5 and 14:34-35, we should start with Paul's absolute prohibition in 14:34-35 as the longer and clearer text, not Paul's incidental comment about women praying and prophesying in 11:5. Warfield says of 14:34-35, "It would be impossible for the apostle to speak more directly or more emphatically than he has done here. He requires women to be silent at the church meetings; for that is what 'in the churches' means, there were no church buildings then. And he has not left us in doubt as to the nature of these church meetings. He had just described them in verses 26ff. They were of the general character of our prayer meetings."[36] In other words, Paul clearly speaks of the public church assembly in 1 Corinthians 14:33b—"As in all the churches of the saints."

Warfield supports this point by comparing 1 Corinthians 14:30 with 14:34—"Note the words 'let him be silent in the church' in verse 30 [also 14:28], and compare them with 'let them be silent in the churches' in verse 34. The prohibition of women speaking covers thus all public church meetings—it is the publicity, not the formality of it, which is the point. And he tells us repeatedly that this is the universal law of the church. He does more than that. He tells us that it is the commandment of the Lord, and emphasizes the word 'Lord' (verse 37)."[37] Thus, a woman is not to speak from the pulpit or address the congregation. In that regard, she is to be silent.

What is "the Law" to which Paul refers when he says women "should be in submission, as the Law also says" (1 Corinthians 14:34)? Some who take the view that Paul only prohibits women from weighing prophecy suggest Numbers 12:1-15,[38] though it is not clear how this supports their

---

36. B.B. Warfield, "Paul on Women Speaking in Church."
37. Ibid.
38. Roy E. Ciampa and Brian S. Rosner, *The First Letter to the Corinthians* (Grand Rapids: Eerdmans, 2010), 727.

case. God rebuked Miriam and Aaron because they undermined Moses, not because Miriam was a woman judging Moses' prophecy. Many in history have thought Paul appealed to Genesis 3:16 and man's rule over woman in the fall. However, it is most likely that Paul appeals to Genesis 1–3 as a whole, which would include Adam's chronological priority and Eve being made as a helper, in addition to Genesis 3:16. This was Paul's practice in two other passages on gender roles, where he appeals to Adam's creation and Eve's deception in 1 Timothy 2:13-14 and Eve being created "for" Adam in 1 Corinthians 11:8-10.[39] Paul draws a similar point from the creation account here in 1 Corinthians 14:34-35 as he does in 1 Timothy 2:8-15, where Adam being formed first is the basis for Paul's prohibition of women teaching and exercising authority over men.

In contrast to the lucidity of 1 Corinthians 14:34-35, 1 Corinthians 11:5 is unclear. It is merely an incidental reference to women praying and prophesying, and Paul never mentions the publicity of such behavior. He also speaks descriptively rather than prescriptively. Warfield raises doubts about the meaning of 11:5—"Precisely what is meant in 1 Corinthians 11:5, nobody quite knows. What is said there is that every woman praying or prophesying unveiled dishonors her head. It seems fair to infer that if she prays or prophesies veiled she does not dishonor her head. And it seems fair still further to infer that she may properly pray or prophesy if only she does it veiled. We are piling up a chain of inferences. And they have not carried us very far."[40] Warfield then argues that there is nothing in 1 Corinthians 11 indicating that it deals with public worship:

> We cannot infer that it would be proper for her to pray or prophesy in church if only she were veiled. There is nothing said about church in the passage or in the context. The word 'church' does not occur until the 16th verse, and then not as ruling the

---

39. George Knight, "The Role of Women in the Church," in *Confessing our Hope*, 192: "by the Law Paul certainly means that that to which he has already adverted in 1 Cor. 11:8 & 9, namely, the teaching of Gen. 2:20-24 and its inherent implications."

40. Warfield, "Paul on Women Speaking in Church."

reference of the passage, but only as supplying support for the injunction of the passage. There is no reason whatever for believing that 'praying and prophesying' in church is meant. Neither was an exercise confined to the church. If, as in 1 Corinthians 14:14, the 'praying' spoken of was an ecstatic exercise—as its place by 'prophesying' may suggest—then there would be the divine inspiration superceding all ordinary laws to be reckoned with. And there has already been occasion to observe that prayer in public is forbidden to women in 1 Timothy 2:8, 9—unless mere attendance at prayer is meant, in which case this passage is a close parallel of 1 Timothy 2:9.[41]

We can add to this the point that the passage preceding 1 Corinthians 11:2-16 deals with an issue *outside* the public church assembly (10:23-33), as was the case since 6:1. The letter transitions *after* 11:2-16 to the public assembly, as Paul then speaks about the Lord's Supper. The text makes this transition clear in 11:17-18—"But in the following instructions I do not commend you, because when you come together it is not for the better but for the worse. For, in the first place, *when you come together as a church*, I hear that there are divisions among you." Paul uses the phrase "when you come together" five times (11:17, 18, 20, 33, 34; cf. 14:23, 26) and specifically speaks of the Corinthians here as coming together "as a church" [ἐν ἐκκλησίᾳ, *en ekklesia*] in 11:18 (cf. 14:19, 28, 35). Further, Paul says in 11:18, "For in the first place, when you come together as a church . . ." The phrase "in the first place" shows Paul is transitioning to a new subject, which is the *public* gathering of the Christian assembly. This clear context of the assembled church is not mentioned at all in 11:2-16. As Gordon Clark says, "The text does not say 'in the church.' Therefore these words should not be inserted. Then when another text says explicitly, Let women keep silence in the church, it follows that 1 Corinthians 11 *cannot* mean 'in the church.' It must refer to some informal gatherings."[42]

---

41. Ibid.
42. Gordon H. Clark, "The Ordination of Women," *The Trinity Review*

There are examples of New Testament prophecy taking place outside publicly assembled worship, such as Agabus's prophecies in Acts 11:28 and 21:9-11. This latter passage even mentions the daughters of Philip who prophesied (Acts 21:9). Yet there is no evidence that these women prophesied in publicly assembled worship. Rather, women prayed and prophesied in private or semi-private gatherings, and they were to have their heads covered to indicate they were under the authority of their husbands. But when it comes to public worship, women are to remain silent.

It is also important to note that many who argue for the weighing of prophecy view of 1 Corinthians 14:34-35 also take 1 Timothy 2:8-15 to prohibit women from teaching or exercising authority over men in public worship. Yet these passages have significant similarities. Here are the two key passages side by side:

> the women should keep silent in the churches. For they are not permitted to speak, but should be in submission, as the Law also says. If there is anything they desire to learn, let them ask their husbands at home. For it is shameful for a woman to speak in church (1 Corinthians 14:34-35).

> αἱ γυναῖκες ἐν ταῖς ἐκκλησίαις σιγάτωσαν· οὐ γὰρ ἐπιτρέπεται αὐταῖς λαλεῖν, ἀλλὰ ὑποτασσέσθωσαν, καθὼς καὶ ὁ νόμος λέγει. εἰ δέ τι μαθεῖν θέλουσιν, ἐν οἴκῳ τοὺς ἰδίους ἄνδρας ἐπερωτάτωσαν· αἰσχρὸν γάρ ἐστιν γυναικὶ λαλεῖν ἐν ἐκκλησίᾳ.

> Let a woman learn quietly with all submissiveness. I do not permit a woman to teach or to exercise authority over a man; rather, she is to remain quiet (1 Timothy 2:11-12).

> Γυνὴ ἐν ἡσυχίᾳ μανθανέτω ἐν πάσῃ ὑποταγῇ· διδάσκειν δὲ γυναικὶ οὐκ ἐπιτρέπω οὐδὲ αὐθεντεῖν ἀνδρός, ἀλλ᾽ εἶναι ἐν ἡσυχίᾳ.

(January/February 1981): 6.

The similarities between these passages are striking:[43]

1. Both use the word "permit" [ἐπιτρέπω] with a negation[44]—women are not permitted to "speak" in 1 Corinthians 14:34, while women are not permitted to "teach" or "exercise authority" in 1 Timothy 2:12.
2. Both require women to refrain from speaking—women are to be "silent" [σιγάω] in 1 Corinthians 14:34, while women are to remain "quiet/silent" [ἐν ἡσυχία] in 1 Timothy 2:11 and 2:12.
3. Both require women's submission—women "should be in submission" [ὑποτασσέσθωσαν] in 1 Corinthians 14:34, while women are to "learn quietly with all submissiveness" [ἐν πάσῃ ὑποταγῇ] in 1 Timothy 2:11.
4. Both place restrictions on women's learning—women are to "ask their husbands at home" if they desire to "learn" [μαθεῖν] anything in 1 Corinthians 14:35, while women are to "learn" [μανθανέτω] quietly with all submissiveness in 1 Timothy 2:11.
5. Both appeal to the creation order—"the Law" in 1 Corinthians 14:34 (probably a reference to Genesis 1–3), and Adam's chronological priority and Eve's deception in 1 Timothy 2:13-14.

It has already been argued that 1 Timothy 2:8-15 prohibits women from teaching or exercising authority over men (chapter 8). If one adopts this position, as complementarians do, it is hard to conclude from the parallels that 1 Corinthians 14:34-35 only prohibits women from weighing prophecy in worship. Yet this is the common position of complementarians.

---

43. Unsurprisingly, some egalitarians use these similarities to support their argument that 1 Corinthians 14:34-35 was an interpolation by scribes, who supposedly adopted similar language from 1 Timothy 2. Payne, *Man and Woman, One in Christ*, 262–263. However, these passages are similar yet tailored to different contexts, which supports them stemming from the same author, not a scribe seeking to imitate Paul. This is comparable to how Paul uses similar language and concepts throughout his epistles.

44. Out of the 17 uses of ἐπιτρέπω in the New Testament, these are the only two where the word is negated—with οὐ in 1 Corinthians 14:34 and οὐκ in 1 Timothy 2:12.

The two passages both speak of women being silent/quiet in public worship. Thus, the weighing of prophecy view of 1 Corinthians 14:34-35 opens the door to minimizing the force of 1 Timothy 2:8-15, as many are doing today.

To the contrary, Warfield sees 1 Corinthians 14:34-35 and 1 Timothy 2:8-15 as reinforcing one another—"What must be noted in conclusion is: (1) That the prohibition of speaking in the church to women is precise, absolute, and all-inclusive. They are to keep silent in the churches—and that means in all the public meetings for worship; they are not even to ask questions; (2) that this prohibition is given especial point precisely for the two matters of teaching and ruling covering specifically the functions of preaching and ruling elders; (3) that the grounds on which the prohibition is put are universal and turn on the difference in sex, and particularly on the relative places given to the sexes in creation and in the fundamental history of the race (the fall)."[45]

Objections to the Public/Private Worship Solution

We must now turn to objections to the public/private worship solution we have been advocating. D.A. Carson is one of the few modern scholars to consider the public/private worship solution, and he gives seven arguments against this interpretation:

1. "Paul thinks of prophecy primarily as revelation from God delivered through believers *in the context of the church*, where the prophecy may be evaluated (14:23-29)."
2. "Distinctions between 'smaller house groups' and 'church' may not have been all that intelligible to the first Christians, who commonly met in private homes. When the 'church' in a city was large enough (as certainly in Jerusalem, Antioch, Ephesus, and possibly Corinth) to overflow the largest private accommodation, it must have been rather difficult, once opposition was established, to find

---

45. Warfield, "Paul on Women Speaking in Church."

a public venue large enough to accommodate *all* the believers of that city; i.e., the house groups in such instances *constituted* the assembly of the church."

3. "The language of 11:16 ('If anyone wants to be contentious about this, we have no other practice—nor do the churches of God.') seems to suggest a *church* concern, not merely the concern of private or small-group piety. The 'we'/'church of God' parallel either means that Paul has never allowed the practice, and the churches have followed his lead; or that Paul and the church in Ephesus (from which he is writing) constitute the 'we' that have not followed the practice, and again the other churches have adopted the same stance. Either way, when Paul adopts the same tone elsewhere (see especially 14:33b, 36), he is talking about conduct *in an assembly*."

4. "The immediately succeeding verses (11:17-34) are certainly devoted to an ordinance designed for the assembly."

5. "If someone points out that 11:2-16, unlike 14:33b-36, does not include the phrase 'in the church,' it must also be observed that 11:2-16 does not *restrict* the venue to the private home or small group."

6. "Whether the restriction in 11:2-16 requires some kind of hat or a distinctive coiffure, it becomes faintly ridiculous in proportion to the degree of privateness envisaged. If the restriction pertains to every venue *except* the church assembly, does this mean the Christian wife must postpone her private prayer until she has hurried to her chambers and donned her headpiece? The restriction is coherent only in a public setting."

7. "Above all, the universality of the promise of Joel, cited at Pentecost, that the Holy Spirit would be poured out on men and women such that both would prophesy as constituent members of the community of the new covenant, seems somehow less than

transparent if the women may display their inheritance only outside the gathered messianic community."[46]

Let us respond to each of these arguments. It should be noted that Carson tends to assume his position and thus "begs the question" in these objections. Contra point 1, saying prophecy and its evaluation "primarily" take place in public worship does not establish that this is what Paul had in mind in 1 Corinthians 11:5. He easily could have been appealing to another setting to support his point. Contra point 2, the type of building in which the church meets does not determine the character of the meeting. Paul distinguishes between public worship and smaller groups, seen in 11:18 (cf. 14:26), "when you come together as a church" [ἐν ἐκκλησίᾳ, literally "in church/assembly"]. So Carson is wrong to assume that Paul's hearers could not understand such a distinction. Contra point 3, Paul's reference to the "churches of God" in 11:16 does not demonstrate he is speaking of public worship throughout 11:2-15. Churches can lay down rules not only for public worship, but also for private worship and women wearing head coverings in general.

Contra point 4, the passage following the discussion of head coverings is about the Lord's Supper during public worship (11:17-34), but Paul distinguishes this from the prior section by saying "when you come together" in 11:17-18. Contra point 5, while Carson is correct that nothing in 11:2-16 "restricts" Paul's instructions about head coverings to private worship, it does not follow that woman's "prophecy" in 11:5 refers to public worship. Contra point 6, the public/private worship view does not hold that Paul is only speaking of women wearing head coverings in private in 11:2-16, as Carson attempts to frame things ("If the restriction pertains to every venue *except* the church assembly . . ."). Rather, Paul in 11:2-16 is speaking of head coverings in general and in 11:5 appeals to women wearing head coverings while praying and prophesying in either private or semi-private settings. Contra point 7, the fact that women prophesied says

---

46. Carson, "'Silent in the Churches,'" in *Recovering Biblical Manhood and Womanhood*, 145–146.

nothing about women prophesying in *public* worship. Carson confuses the Christian "community" with assembled public worship.[47]

In summary, none of Carson's arguments demonstrates that Paul has public worship in view when he mentions women praying and prophesying in 1 Corinthians 11:5. Moreover, Carson's own position is untenable. While he thinks the weighing of prophecy view best fits both the "flow" and "structure" of the passage, he recognizes the major objection is that it is inconsistent for Paul to permit women to prophesy but forbid them to weigh prophecies. Carson says this objection "carries little weight *provided* that such prophecy does not have the same authority status that the great writing prophets of the Old Testament enjoyed," [48] thus distinguishing between the nature of New Testament and Old Testament prophecy. This error has already been refuted.

However, Carson also ignores the problem that the weighing of prophecy view results in women prophesying in public worship while being prohibited from asking questions there ("let them ask their husbands at home," 1 Corinthians 14:35). Carson takes these questions to refer to prophecies and sees them as prohibited, along with weighing prophecy, under the category of authoritative "teaching" (1 Timothy 2:12).[49] Yet it is not clear how asking a question falls under such a prohibited category. Carson's view results in the absurd conclusion that both asking questions and weighing prophecy are of higher authority than prophecy itself. In the end, Paul's broad prohibition is just too much for Carson's reading. The weighing of prophecy view stretches words beyond their meaning, as it takes the prohibition on women's "speech" to refer to "weighing prophecy"

---

47. I credit Michael Merlowe's "Excursus on 1 Corinthians 11:5" for guiding my thinking here. His article can be accessed at http://www.bible-researcher.com/women-prophesying.html.

48. Carson, "'Silent in the Churches,'" in *Recovering Biblical Manhood and Womanhood*, 153. Carson adds, "'[P]rophecy' in the New Testament is an extraordinarily broad category, extending all the way from the product of the pagan Muse (Titus 1:12) to Old Testament canonical prophecy. In common church life, it was recognized to be Spirit-prompted utterance" that was "necessarily inferior in authority to the deposit of truth represented by the Apostle Paul (14:37-38)."

49. Ibid., 152.

but not the act of speaking a "prophecy." Yet women speaking a prophecy in public worship is the exact opposite of Paul's command for women to be "silent."

Dan Doriani also criticizes the public/private worship solution by arguing that it "does not adequately harmonize 14:26 and 14:35."[50] 1 Corinthians 14:26 says, "When you come together, each one has a hymn, a lesson, a revelation, a tongue, or an interpretation." Doriani asks, "How can Paul say everyone has a hymn or word of instruction in 14:26 and also say women must be silent in 14:35 if there is no qualification or limit on that silence?"[51] This is not a difficult problem, as 14:35 should guide our understanding of 14:26. If Paul forbids women from speaking publicly in worship in 14:35, then either (1) "each one" in 14:26 refers only to men, or (2) Paul includes women in the generic "each one" in 14:26 and then waits to prohibit such speech by women in 14:35.

The public/private worship distinction between 1 Corinthians 11:5 and 14:34-35 makes good sense of these passages. However, even if this were incorrect, it is still possible that the delayed-condemnation solution reconciles these texts. Paul never approved of women praying and prophesying in the public church assembly but only made a mere *incidental* reference to women praying and prophesying in 1 Corinthians 11:5. Either way, 1 Corinthians 14:34-35 is far clearer than 11:5, and the clearer passage should guide our interpretation, not vice-versa. As James Greenbury says, "An enormous amount of weight is being placed on this one verse [1 Corinthians 11:5]. This approach does not assign at least equal weight to 1 Timothy 2:8-15 and 1 Corinthians 14:34-35, as to interpreting 1 Corinthians 11:5 . . . Instead of allowing our doctrine to be shaped by passages that merely *allude* to a subject, we should draw our teaching primarily from *preceptive* passages."[52]

---

50. Dan Doriani, *Women and Ministry*, 82.
51. Ibid.
52. James Greenbury, "The Contribution of 1 Timothy 2:8-15 and 1 Corinthians 11:5 to the Discussion Concerning Women Speaking in Church," *Presbyterion* 44/2 (Fall 2018): 71–72.

Not Paul's Words? Two Attempts to Dismiss Paul's Prohibition

A final issue must be addressed regarding 1 Corinthians 14:34-35, as several modern scholars recognize Paul's clear prohibition of women speaking publicly in church and thus seek to argue that Paul did not really say this. These scholars recognize the inadequacy of the modern weighing of prophecy interpretation of 1 Corinthians 14:34-35, but they are unwilling to accept the historic reading that prohibits women from speaking publicly in church. There are two proposed solutions that fall into this camp: (1) 1 Corinthians 14:34-35 is a scribal interpolation and not Paul's actual words (argued by Gordon Fee and Philip Payne); and (2) Paul quotes the Corinthians in 14:34-35 and then refutes them (argued by Kirk MacGregor and Lucy Peppiatt).

Beginning with the interpolation charge, Gordon Fee recognizes the absolute nature of Paul's prohibition of woman speaking in church, citing that there is not only a negative command ("not to speak") but a positive one ("be silent"). Since some manuscripts place 14:34-35 after 14:40, Fee has run with this and argued against the authenticity of these verses. Fee says there is "substantial evidence" that these "intruding" and "thoroughly un-Pauline" words are "not authentic."[53] Fee's argument can be summarized as follows.

First, Fee argues that 1 Corinthians 14:34-35 is transcriptionally improbable because a scribal gloss best explains how these verses ended up in two different places (14:34-35 and 14:40). Fee appeals to Bengel's first principle that the textual form that best explains all other forms is most likely the original. Fee argues that there is no good explanation as to why scribes placed these verses in one place and transposed them to the other. As for the proposed explanation that a second-century scribe transposed the text "to find a more appropriate location," Fee calls this a "shot in the dark" because such "displacement" does not make better sense in either place.[54]

---

53. Gordon Fee, *The First Epistle to the Corinthians* (New International Commentary on the New Testament; Grand Rapids, MI: Eerdmans, 2014), 772.
54. Ibid., 783.

Second, Fee argues that the passage makes better sense without 14:34-35, and therefore the improbable textual authenticity also adequately addresses the intrinsic improbability. If authentic, these verses would have to be understood as an "intruding afterthought to the present argument." Further, the authenticity of 14:34-35 would require reconciliation with the "contradiction" of Paul's earlier words regarding "every woman who prays or prophesies" (11:5), where it is "assumed without reproof that women *pray* and *prophesy* in the assembly."[55] Fee thus concludes, "On the whole, therefore, the case against these verses is so thoroughgoing, and finding a viable solution to their meaning so difficult, that it seems best to view them as an interpolation."[56]

In response to Fee's interpolation argument, it must be stated that the burden is on Fee to show that this passage of Scripture is inauthentic and thus a scribal addition. The fact that *zero manuscripts lack 1 Corinthians 14:34-35* has led most other textual scholars to conclude they are authentic. The universal witness of these verses means a scribal addition would have had to take place in the earliest manuscripts (or even the original manuscript!), which is highly unlikely. Thus, while there is uncertainty as to how 14:34-35 became located in two different places in the manuscripts, Fee's interpolation "solution" still does not explain why these verses exist and how they got into the text so early. It is perfectly reasonable to think that a scribe either purposely or accidentally moved these verses to a different place in the passage. Another option is that Paul himself added 14:34-35 in the margin of his letter and then later copyists placed the marginal words in two different places.[57] Regardless, even if we do not know exactly how 14:34-35 ended up in two different locations in the manuscripts, these explanations are no more improbable than Fee's claim that one of the very earliest scribes made up these verses in Greek on his

---

55. Ibid., 784–785.
56. Ibid., 788.
57. See E. Earle Ellis, "The Silenced Wives of Corinth (1 Cor. 14:34-5)," in *New Testament Textual Criticism, Its Significance for Exegesis: Essays in Honour of Bruce M. Metzger* (eds. E.J. Epp and G.D. Fee; Oxford: Clarendon, 1981), 213–220.

own in the margin and then later scribes inserted them in two different places.

Fee's argument mostly relies on his second point of intrinsic improbability, namely the fact that he does not think 14:34-35 makes sense of the passage. But Paul's prohibition of women speaking publicly in worship makes good sense—Fee just does not like it. Earlier in the chapter, Paul gives instructions for tongues and prophecy, and here he regulates such practices by affirming the practice of the churches, that women are not to speak publicly in worship. Fee alleges a "contradiction" with 11:5, but we have already dealt with this issue. Conveniently, Fee does not mention the text critical principle *lectio difficilior potior,* that the most difficult reading is to be preferred, as scribes tended to smooth out passages, not make them harder. Of course, this principle goes entirely against Fee's concerns over making sense of the flow of the passage and reconciling it with 11:5. It is hard to avoid the conclusion that Fee just does not like what 14:34-35 says and he seeks to escape the apostle's command by dismissing it as a scribal interpolation.[58]

Is Paul Quoting the Corinthians?

Other interpreters, such as Kirk MacGregor and Lucy Peppiatt, recognize the plain meaning of 1 Corinthian 14:34-35 (that it prohibits women from speaking publicly in church), but they seek to evade Paul's command by

---

58. Philip Payne adopts Fee's interpolation position in *Man and Woman, One in Christ*, 217–267. Payne adds the argument that two dots ("distigmai") in Codex Vaticanus mark this passage as an interpolation, but this is highly tenuous. The distigmai may have been used by a scribe to mark a textual variation rather than an interpolation, and there is debate over when these distigmai were added. James Hamilton ably critiques Payne in his review in the *Journal of the Evangelical Theological Society* 54/1 (2011): 177–179. See also Curt Niccum, "The Voice of the Manuscripts on the Silence of Women: The External Evidence for 1 Cor 14:34-35," *New Testament Studies* 43 (1997): 242–255; J. Edward Miller, "Some Observations on the Text-Critical Function of the Umlauts in Vaticanus, with Special Attention to 1 Corinthians 14:34-35," *Journal for the Study of the New Testament* 26 (2003): 217–236.

arguing these words are actually Paul's quotation of a prior letter from the Corinthian church—a "quotation-refutation."[59] In this case, Paul would be quoting the Corinthian men as saying "women should keep silent in the churches," to which Paul responds, "Or was it from you that the word of God came? Or are you the only ones it has reached?" (1 Corinthians 14:36). Throughout 1 Corinthians, Paul responds to issues the Corinthians raised in a prior letter, and chapter 14 falls under the section "concerning spiritual gifts" (12:1; similar to 7:1, 25; 8:1; 16:1, 12).

However, MacGregor's quotation-refutation interpretation runs into several problems. First, as noted above, 1 Corinthians 14:34-35 parallels Paul's words in 1 Timothy 2:11-14. Thus, it is unlikely he is now quoting the Corinthians with similar words to his own elsewhere. Second, if 14:33b ("As in all the churches of the saints") goes with 14:34-35 as most commentators hold, it does not make sense for a quotation to follow. Rather, it supports Paul giving a general rule for the churches. Third, MacGregor's argument in part rests on the contextual evidence that 14:34-35 contradicts 11:5, a problem we dealt with above. Fourth, MacGregor takes Paul as only rebuking *men* who held this prohibition on women speaking in church, arguing that "only ones" [μόνους] in 14:36 refers only to "men." However, the masculine plural would also be used to rebuke the entire church of men and women, so this argument carries no weight.

Fifth, 14:34-35 does not fit Paul's other quotations of the Corinthians, which are short and followed by a detailed response to the Corinthians' erroneous belief. MacGregor attempts to show grammatical similarities between 14:34-35 and other Corinthian quotations. However, as Carson correctly notes, "the instances that are almost universally recognized as quotations (e.g. 6:12; 7:1b; 8:1b) enjoy certain common characteristics: (i) they are short (e.g., 'Everything is permissible for me,' 6:12); (ii) they are usually followed by sustained qualification (e.g., in 6:12 Paul goes on to add 'but not everything is beneficial . . . but I will not be mastered by anything'—and then, following one more brief quotation from their letter,

---

59. Kirk R. MacGregor, "1 Corinthians 14:33b-38 as a Pauline Quotation-Refutation Device," *Priscilla Papers* 32/1 (Winter 2018).

he devotes several verses to the principle he is expounding); (iii) Paul's response is unambiguous, even sharp."[60] 1 Corinthians 14:34-35 does not fit the first two characteristics, as it is a longer passage, not short, and this would be a complete refutation of the Corinthians' words with no sustained qualification. Only the third characteristic would fit, as 14:36 can be read as a sharp response ("Or was it from you that the word of God came? Or are you the only ones it has reached?"). However, this would leave Paul providing a mere rebuke with no alternative to the Corinthians' prohibition of women speaking in church. Moreover, Carson notes that "in every instance in the New Testament where the disjunctive particle [ἤ] in question is used in a construction analogous to the passage at hand [1 Corinthians 14:34-35], its effect is to reinforce the truth of the clause or verse that precedes it"[61] (e.g. Romans 3:29). Thus, Paul's words in 14:36 should not be understood as a rebuke of a Corinthian quotation, but rather as a call for the Corinthians to embrace the church's teaching that women are not to speak publicly in church (14:34-35).

Lucy Peppiatt also argues for a quotation-refutation, or what she calls a "rhetorical reading" of 1 Corinthians 14:34-35. While her work focuses on 1 Corinthians 11:2-16, she also thinks 14:34-35 is a Corinthian quotation. Her reason for holding this is that "[t]raditional explanations are riddled with inconsistencies when read within the Corinthian correspondence as a whole, and with Paul's other letters."[62] However, Peppiatt also holds that 1 Corinthians 11:5 is a Corinthian quotation to which Paul responds,[63] which ironically removes the alleged inconsistency with 14:34-35. For if Paul did not affirm women prophesying in 1 Corinthians 11:5 but was quoting the Corinthians, this would strongly support the delayed-condemnation solution in reconciling 11:5 with 14:34-35. In the end, Peppiatt does not provide convincing arguments for reading portions of

---

60. Carson, "'Silent in the Churches,'" in *Recovering Biblical Manhood and Womanhood*, 148.

61. Ibid., 151.

62. Lucy Peppiatt, *Women and Worship at Corinth: Paul's Rhetorical Arguments in 1 Corinthians* (Eugene, OR: Cascade Books, 2015), 109.

63. Ibid., 139.

11:2-16 or 14:34-35 as quotations, and she admits this rhetorical reading can only by pieced together by "clues."[64]

Yet Peppiatt also makes a fatal admission that how we read Paul, which includes her reading quotations into these passages, "depends on who we believe Paul to be." She asks, "Was Paul a misogynist? Was he just committed to a gentle patriarchy? Was he confused? Or was he a radical? Our prior conceptions of him will clearly affect our reading of his letters."[65] Peppiatt is quite open that she is unwilling to follow the "traditional approach" to 1 Corinthians 11:2-16 because it "leaves the reader with very few options for rescuing Paul from misogyny, or inconsistency, or bad theology, or all three."[66] This passage teaches "subordination and inequality,"[67] and disagreement over its meaning is an "'exegetical embarrassment' for the church."[68] She even holds that 1 Corinthians 11:7-9 is a "corrupted form of Genesis 1:26-27."[69] It is clear that Peppiatt's quotation proposal in 11:2-16 and 14:34-35 is not driven by the text of Scripture but by her desire to rescue Paul from hierarchical views of man and woman.

Embracing the Plain Teaching of Scripture

Both the interpolation and quotation arguments fail to withstand scrutiny. However, these arguments reveal an important point, which is that *many modern scholars find the weighing of prophecy interpretation of 1 Corinthians 14:34-35 to be unconvincing.* These scholars take these words at face value, as a prohibition on women speaking publicly in church, and they either think this contradicts 11:5 or, more likely, they are unwilling to accept the plain reading of the passage. Thus, these scholars are willing to go to great lengths to explain away what 1 Corinthians 14:34-35 plainly says—that women are prohibited from speaking publicly in worship.

---

64. Ibid., 137.
65. Ibid., 133.
66. Ibid., 33.
67. Ibid., 65.
68. Ibid., 107.
69. Ibid., 100.

The following conclusion remains. Honest liberal scholars reject 1 Corinthians 14:34-35 as a "sexist" command. Dishonest liberals dismiss the passage as an interpolation or Corinthian quotation. Modern complementarians escape Paul's words by limiting the prohibition to the weighing of prophecy. But those who embrace the plain meaning of the passage prohibit women from speaking publicly in worship—and they do not cater to the unbelieving world.

Chapter 10

MASCULINE AUTHORITY IN THE CHURCH

THE PRIMARY ARGUMENT of the previous two chapters has been that only men can serve as pastors and elders in the church. However, the prior exegesis of 1 Timothy 2:8-15 and 1 Corinthians 14:34-35 has gone further by arguing that women may not speak publicly in assembled worship or teach theology to men. There are many complementarians who disagree with these latter conclusions. Some think 1 Corinthians 14:34-35 still allows for women to prophesy and lead prayer in church (citing 1 Corinthians 11:5), and some think the restriction in 1 Timothy 2:8-15 is limited to the role of elder and thus permits women to occasionally teach and preach Scripture to men.

May a Woman Do Anything an Unordained Man May Do?

This limiting view of 1 Timothy 2 takes Paul to only prohibit women from an authoritative teaching (such as that exercised by elders) and not teaching in general. This line of thinking has led to the claim that "a woman may do anything in the church that an unordained man may do." This was Tim Keller's position at his church, seen in the words of his wife Kathy Keller—"That is the difference between public communication of information, exhortation, or explanation (all permitted to both unordained men and women) and teaching with authority, which is the province of ordained elders. Stated the way we do at Redeemer: anything that an unordained man is allowed to do, a woman is also allowed to do . . . Women are encouraged to be active, verbal participants in the life of the church—teaching, exhorting, encouraging, and contributing in every way except in the office of elder."[1]

Even complementarian theologian John Frame thinks 1 Timothy 2 only prohibits women from holding the office of elder and thus concludes that a woman may preach a sermon or teach Sunday school to men. Similar to Keller, Frame says, "In general, a woman may do in the church anything an unordained man may do."[2] Frame goes so far as to conclude that some women scholars can teach the Bible to men training for the pastorate in seminary—"I think that women may contribute much to the church as biblical scholars, and it is appropriate for women who are expert in Scripture and other relevant fields to instruct men preparing for ordination. I have no objection to women as seminary professors. I do believe that most seminary professors should be ordained males, for I think that that teaching should come, for the most part, from elders, those authorized to speak for the church."[3] Thus, Frame qualifies his approval of women seminary professors by saying it should not be normative. Yet he still opens the door to women teaching the Bible to men in a variety of settings.

Complementarian Thomas Schreiner thinks 1 Timothy 2 applies more broadly by prohibiting women from preaching sermons to men and teaching men in Sunday school settings, but even he thinks women may otherwise speak publicly in worship—"there is no scriptural basis to prevent women from serving Communion or from leading in prayer or Scripture reading when we gather to worship."[4] Schreiner thus adopts the

---

1. Kathy Keller, *Jesus, Justice, and Gender Roles* (Grand Rapids, MI: Zondervan, 2012), 21, 29.
2. John Frame, *The Doctrine of the Christian Life* (Phillipsburg, NJ: P&R Publishing, 2008), 640.
3. Ibid.
4. Thomas R. Schreiner, "A Response to Craig Blomberg," in *Two Views on*

mindset that Christians should push women into as many positions as possible—"complementarians need to work especially hard at including women in ministries that are permitted by Scripture."[5] Wayne Grudem also takes the position that women can pray and read Scripture in publicly assembled worship, as well as perform baptism and serve Communion.[6] Grudem hopes churches can examine their traditions to "see if there are more areas of ministry they could open to women."[7] Thus we see how important the interpretation of 1 Corinthians 14:34-35 becomes. The modern particular-speech solution opens up the door for women to speak publicly in church. (Schreiner thinks 1 Corinthians 14:34-35 only prohibits women from asking questions,[8] while Grudem takes the more common view that it only prohibits women from weighing prophecy.[9])

In response to these claims, we will appeal to the prior exegesis of 1 Timothy 2:8-15 showing that the creation order prohibits women from preaching and teaching the Bible and theology to men, as well as the exegesis of 1 Corinthians 14:34-35 showing that women are not permitted to speak publicly in assembled worship. Teaching, and preaching in particular, is an *authoritative task* that belongs to men, especially the elders of a church. However, public prayer and Scripture reading are also authoritative tasks, as prayer leads the congregation before God and reading Scripture brings God's authoritative Word to the congregation. Both tasks involve public speaking that is prohibited to women. Along with serving the Lord's Supper and performing baptisms, these are all tasks that primarily belong to the elders and are thus reserved for men. We should not adopt the modern feminist mindset that seeks to push women into as many positions as possible. Paul did not prohibit women from teaching

---

Women in Ministry (ed. James R. Beck; Grand Rapids, MI: Zondervan, 2005), 190.

5. Ibid.

6. Wayne Grudem, *Countering the Claims of Evangelical Feminism: Biblical Responses to the Key Questions* (Colorado Springs: Multnomah, 2006), 62.

7. Ibid., 53.

8. Schreiner, "A Response to Craig Blomberg," in *Two Views on Women in Ministry*, 192.

9. Grudem, *Countering the Claims of Evangelical Feminism*, 144.

men with the exception that they may get behind the pulpit occasionally or train men in a seminary classroom. If Paul wanted to limit his prohibition to the office of elder, he could have said, "I do not permit a woman to be an elder." Instead, he used broad language that prohibits women from the tasks of "teaching" and "exercising authority," and he forbade them to "speak" in the public assembly.

May a Woman Still Preach a Sermon?

We should address a more recent argument that seeks to allow women to preach sermons by making a distinction between "teaching" and "preaching a sermon." This is advocated by John Dickson in his booklet *Hearing Her Voice: A Biblical Invitation for Women to Preach*.[10] Dickson argues that Paul's specific use of "teaching" (διδάσκω, *didasko*) refers to the task of passing down apostolic doctrine, which is distinguished from other tasks such as "prophecy" and "exhortation." In defense of this distinction, he appeals to Romans 12:4-8, which lists "gifts that differ"—prophecy, service, teaching, exhortation, generosity, leadership, and mercy. Dickson then argues that a modern sermon (the exposition and application of Scripture) is not strictly "teaching" (the passing down of oral apostolic doctrine) and has more in common with "prophecy "and "exhortation." Since Paul in 1 Timothy 2:12 only prohibits women from "teaching," women are thus allowed to give a sermon. Dickson's argument can be summarized as follows: (1) Women are only prohibited from teaching, not prophecy and exhortation; (2) A sermon is not teaching, but more akin to exhortation; (3) Therefore, women may preach sermons to men.

No one can claim that the feminist spirit lacks ingenuity. However, this argument runs into several problems. For the sake of argument, we are assuming a less restrictive view of 1 Corinthians 14:34-35. If the prior exegesis of that passage is correct, women are prohibited from speaking

---

10. John Dickson, *Hearing Her Voice: A Biblical Invitation for Women to Preach* (Grand Rapids, MI: Zondervan, 2014).

publicly in the assembled congregation and Dickson's argument is moot. However, there are two other reasons Dickson's argument fails.

First, *Paul does not make a strict separation between "teaching" and "exhortation."* Dickson says that "exhortation" is based on the Scriptures, but he argues for an extremely narrow view of "teaching" that only involves the "specific activity" of "preserving and laying down the tradition handed on by the apostles."[11] While this point could be refuted easily by appealing to the Old Testament use of "teaching" for expositing Scripture passages (e.g. Deuteronomy 4:1-14; 2 Chronicles 17:9; Ezra 7:10; Nehemiah 8:8), we must focus on Paul's writing specifically because Dickson limits his definition of "teaching" to Paul's use of the term. However, it should not be ignored that this use of "teaching" in the Septuagint would have served as background to Paul's understanding.

Yet even in Paul's writings there is a connection between "teaching" and the use of Scripture. In fact, there is a connection between "teaching" and "exhorting" where both involve Scripture. The two are not separate actions but are related. In 1 Timothy 4:13, Paul says to Timothy, "Until I come, devote yourself to the public reading of Scripture, to exhortation, to teaching." Literally, this says "pay attention to the reading, to the exhortation, to the teaching" [πρόσεχε τῇ ἀναγνώσει, τῇ παρακλήσει, τῇ διδασκαλίᾳ]. Thus, Paul lists three different tasks. However, these tasks are connected and all relate to the Scriptures. What is Timothy to "read"? This is an obvious reference to the Scriptures. Are we really to understand that the "exhortation" also refers to the Scriptures but the "teaching" does not? Anticipating this argument, Dickson responds, "I am not denying that 'teaching' in 1 Timothy 4:13 is *related* to the Old Testament Scriptures . . . But this does not make teaching identical with exposition of Scripture."[12] However, teaching does not have to be "identical" with expositing Scripture in order to undermine Dickson's argument. If "teaching" is connected with the exposition of Scripture (and not merely laying

---

11. Ibid., 12.
12. Ibid., 52.

down the apostolic tradition), and if Paul prohibits women from teaching men, then women may not exposit Scripture to men.

"Teaching" and "exhortation" are also both linked with Scripture in 2 Timothy 4:1-2, where Paul says to Timothy, "I charge you in the presence of God and of Christ Jesus, who is to judge the living and the dead, and by his appearing and his kingdom: *preach* the word; be ready in season and out of season; reprove, rebuke, and *exhort*, with complete patience and *teaching*." The command to "preach" has a clear connection to the Scriptures ("the word"), while the command to "exhort" is tied with teaching—"with complete patience and teaching" [ἐν πάσῃ μακροθυμίᾳ καὶ διδαχῇ]. These activities cannot be separated. Preaching the Scriptures involves rebuking and exhorting and, yes, even teaching.

Contrary to Dickson, "teaching" for Paul is more than the mere passing down of apostolic doctrine, but also includes instruction and exhortation in the Scriptures. Dickson claims, "I am not creating a hard distinction between teaching and exhorting, but I am observing that, whereas teaching is principally about laying something down in fixed form, exhorting is principally about urging people to obey and apply God's truth."[13] Thus, he denies separating teaching and exhorting. But such a denial will not do. His entire argument is based on such a separation, and this separation does not hold up under examination.

Second, *Paul links "teaching" to the office of elder*. The Bible clearly states that "teaching" is a task that belongs to elders. Elders must be "able to teach" [διδακτικόν] (1 Timothy 3:2), and "elders" who labor in "preaching and teaching" (literally "in word and teaching") should be "considered worthy of double honor" (1 Timothy 5:17). Yes, elders are teaching and passing down the apostolic doctrine handed down from the apostles. But this apostolic doctrine is laid down for us *in the Scriptures*. The Bible contains the apostolic doctrine in both the Old and New Testaments, and "teaching" of this doctrine is the essential task of church leaders, continuing beyond the apostolic age. It is doubtful Dickson would argue that elders are only to "teach" apostolic doctrine and not exposit Bible texts.

---

13. Ibid., 65.

Yet there is nothing in Paul's requirement or description of elders that is limited to the "exhortation" of the Bible. Rather, Paul speaks of elders "teaching" the Scriptures.

This becomes a problem for Dickson, as he admits that the apostolic tradition is laid down in the Bible—"A sermon doesn't usually preserve and lay down the apostolic traditions; it expounds and applies the biblical text in which those traditions are already preserved and laid down."[14] Dickson does not use the word "teach" here, but that is exactly what he is describing. The apostolic tradition is laid down in the Bible, and elders have the duty of expositing the Bible so as to pass down the apostolic tradition. These things cannot be so neatly separated. Further, while Scripture does not give a prohibition of non-elders preaching sermons, this task is particularly tied with the role of elders. A church may want an unordained man to preach to test and practice his gift, but it should not be the ordinary practice for unordained men to preach sermons. Following this logic, there is no reason that a woman should engage in this same task.

Pastoring Is a Masculine Task

Something that is often left out of the discussion of whether women may be elders is the nature of the tasks of the elder. Egalitarians assume that women may do anything men may do, including preaching and ruling. Apart from rejecting the teaching of 1 Timothy 2:8-15, egalitarians fail to understand that these are by nature masculine tasks. As seen in the discussion of gender roles in creation (chapter 5), man was given the tasks to provide and protect—"work" and "keep" (Genesis 2:15). We saw that these can also be translated "serve" and "guard" and that they relate to providing and protecting. *These are the same tasks given to pastors,*[15] only in relation to the church instead of the garden or a man's wife. Pastors are to provide for and protect their flock. Let us examine both of these tasks.

---

14. Ibid., 48.
15. I am using the word "pastor" here to refer specifically to the teaching elder, as ruling elders are not as involved in the preaching and teaching of God's Word.

First, pastors are to *provide* for God's people by teaching them His Word (Ephesians 4:11; 1 Timothy 3:2; 5:17; Titus 1:9). Pastors must feed the sheep, and they do this by preaching and teaching. Pastors must teach the Word by reading Bible texts, explaining what the text means, and connecting the text to other passages of Scripture and ultimately to Christ. This teaching should lead to exhortation, as pastors call Christians to believe, repent, and obey God's Word. *Preaching is a masculine task* that carries authority from both God and the church. A preacher is "sent" from God (Romans 10:14-15), as he is commissioned and authorized to preach His Word.

Christian preaching is didactic exhortation. And such an authoritative task belongs to men. This is why teaching in the Old Testament was done by the male Levites (Deuteronomy 21:5; 33:10; 2 Chronicles 17:7-9; 35:3; Nehemiah 8:7-9; Malachi 2:4-7). And in the new covenant, God has reserved the task of preaching and teaching His Word for qualified men, usually teaching elders (1 Timothy 5:17). Man's nature should not be ignored in this reasoning. A man's body is better suited for communicating authority, seen in his deeper voice and larger body. A woman's body is not built for communicating authority but is designed to bear and nurse children. As Dabney says, "Woman is excluded from this masculine task of public preaching by Paul, not because she is inferior to man, but simply because her Maker has ordained for her another work which is incompatible with this."[16]

Second, pastors are to *protect* God's people from sin, false teaching, and attacks from Christ's enemies. Pastors are "overseers" of the church (Acts 20:28; 1 Timothy 3:1-2; Titus 1:7) who are to "shepherd" the flock by "exercising oversight" (1 Peter 5:2). Pastors are given the task of governing and ruling the church (1 Timothy 3:4-5; 5:17), as ruling is a masculine task. Thus, God has not given women rule in the home, church, or civil government. The Bible requires an elder to "manage" his household well because this is a measure of his ability to rule in the church of God (1

---

16. R.L. Dabney, "The Public Preaching of Women," in *Discussions*, vol 2 (1891; repr., Harrisonburg, VA: Sprinkle Publications, 1982), 110.

Timothy 3:4-5). A man's ability to manage his household is also a measure of his ability to rule in civil government.

Pastors must shepherd the flock, and that includes protecting the flock from wolves. There are many wolves in sheep's clothing who teach what is contrary to the faith (Matthew 7:15). Thus, Paul spoke to the Ephesian elders before leaving them, "Pay careful attention to yourselves and to all the flock, in which the Holy Spirit has made you overseers, to care for the church of God, which he obtained with his own blood. I know that after my departure fierce wolves will come in among you, not sparing the flock; and from among your own selves will arise men speaking twisted things, to draw away the disciples after them" (Acts 20:28-30).

Masculinity defends the truth, and it is the men who must stand up against the wolves and protect the flock. Men must "contend for the faith that was once for all delivered to the saints" (Jude 3). Paul implicitly connects masculinity and defending the faith when he prohibits women from teaching on the basis that Eve was deceived and Adam was not—"For . . . Adam was not deceived, but the woman was deceived and became a transgressor" (1 Timothy 2:13-14). This is not to say that men are never deceived. Obviously, there are many men who are false teachers and members of cults. Yet Paul seems to indicate that women are more prone to deception because God designed women to follow. Women are not suited for shepherding, and thus women are not to teach men.

Contending for the faith, defending the truth, and protecting the flock—these are manly tasks that belong to elders. Thus, God has reserved the office of elder for men. Women have important tasks in life, but they are different from those of men. Biblical leaders were tough men. Pastors are shepherds and guardians. Nice men will not cut it. We need masculine men to lead Christ's church—men who will fight for truth and guard the flock.

Sadly, the feminization of the church has made many pastors soft. They are afraid of preaching the hard truths of Scripture and calling out the sins of the congregation because they do not want to upset anyone. Many pastors also shy away from a forceful tone and authoritative voice for this reason. It is easier to skip over hard passages, tell stories, and speak softly in order to keep the peace. Granted, it does not help when congregants get easily offended and can easily leave the church (or seek to get the pastor fired). Yet it is the task of the shepherd to fulfill his duty regardless of the outcome. It is better to be fired for faithfully preaching God's Word than to abdicate one's duty just to keep a paycheck. Moreover, good fruit comes from faithful preaching—the Spirit may work on the hearers and the church will be blessed.

Sadly, many complementarians today want to affirm that women are as capable of the tasks and roles given to men, as if a woman can be just as good a pastor and preacher as a man. Even John Piper states that "leadership and submission" do not have anything to do with "muscles and skills" and are "not a matter of capabilities and competencies."[17] This is false. God did not design women to lead, and He did not orient woman's nature to exercise the godly authority requisite for preaching His Word. This is not an insult to women. It is merely an affirmation that men and women are different. Men are better suited for the tasks God has given them, including ruling and preaching, and women are better suited for the tasks God has given them, including nurturing. These are good differences to be embraced. We must reject egalitarianism in all forms, including the claim that men and women are equally capable of the same tasks and functions.

The Continuity of Male Rule in the Old and New Testaments

All of this finds continuity with the practice of the Old Testament. Though we are members of the new covenant, it is built upon the promises of old. And gender roles have always been built on the creation order. The positions of rule in the church were held only by men in both the Old Testament (priests and elders) and in the New Testament (apostles and elders).

Contrary to Roman Catholic theology, New Testament clergy do not fulfill the role of Old Testament priests. Jesus is our Great High Priest (Hebrews 4:14) who made a final sacrifice for sin on the cross (Hebrews 7:27). However, it is still important that only men were priests in the Old

---

17. *Recovering Biblical Manhood and Womanhood*, 25.

Testament, and it was the priests who were the teachers of Israel (Leviticus 10:11; Deuteronomy 33:10; 2 Chronicles 17:7-9; 35:3; Nehemiah 8:7-9; Malachi 2:4-7). New Testament elders find a close approximation in the Old Testament elders (e.g. Exodus 19:7), and the New Testament uses the same word for "elder" as that used in the Septuagint (πρεσβύτερος, *presbuteros*). Just like the New Testament, Old Testament elders were all men.

Thus, we have the fact that the Old Testament teachers and rulers were men (priests and elders). Another way to say this is that the Old Testament offices corresponding to the New Testament elder were only held by men. What changed about human nature and God's design so that women can now take on a role always reserved for men? We can add to this that in the New Testament, Jesus chose 12 men to serve as apostles. We also have Paul's teaching that elders must be men (1 Timothy 3; Titus 1) and that only men may teach and exercise authority over men (1 Timothy 2). There is strong continuity between the testaments regarding male-only leadership, not discontinuity as egalitarians contend.

Grape-Juice Christianity

These arguments put forth in this and the prior two chapters are why the church has historically not allowed women to be elders. The fact that male-only church leadership has almost always been practiced is not alone determinative, but it should keep the burden of proof on those advocating for women elders. Similar to the recent practice of substituting grape juice for wine (also a departure from 1800 years of church tradition), there should be an *explicit biblical basis* for changing the church's practice. The church can err, but it is unlikely considering the consensus on this issue among different traditions for such a long period of time.

The link between the novel practices of grape juice and women pastors should be pressed further. They are both connected in that the 19th-century temperance and feminist movements overlapped. Many feminists opposed the use of alcohol (and wanted it legally banned), and many prohibitionists were feminists. Both of these movements undermined the authority of the Bible, a book that is thoroughly patriarchal and happily affirms the goodness of alcohol, particularly in its use in the Lord's Supper. The predominance of grape juice as the element used in Communion in most Protestant churches today is symbolic of the weakness and effeminacy of the modern church. We are living in an age of grape-juice Christianity.

Those who insist on permitting women to be pastors cannot do so on the basis of Scripture or church practice. They are merely caving to unbelieving cultural pressure. It is therefore no surprise that churches allowing women to be pastors and elders are also caving on other cultural issues. The question of whether women may serve in church leadership turns on whether God allows the practice. And the Bible's answer is a resounding no. God has established men as the rulers in the home, church, and society. Ruling in the church, along with preaching and teaching, are authoritative tasks reserved for men.

Chapter 11

MASCULINE AUTHORITY BEYOND THE HOME AND CHURCH

CONSERVATIVES WITHIN THE modern church have responded to feminism by affirming male leadership in the home and church. But most have stopped there. For the majority of those who call themselves complementarians, anything outside the home and church is off limits from consideration and is left to the domain of the feminists. The result is that women now fill all positions in society traditionally reserved for men, including those that involve physical force. Women fill positions of high office in civil government, such as mayor, governor, and president. And women are welcomed—and even encouraged—to become police officers and soldiers.

This is a sure change from historic Christian practice. Many Christians today are unwilling to speak against women in these positions because the Bible is not as explicit here as it is on male rule in the home and church. However, this position errs in two ways. First, it fails to take into account the passages that do speak on women in the military and women in political office. Second, it fails to acknowledge that *the creation order applies to men and women wherever they are*, not just the home and church. The God-designed differences between men and women carry over to all of life. A woman and her nature, including her body, is still different from a man and his nature outside the home and church. Limiting gender roles to home and church creates a dichotomy between Christianity and the world around us, as if the two can be completely separated.

The church's failure to speak on these issues has led to the world becoming feminized at an even faster rate, as Christians have joined unbelievers in accepting women in positions of combat and high civil office. These Christians, seeing the inconsistency, are in turn more open to egalitarian practices in the home and church. Add on the feminized world's pressure for the church to "modernize," and it is no surprise Christians are caving to feminism in all spheres of life.

The Creation Order Applies Everywhere

We have already demonstrated that gender roles are rooted in creation (chapters 5 and 6). God made man to provide for, protect, and lead his wife and children, and He made woman to support her husband, bear children, and care for the home. Based on this creation order, we know that husbands have authority in marriage (chapter 7) and that only men can serve as elders in the church (chapters 8, 9, and 10). In speaking on male headship, Paul appealed to Eve being made "for" Adam (1 Corinthians 11:9). And in prohibiting women from teaching and exercising authority over men in the church, Paul appealed to Adam being formed first and Eve being deceived (1 Timothy 2:12-14).

Why then does the creation order not apply outside of marriage and the church? Does God's differing design of men and women have no implications for other areas of life? A woman is still a woman when running for political office. The same nature that prohibits her from having authority in the home and church is the same nature that she carries into public life. A woman does not have authority over her husband, and she cannot be a leader of Christ's church. But according to modern Christian thinking, she can have civil authority over men in her city and neighborhood. The Apostle Peter says a woman is the "weaker vessel" and should therefore be treated with understanding and honor by her husband (1 Peter 3:7). But according to the modern Christian, she can carry that weakness onto the battlefield and into a crime bust.

1 Timothy 2 is an important passage on this subject. Paul's prohibition in 1 Timothy 2:12 targets women teaching Scripture and theology to men and exercising authority in the church over men. However, its application should not be limited to teaching and ruling in the church. For the creation order that leads Paul to prohibit women from teaching and ruling men in the church is the same creation order that regulates all of life. And one thing the creation order teaches is that the nature of authority is masculine.

Thus, the criticism of narrow complementarianism by egalitarian Michael Bird has merit—"I think it is worth pointing out that complementarians themselves toned down the full implications of their view, and herein is the weakness of their position . . . A woman can write a commentary on Hebrews to be read by men but cannot preach or teach on Hebrews. A woman can be president, a prime minister, a CEO, a general, or a police officer, but she cannot serve as a pastor."

Bird continues, "The problem I have here is that some complementarians appeal to Genesis and the order of creation to show that it is inherently wrong for a woman to be in a position of authority over a man, and yet they only apply that restriction to church life or Sunday worship . . . If it is such a clear violation of God's ordering of creation for a woman to have authority over a man, then this should apply to all spheres of life whether it is business, government, politics, civil service, or church because God is sovereign over all institutions, and all of life is lived before God and under God."[1]

We should respond to Bird with a hearty "amen." He is spot on in his criticism of narrow complementarianism. It is inconsistent in its application of the creation order, acting as if we can bifurcate the church and the rest of society. Bird says his criticism only applies to "some" complementarians, though it is probably accurate to say it applies to the *vast majority* of them. Even the prolific complementarian author Wayne Grudem has

---

1. Michael F. Bird, *Bourgeois Babes, Bossy Wives, and Bobby Haircuts* (Grand Rapids, MI: Zondervan, 2012), 41.

said that women may exercise authority over men in politics and business and has said that he would be "fine" with a woman president.² John Piper has been one of the few complementarians who has argued for a broader and more all-encompassing application of biblical gender roles, saying that only men should serve as presidents and police officers.³

Bird's solution is to abandon complementarianism completely for some form of egalitarianism. However, the alternative solution is to maintain consistency by adhering to a broader and more comprehensive complementarianism that applies the creation order to all of life. That will be the approach advocated here.

The Reformed Two Kingdoms Dichotomy

Where does such bifurcated complementarian thinking come from? There are likely multiple contributing philosophies, but surely the Reformed two kingdoms view (known as R2K for short) has contributed significantly to this dichotomy. R2K distinguishes between two kingdoms, the "common kingdom" and the "redemptive kingdom." The R2K common kingdom is founded on the Noahic covenant (Genesis 8:20–9:17). All people are part of the common kingdom, and it includes the areas of civil government, family, education, and art. Jesus rules this civil kingdom as creator and sustainer, and it is guided by general revelation, namely natural law. In contrast to the common kingdom, the R2K redemptive kingdom is founded on the Abrahamic covenant (Genesis 15, 17). Only Christians are part of the redemptive kingdom, and it includes the church and its

---

2. According to Philip Payne, Grudem said this at a lecture at Wheaton College's Blanchard Hall, April 13, 2005. Payne, *Man and Woman, One in Christ*, 403. See also Grudem, *Evangelical Feminism & Biblical Truth* (2004), 140, discussed below.

3. Piper provides "guidelines" rather than a "list" of what positions men and women can take on, and he concludes that women should not fill roles that involve "personal" and "directive" influence over men. He gives the example of a drill sergeant. John Piper, *What's the Difference?* (Wheaton, IL: Crossway, 2001).

mission. Jesus rules this spiritual kingdom as redeemer, and it is guided by special revelation, namely the Bible.[4]

Proponents of the modern Reformed two kingdoms claim to follow the "two kingdom" theology of the Protestant Reformers, but this is not the case. The R2K model is better termed as the *radical* two kingdoms because of its *departure* from the two kingdoms doctrine of Reformers like Martin Luther and John Calvin. Those men spoke of "this age" and "the age to come," in contrast to the "common kingdom" and "redemptive kingdom" of the R2K scheme. The Reformers' eternal kingdom ("the age to come") referred to the invisible church, whereas the temporal kingdom ("this age") included *both the state and the visible church*. In other words, the Reformers did not make the sharp state-church divide found in the R2K scheme.[5] (The Reformers advocated a form of theocracy, not the modern American disestablishment of state churches. Calvin equated natural law with the Ten Commandments, which led him to the position that the state should prohibit even blasphemy and idolatry.[6]) The R2K scheme

---

4. For more on this subject, see David VanDrunen, *Living in God's Two Kingdoms: A Biblical Vision for Christianity and Culture* (Wheaton, IL: Crossway, 2010). For a fuller critique of R2K, see Zachary Garris, "Should We Seek a Christian Government? Part 1—A Critique of the Reformed Two Kingdoms," *KnowingScripture.com* (November 5, 2019), https://knowingscripture.com/articles/should-we-seek-a-christian-government-part-1-a-critique-of-the-reformed-two-kingdoms.

5. See John Calvin, *Institutes of the Christian Religion* (trans. Ford Lewis Battles; Louisville, KY: Westminster John Knox Press; 2006), 847–849 [3.19.15], 1485–1488 [4.20.1–2].

6. Ibid., 367–368 [2.8.1]: "That inward law, which we have above described as written, even engraved, upon the hearts of all, in a sense asserts the very same things that are to be learned from the two Tables." Ibid., 1488–1489 [4.20.3]: "It [civil government] does not, I repeat, look to this only, but also prevents idolatry, sacrilege against God's name, blasphemies against his truth, and other public offense against religion from arising and spreading among the people; it prevents the public peace from being disturbed; it provides that each man may keep his property safe and sound; that men may carry on blameless intercourse among themselves; that honesty and modesty may be preserved among men. In short, it provides that a public manifestation of religion may exist among Christians, and that humanity be maintained among men."

has implications for civil government because it pits the state against the church. They are two separate institutions, and they are governed by two different rules—the state by natural law and the church by Scripture.

How does this apply to gender roles? R2K proponents are happy to affirm male leadership in the home and church because Scripture explicitly teaches these things, and Scripture guides Christians. So far, so good. But where R2K runs into trouble is that its proponents are often unwilling to apply Scripture to the civil sphere. So even if the Bible mocks women governors (Isaiah 3:12) and forbids women from being soldiers (Deuteronomy 22:5), those passages cannot be applied to such persons because governors and soldiers are part of the civil realm. Civil government and military are only guided by natural law.

Of course, natural law still teaches that women should not be soldiers. Women's bodies are different from those of men and are not suited for war. Considering that soldiers are usually young, this means female soldiers are women of child-bearing age. These are mothers (or should-be mothers) who should be protected from harm by men, not thrown into harm's way in combat. Yet men suppress the truth (Romans 1:18-20), and that includes natural law. Thus, people today even reject nature's obvious teaching that women should not serve in combat. This suppression of natural law does not mean Christians should reject natural law arguments. Rather, the point is that we should not *limit* ourselves to natural law arguments. We have a clearer guide than natural law, namely Scripture, to guide us in these things. As Calvin says, "Accordingly (because it is necessary both for our dullness and for our arrogance), the Lord has provided us with a written law to give us a clearer witness of what was too obscure in the natural law."[7] Men may still suppress the truth of the Bible, but it may also cut to the heart. There is no reason to hold back the power of God's Word (1 Thessalonians 1:5).

The Reformed two kingdoms view has created a radical divide between the church and the world around us. It has also formed a dichotomy between creation and redemption. Even though R2K holds that Jesus rules

---

7. Calvin, *Institutes of the Christian Religion*, 368 [2.8.1].

the common kingdom as creator, it has failed to apply creational gender roles to that kingdom, in part because of its refusal to use Scripture to speak to the common kingdom. More than this, R2K has encouraged the modern Christian to accept the absurd position that a woman can lead a nation but not her home or church. How does this work? It is best just not to think about it. That is the world out there, and God has nothing to say about it.

Yet that is not how Christianity works. God orders all of life, and He has given instructions for all spheres, including the civil sphere. Jesus has "all authority in heaven and on earth," and His disciples are to teach His commandments to the nations (Matthew 28:18-20). A Christian people will seek to shape the civil government according to God's design as laid down in His Word. The Bible does not make the R2K church-state dichotomy, and it does not make the R2K creation-redemption dichotomy. Is not Christ redeeming His creation? Of course He is. Christ redeems marriage, family, education, government, art, and more because He redeems all things through the work of His church. This is why Christ's apostles give extensive instructions for the Christian family (e.g. Ephesians 5 and 6). Jesus is redeeming and perfecting the created order.

Civil Government Is Modeled on—and Is an Extension of—the Home

Assuming we should apply the Bible to the civil realm (and we should), where does that leave us? While the Bible is not a civics textbook, it does have plenty to say about civil government, including that women should not hold civil office. The first point in support of this is that *civil government is an extension of the family*. The Fifth Commandment deals with authority structures, starting with the family. Parents have authority over their children (Ephesians 6:1-2), and husbands have authority over their wives (Ephesians 5:23). From this structure flow both the church and state. The church is the outgrowth of the family for spiritual government, while the state is the outgrowth of the family for civil government. As

Benjamin Morgan Palmer says, "[I]n the Family are to be found both the State and the Church in embryo, perpetuated as they both are, through its continuance, until the end of time."[8]

Both the church and state are composed of the family unit (and not just individuals), and both carry authority over families so long as such authority is properly exercised according to God's design. When it was just Adam and Eve, Adam as the head of the family had all governing authority. But when Adam's descendants multiplied, there was need for oversight among the several families living together. Civil government grew out of this family structure. Just as a family needs an authority (and God has made the husband such), so the collection of families needs an authority to provide rules for living and to execute justice in conflicts. Societies throughout history have established this through rulers such as elders, governors, and kings.

We see civil government arise in Old Testament Israel with the elders (Exodus 3:16; 4:29), all of whom were men. We later see Israel's republic replaced by a monarchy, and Israel was ruled by a king, not a queen (Deuteronomy 17:14-20; 1 Samuel 8). Yet even this monarchy reflects the family model. Instead of a group of appointed fathers holding civil authority, one father held civil authority. Thus, Israel's government was based on the family.

The implication of this is that only men may rule in civil government. When we examine the family model, Scripture is clear that man is the head of the household, not woman. If a woman cannot lead in her own home, how can she lead in civil government? A woman civil ruler also introduces an absurd situation, as *a woman who holds civil office holds authority over her own husband.* (The only exception would be a widow or divorcee, both unideal circumstances.) This should not be. The same nature that prohibits a woman from exercising familial authority prohibits her from exercising civil authority. Moreover, the Apostle Paul instructs wives to submit to their husbands "in everything" (Ephesians 5:24). Surely this submission includes the political and civil realm.

---

8. B.M. Palmer, *The Family in its Civil and Churchly Aspects*, 209.

The same is also true of the church. The church, like the state, is an extension of the family. (There are similarities between church and state, especially when one compares republican civil government with Presbyterian church government.) This provides a further argument against women leaders in the church. Since man is the head of woman in the family, and since both church and state are extensions of the family, therefore women may not lead in the home or the church. Yet many Christians who affirm that women may not lead in the home or church (complementarians) turn around and permit women to lead in civil government. Such a position disconnects the family from the rest of society. Yet the family is the foundational unit in society. Both state and church are built upon it, with each having different purposes. There are three primary sphere's in this world (family, church, state), with the family being foundational.

We can add to this the argument that a woman's domestic responsibilities should keep her out of civil government. The home is the woman's sphere, and civil duties distract from home duties. Commenting on Titus 2:4-5, R.L. Dabney says, "Does not the apostle here assign the *home* as the proper sphere of the Christian woman? That is her kingdom and neither the secular nor the ecclesiastical commonwealth. Her duties in her home are to detain her away from the public functions."[9] God is a God of consistency—"a wise God designs no clashing between his domestic and political and his ecclesiastical arrangements."[10]

Countering Arguments for Women Leading in Society

Egalitarian Bible scholar R.T. France does not think male leadership is the ideal, and he questions whether male headship in marriage can be applied to broader society. France says, "Male leadership may be a reality in the first-century world, but it is not presented to us [as] an ideal for human life in general, other than in the marriage relationship, and it is at least a

---

9. R.L. Dabney, "The Public Preaching of Women," in *Discussions*, vol 2 (1891; repr., Harrisonburg, VA: Sprinkle Publications, 1982), 106.

10. Ibid., 112.

valid question whether it is acceptable to extrapolate from marriage to the wider structures of society."[11] As has been previously argued, Scripture does present male leadership as the ideal in the home, church, and society. And France does not provide an alternative to understanding civil government as an extension of the home.

France also rejects the argument that if the Bible prohibits women from leadership in the church, then they should not lead in society—"What God intends for society and what he intends for the church are not necessarily the same."[12] But appealing to the differences between God's intentions for the church and society does not settle the issue. Yes, God has intended the church, and not society or civil government, to preach the Word and administer the sacraments. But on what basis would God prohibit women from ruling in the church but not in society? The contention thus far is that God has made men to lead in both spheres.

Bible scholar Gordon Hugenberger, who affirms male headship only in the home, argues that a wife's submission to her husband has no bearing on her role in society—"a wife's responsibility to be submissive is precisely limited to familial concerns and as such would not necessarily prohibit her from being the president of the company where her husband is employed or of the country where her husband resides."[13] (Hugenberger also thinks a husband's headship does not prohibit his wife from being his pastor; see chapter 8.) He appeals to Deborah as having political authority over her husband Lappidoth,[14] but as will be shown below, her civil authority was not so clear. Hugenberger provides the following analogy to support his

---

11. France, *Women in the Church's Ministry*, 37.
12. Ibid., 36.
13. Hugenberger, "Women in Church Office: Hermeneutics or Exegesis? A Survey of Approaches to 1 Tim 2:8-15," *JETS* 35 (1992): 359.
14. Ibid., 359: "presumably Deborah was a submissive wife to her husband Lappidoth in terms of their domestic life, while in the political sphere she was a judge over Israel, including her husband. In a similar manner it may be that a requirement to be submissive in the familial sphere would not necessarily require submission in the ecclesiastical sphere (a man's slave could conceivably be his elder at church, etc.)."

argument that a woman can be under the submission of her husband yet have authority over him in other situations:

> although Rom 13:1-2 exhorts believers to "be subject (*hypotassestho*) to the governing authorities," using the same terminology as Paul applies to wifely submission, it is doubtful that this command would prohibit a believer from being an elder of a church where a senator, president or king might be in attendance. Naturally, special wisdom and care would be required by such an elder not to allow his rightful ecclesiastical authority to tempt him to challenge or compromise the rightful political authority of his church member (such as by threatening excommunication unless taxes are reduced, etc.).

The problem with Hugenberger's argument is that he ignores the differing *natures* of men and women, assuming that God's design for women to submit to husbands has no bearing on the rest of their lives outside the marriage relationship. Thus, he limits the husband's authority over his wife to the home, as if a man's authority over his wife ends once they step onto the employer's property. In the case of his example above, a president may hold civil authority over his church elders at the same time that his elders hold ecclesiastical authority over the president. This is because *a president and elders have limited authority over one another*. They have concurrent authority in their proper spheres, the president in the civil realm and the elders in the ecclesiastical realm.

But a husband does not have such limited authority, as if he is only head of his wife when they are in the home. Rather, the husband's headship extends over *everything* his wife does, whether in church or in civil society. As Paul says, wives are to submit to their husbands "in everything" (Ephesians 5:24). Thus, a wife may not exercise authority over her husband as an elder or as a civil ruler. In contrast, a president is not the head of all citizens but the *civil* authority over citizens, and even then in a limited capacity (his powers are limited by the Constitution and other branches of government). In other words, a husband's authority over his wife is much broader than a civil ruler's authority over his constituents.

Sadly, even many complementarian scholars argue that women may hold civil office. Wayne Grudem argues that the Old Testament model of male leadership in civil government does not apply to modern civil government because Israel was a mix of church and state—"There was no distinction between civil government and church government as we have in the New Testament age . . . Therefore we cannot assume that the general pattern of restricting *civil government* leadership over the people of God to men would also apply to the New Testament age."[15] This argument rests on a radical distinction between Israel and the church, as if Christ does not also rule over civil government today. Yet Christ has authority over all nations (Matthew 28:19).

Moreover, Grudem's logic could be extended the other direction to mean that since civil government and church government were mixed in the Old Testament, then we cannot assume that Israel's pattern of restricting *church* leadership to men applies today. Yet this is something Grudem would surely reject. Grudem's arguments for women in civil leadership are brief, and he does not account for the arguments from the family model of civil government and the differing natures of men and women.

Calvin and Knox on Women Civil Rulers

The attempt to limit gender roles to the home and church is dualistic in that it pits the religious against the secular. But God has designed men to be men in all of life, and He has designed women to be women in all of life—in the home, church, and society. Women do not get to act like men just because they have stepped outside the home into broader society. A woman takes her womanly nature with her wherever she goes, and a man takes his manly nature with him wherever he goes.

Both John Calvin and John Knox followed this very reasoning. In commenting on Paul's prohibition of women teaching men in 1 Timothy

---

15. Wayne Grudem, *Evangelical Feminism & Biblical Truth* (2004), 140.

2:12, Calvin says the prohibition is rooted in woman's nature—"why they [women] are forbidden to teach, is, that it is not permitted by their condition. They are subject, and to teach implies the rank of power or authority." Calvin considers the counterargument that teachers are also subject to authority—"Yet it may be thought that there is no great force in this argument; because even prophets and teachers are subject to kings and to other magistrates." Calvin responds that a woman's very nature is different—"I reply, there is no absurdity in the same person commanding and likewise obeying, when viewed in different relations. But this does not apply to the case of woman, who by nature (that is, by the ordinary law of God) is formed to obey; for γυναικοκρατία (the government of women) has always been regarded by all wise persons as a monstrous thing; and, therefore, so to speak, it will be a mingling of heaven and earth, if women usurp the right to teach. Accordingly, he bids them be 'quiet,' that is, keep within their own rank."[16]

This argument is worth unpacking. First, Calvin states that women are not permitted to teach in the church because of their "condition" as those who do not have authority. Then he counters the argument that this cannot be because church leaders (teachers and prophets) are also subject to the civil authority (kings and magistrates), essentially the argument that Hugenberger makes. Calvin responds that "there is no absurdity in the same person" having authority ("commanding") and being under authority ("obeying") "when viewed in different relations." But this does not apply to woman because she "by nature . . . is formed to obey." In other words, woman's very nature is different from that of man, and woman's nature prohibits her from ruling in both the ecclesiastical and civil realms.

Like Calvin, John Knox also appealed to the differing nature of woman as to why she should not function as a civil ruler. Knox wrote his infamous work, *The First Trumpet Blast Against the Monstrous Regiment of Women*, when the wicked Bloody Mary (r. 1553–1558) ruled and persecuted Protestants, and this brought Knox trouble when the Protestant

---

16. John Calvin, *Commentaries on the Epistles to Timothy, Titus, and Philemon*, 68.

Elizabeth came to the throne in 1558. Though there may be exceptional cases of decent women rulers, this does not overcome Knox's argument that woman's nature is not fit for rule. Applying Paul's prohibitions on women in the church in 1 Timothy 2 and 1 Corinthians 14, Knox says, "For he that takes from woman the least part of authority, dominion or rule, will not permit unto her that which is greatest: But greater it is to reign above realms and nations, to publish and make laws, and to command men of all estates, and finally to appoint judges and ministers, than to speak in the congregation."[17]

Knox concludes that "a woman promoted to sit in the seat of God, that is, to teach, to judge or to reign above man, is monstrous in nature, contumelious to God, and a thing most repugnant to his will and ordinance."[18] Thus, Knox makes the case that reigning in the civil realm involves greater authority in some sense than speaking in church. And if Paul prohibits women from speaking publicly and teaching in church based on their nature, then certainly women are not permitted to rule nations. It is contrary to the very nature of woman.

Women Governing in the Bible (Including Deborah)

We shall now turn to what the Bible says about women ruling in civil government, as our detractors will quickly bring up the example of Deborah. It must first be stated that almost all the governing authorities in Scripture were men. Israel's elders, kings, and priests were all men. There were no women governors or representatives. Women did not hold office in Israel—with two possible exceptions.

The first exception is the two women rulers in Israel's history—Jezebel, the wife of King Ahab (1 Kings 21:1-29; 2 Kings 9:1-37), and Athaliah, the mother of King Ahaziah (2 Kings 11:1-20; 2 Chronicles 22:10–23:15).

---

17. John Knox, *The First Blast of the Trumpet Against the Monstrous Regiment of Women* (ed. Edward Arber; London, 1880), 18. I modernized the old English spelling.
18. Ibid.

Yet neither Jezebel nor Athaliah was the king of Israel. They usurped rule (and ruled quite poorly). Athaliah was a murderer (2 Kings 11:1-3) who is referred to as the "wicked woman" (2 Chronicles 24:7), while Jezebel murdered the prophets (2 Kings 9:7) and her name is connected with false teaching, sorcery, and sexual immorality (Revelation 2:20). Thus, rather than establishing a case for woman's rule in society, these examples associate women in leadership with apostasy and societal decline.

The second and most notable exception to only men holding office in Israel is Deborah, who was a judge in Israel. Egalitarians often cite Deborah as an example of women in leadership, as she was a godly woman who was both a judge and prophetess (Judges 4:4-5). However, Deborah's position is more complex than egalitarians portray. In the Book of Judges, judges were not primarily civil leaders but military heroes. And Deborah was not even a typical judge by the book's own standards. Thus, Deborah does not establish the principle that women may serve as civil leaders.

Let us examine this point further. There are two reasons that Deborah was not a typical judge in Israel. First, *Deborah is not described in the same way as the male judges*. Deborah is not described as "saving" Israel like some of the other judges (Judges 3:9, 31; 10:1; 13:5), and the phrase "Yahweh raised up" is not used for Deborah as in the case of some of the male judges (Judges 3:9, 15). The author of Judges does not mention the "Spirit of the LORD" working in Deborah as with several of the male judges (Judges 3:10; 6:34; 11:29; 13:25; 14:6, 19; 15:14). In fact, Deborah is only described as "judging Israel at that time" (Judges 4:4), which was a time when Israel "did what was evil in the sight of the LORD" (4:1). Therefore, the context suggests that Israel having a woman judge like Deborah was not the ideal situation.

Second, *Deborah did not serve as a military leader, which was the primary role of the judges*.[19] The introduction of Judges specifies the role of

---

19. Hugenberger argues that the judges were elders: "In support of the supposition that the 'judges' of the book of Judges, including Deborah, were in fact elders, cf. Deuteronomy 1, which melds together Exodus 18 (the appointment of the judges) and Numbers 11 (the appointment of the seventy elders) with the implication that these two chapters record the same event." Hugenberger, "Women in

the judges as those Yahweh "raised up" to "save/deliver" Israel from their enemies (Judges 2:16, 18; cf. 3:9, 15, 31; 10:1; 13:5). Men like Jephthah and Samson were courageous military leaders who delivered Israel through warfare. But Deborah was not a military leader.[20] Rather, she urged Barak to fight—"Has not the LORD, the God of Israel, commanded you, 'Go, gather your men at Mount Tabor . . . and I will give him [Sisera] into your hand'?" (Judges 4:6-7). Yet Barak refused unless Deborah went with him—"If you will go with me, I will go, but if you will not go with me, I will not go" (4:8). Deborah the prophetess then foretold that "the road" on which Barak was going would not lead to his "glory," as Yahweh would "sell Sisera into the hand of a woman" (4:9), who is later revealed to be Jael (4:21-22; 5:24). The story of Barak's abdication suggests that the men were not leading in Israel as they should have been. It also shows that Barak fulfilled the military role of a judge, not Deborah.

On the whole, the Book of Judges shows just how sinful Israel was at the time, and it is best to read the text descriptively rather than prescriptively. Deborah was a great woman, but she is no model for women serving in civil or ecclesiastical leadership. She had no military function like the other judges, and she might have been only serving as judge because of the failure of the men in Israel during those evil days. Calvin says that God raised up Deborah "to spite men, as if he wished to shame them, since none were worthy of discharging this responsibility," as this was a period "when the church was in bondage and devoid of hope."[21] All of this would

---

Church Office": 359. However, the identity of the judges as elders does not fit the context of the Book of Judges. The judges there were clearly military leaders sent to "deliver" Israel. Furthermore, Hugenberger's claim does not help his case for women rulers, as all three passages he mentions identify the judges and elders as "men" (Exodus 18:25; Numbers 11:16; Deuteronomy 1:13). Even if he were correct in identifying Deborah as an "elder," this would prove she was a deviation from the original appointment of men for this position.

20. One could counter that Samuel was a judge (1 Samuel 7:6, 15) who also was not a military leader. However, Samuel was not mentioned in the context of the Book of Judges and its definition of judges as military leaders (Judges 2:16, 18). Moreover, Samuel showed himself to be a warrior when he executed Agag after Saul's failure to do so (1 Samuel 15:9, 32-33).

21. John Calvin, *Sermons on 1 Timothy*, 282.

explain why when later books of the Bible cite God's sending of the judges, they actually mention *Barak* instead of Deborah:

> And the LORD sent Jerubbaal and *Barak* and Jephthah and Samuel and delivered you out of the hand of your enemies on every side, and you lived in safety (1 Samuel 12:11).

> For time would fail me to tell of Gideon, *Barak*, Samson, Jephthah, of David and Samuel and the prophets (Hebrews 11:32).

Deborah is never held up in Scripture in the same way as the other judges in Israel. She was not a civil ruler, but instead calls herself a "mother in Israel" (Judges 5:7).

The Bible also mentions female rulers outside of Israel. The most famous is the Queen of Sheba, who heard of Solomon's fame and came to test him with hard questions (1 Kings 10:1-13; 2 Chronicles 9:1-12) and exchanged gifts with him, but there is no comment on whether a female ruler was normative. We know little of her situation, whether she acted on behalf of her husband the king or whether the king was dead and she was the sole ruler. The same is true for Queen Candace of the Ethiopians (Acts 8:27). We know little of the other queens in the Bible, except that many of them had the title "queen" by marriage to the king and that the man was the head of the kingdom. This includes queens such as Tahpenes (1 Kings 11:19-20), the unnamed queen of Chaldea (Daniel 5:10-12), the unnamed queen of Persia (Nehemiah 2:6), Queen Vashti of Persia (Esther 1:9-17), and Esther, the Jewish queen of Persia (Esther 5:2; 7:1-8).

So yes, the Bible mentions women rulers in Israel and abroad. But the two women rulers in Israel, Jezebel and Athaliah, were wicked, and Deborah was not even a typical judge. Thus, *we should not reason from these examples that God designed women to rule and exercise civil authority*. Such a claim would go against all the other teachings of Scripture regarding the nature of man and woman. In answering the objection that there were biblical examples of women rulers, Calvin says,

> If any one bring forward, by way of objection, Deborah (Judges 4:4) and others of the same class, of whom we read that they were at one time appointed by the command of God to govern the people, the answer is easy. Extraordinary acts done by God do not overturn the ordinary rules of government, by which he intended that we should be bound. Accordingly, if women at one time held the office of prophets and teachers, and that too when they were supernaturally called to it by the Spirit of God, He who is above all law might do this; but, being a peculiar case, this is not opposed to the constant and ordinary system of government.[22]

Thus, Calvin argues that even if God called women to rule (or even teach) on exceptional occasions, this does not make it normative. This would be a special or "peculiar" case. Yet the "ordinary" system of government is still male rule. Of course, we have argued thus far that Deborah was not a normal judge and that God never called women to hold office in civil government. The point is that even if there were an exception, it does not overturn the rule that God did not design women to lead in civil government.

Civil Authority Is Masculine

So far we have seen that men and women still have differing natures outside of the home and church and that civil government is an extension of the home. Since God has given men authority in the home, only men are to hold positions of authority in civil government. The Bible does mention women rulers, but when it does so, it speaks descriptively, not prescriptively. And Scripture never speaks of women in civil leadership as good or normative.

Further, when the Bible gives requirements for civil magistrates, it only has men in view. Exodus 18:21 says, "Moreover, look for able *men* from

---

22. John Calvin, *Commentaries on the Epistles to Timothy, Titus, and Philemon*, 67.

all the people, *men* who fear God, who are trustworthy and hate a bribe, and place such *men* over the people as chiefs of thousands, of hundreds, of fifties, and of tens." Deuteronomy 1:13 says, "Choose for your tribes wise, understanding, and experienced *men*, and I will appoint them as your heads." Both of these verses use the Hebrew word for men [אֲנָשִׁים, *anashim*], not women.

Moreover, Scripture uses the word "shepherd" [רעה] to refer to political and military leaders (e.g. 2 Samuel 7:7; 1 Chronicles 17:6; Jeremiah 2:8; 3:15; 10:21; 22:22; 23:1-4; 25:34-36; 50:6; Ezekiel 34:2-10; Isaiah 56:11; Micah 5:4; Zechariah 10:3; 11:5-17). Shepherding is a manly task that requires authority and physical strength. There is a link between "shepherding" and "ruling," seen in the rule of the Lord Jesus, who is described as the good shepherd (John 10:11, 14; Hebrews 13:20; 1 Peter 2:25; Revelation 7:17). Jesus is the "ruler who will shepherd" God's people (Matthew 2:6; citing Micah 5:2). This link between rulers and shepherds demonstrates that ruling is a masculine task.

It should thus come as no surprise that there is even a passage in Isaiah where God *mocks* women rulers:

> My people—infants are their oppressors, and women rule over them. O my people, your guides mislead you and they have swallowed up the course of your paths (Isaiah 3:12).

There are some challenges to this verse, particularly the first clause. Hugenberger says the Hebrew text appears to be corrupt,[23] in part because the Septuagint reads differently. The Hebrew literally says, "My people, their oppressors, he acts severely, and women rule over them." Since the subject and verb do not agree ("oppressors" is plural, "acts severely" is singular), most versions slightly emend the text from the singular "acts

---

23. Hugenberger, "Women in Church Office": 359: "[T]he MT of Isa 3:12, in addition to its troublesome vocabulary, appears to be textually corrupt (cf. *BHS*; LXX). Compare the preferable rendering of the NEB: 'Money lenders strip my people bare, and usurers lord it over them' (cf. also TEV)."

severely" [מְעוֹלֵל] to "children/infants" [עוֹלְלִים]. The vast majority of translations read similarly to the ESV, including the NASB and KJV.

However, the NET Bible offers an alternative emendation of three Hebrew words, including emending "women" [נָשִׁים, *nashim*] to "creditors" [נֹשִׁים, *noshim*]. The NET thus reads, "Oppressors treat my people cruelly; creditors rule over them." However, this more complex emendation is unnecessary, and the NET notes even offer an alternative translation similar to the ESV.

Weight should be given to the Hebrew Masoretic Text (MT), and we should limit emendations of the text. In this case, it is unnecessary to emend "women" to "creditors," and the reference to women ruling Israel makes sense of the passage. The context in Isaiah 3 concerns God's judgment on Judah and Jerusalem, and God is clearly mocking His people for producing weak leaders and being led by them. A similar statement is found earlier in Isaiah 3:4—"And I will make boys their princes and infants shall rule over them." Both Isaiah 3:4 and 3:12 speak of non-men leading Israel. Of course, this is not to say infants, boys, and women are not valuable to society. Rather, the point is that these groups are not fit to rule. The obvious implication is that only *men* are made to rule.

It is not certain whether Isaiah was describing a situation where women actually ruled over Israel or whether he was insulting weak men rulers by calling them women. Alec Motyer suggests this could refer to the royal harem, with the king's wives manipulating him.[24] E.J. Young suggests the harem as a possible influence, but he thinks it describes weak men— "The prophet probably does not intend to describe an actual situation in which women were ruling over the nation, but rather would suggest that the rulers were weak as women. Those who are the rulers are weak men and have no more authority than a child. They are possibly influenced by women who were members of the harem."[25]

---

24. J. Alec Motyer, *The Prophecy of Isaiah: An Introduction & Commentary* (Downers Grove, IL: InterVarsity Press, 1993), 62.

25. Edward J. Young, *The Book of Isaiah*, vol 1 (Grand Rapids, MI: Eerdmans, 1965), 156.

The Celebration of Women Warriors

A woman soldier is even more abominable than a woman in civil government. This is because a woman subverts her nature to an even greater extent when acting as a soldier. Instead of assuming authority as in civil government, a woman soldier assumes the role of protector. Yet protection is a task that God has explicitly given to men. This is doubly bad when women rise to positions of authority in the military, such as general. A woman soldier defies her nature and physical makeup. A woman does not have a body made for strenuous manual labor, let alone physical combat. Women are not only much weaker than men on average, but women's bodies are built for bearing children. This is not to insult women. Rather, it is a call to *honor* women. God has made woman a life-giver, not a life-taker.

Despite these obvious facts, women have made their way into the military and combat in the West in recent years. In the United States, women were permitted to serve as regular members of the military in 1948, though they were excluded from combat positions. Women were admitted to the academies in 1976, and aviation combat positions were opened to them in 1993. Though the Pentagon affirmed that women were prohibited from ground combat in 1994, this ban was lifted in 2013, and now the United States permits women to serve in all combat roles.

This is bad strategy for an effective military, as women are not suited for combat. Women do not compare to men physically, and it is foolish to lower physical fitness standards for woman soldiers in the name of political correctness, as some have done. Younger women have the additional disruption of monthly bleeding. Further, women are a distraction to the male soldiers, who feel the natural instinct to provide special protection for women in danger and sometimes take sexual interest in them. In fact, women serving as soldiers has introduced the problem of men sexually assaulting women in the military. This is not to defend the men engaging in such wicked behavior, but rather it is to say that *this situation is entirely avoidable*. Male soldiers are often rough characters, and it is unwise to put women in barracks with aggressive and female-deprived men. And if women soldiers are concerned about sexual assault by their fellow male soldiers, they should be even more concerned about falling into the hands of enemy combatants. These are just some of the many extra-biblical reasons why women should not serve in combat.[26] Women are a distraction to men soldiers, and the addition of women soldiers only makes for a weaker and less effective military.

Sadly, it is rare to hear pastors speak out against women soldiers. Yet worse than this is the *celebration* of female warriors taking place in Christianity. It is no secret that Hollywood has pushed women warriors in action movies, with the ultimate feminist icon being Wonder Woman. But instead of pushing back against this trend, Christian publications have endorsed the practice. When the movie *Wonder Woman* came out in 2017, the formerly-respectable *Christianity Today* published the piece, "Why We Need Wonder Woman."[27] And what was supposed to be a conservative group, *The Gospel Coalition*, published an article, "'Wonder Woman': A Peculiar and Unexpected Heroine," in which the author praises the movie as one that "elevates both men and women," with no criticism of female warriors.[28]

The Bible Condemns Women Soldiers

This is an embarrassment to Christianity. The biblical case against women warriors is as clear as day. In addition to the obvious bodily differences between men and women, we have creation's teaching that Adam was to "guard" the garden (Genesis 2:15), which included his wife whom God created after him. God designed men to protect the women in their lives.

---

26. See Kingsley Browne, *Co-Ed Combat: The New Evidence That Women Shouldn't Fight the Nation's Wars* (New York: Sentinel, 2007).

27. Alicia Cohn, "Why We Need Wonder Woman," *ChristianityToday.com* (June 2, 2017), https://www.christianitytoday.com/women/2017/june/why-we-need-wonder-woman.html.

28. Gina Dalfonzo, "'Wonder Woman': A Peculiar and Unexpected Heroine," *TheGospelCoalition.org* (June 6, 2017), https://www.thegospelcoalition.org/article/wonder-woman-a-peculiar-and-unexpected-heroine/. Unsurprisingly, the author was also an associate editor at *Christianity Today*.

However, we also have explicit teaching in the Old Testament that only men are to be soldiers. It is proper to appeal to the Old Testament, for as Paul says, "*All Scripture*" is "profitable for teaching" (2 Timothy 3:16) and "*whatever* was written in former days was written for our instruction" (Romans 15:4). So here are three reasons from Scripture why only men should serve as soldiers.

First, *God only instructed the men in Israel to go to war.* This is seen in the opening of the Book of Numbers, where God instructed Moses to take a census of Israel:

> Take a census of all the congregation of the people of Israel, by clans, by fathers' houses, according to the number of names, every male, head by head. From twenty years old and upward, all in Israel who are able to go to war, you and Aaron shall list them, company by company. And there shall be with you a man from each tribe, each man being the head of the house of his fathers (Numbers 1:2-4).

This census of Israel was of every "male" [זָכָר, *zachar*] over the age of 20 who was "able to go to war" (see also Numbers 26:1-51; 32:27). God did not regard women as soldiers in Israel, and He only instructed men to fight wars.

Second, *the examples of soldiers in Scripture are always men.* In the ancient world, men had to be able to fight. Thus, most of the great spiritual leaders in Israel were also soldiers. Abraham, Moses, Joshua, and David were all warriors, not their wives and daughters. The male Levites were not just priests, but warrior-priests. Yahweh "is a man of war," not a woman of war (Exodus 15:3; cf. Isaiah 42:13). God appeared to Joshua as a man and identified Himself as "the commander of the army" of Yahweh (Joshua 5:13-15). War involves the masculine task of fighting, so it is no surprise that Scripture mocks male soldiers by calling them women—"Behold, your troops are women in your midst" (Nahum 3:13; cf. Jeremiah 50:37; 51:30). Women are not to fight as soldiers, for combat is a manly task.

The witness of Scripture is consistent on this point. Abraham took only men to go with him to rescue Lot (Genesis 14:14-15). Moses called only for men to attack the Midianites (Numbers 31:3). Kings only took men for war (1 Samuel 8:11). And David's mighty men were all men (2 Samuel 23:8-37). Men were called to fight for their children and "wives," not women for their husbands (Nehemiah 4:14). Only men were soldiers in the Bible (Deuteronomy 20:5-8; 24:5; Joshua 6:3-9; 8:3; Judges 7:7; 20:8-11; 1 Samuel 11:8; 2 Samuel 24:9; 2 Kings 24:14-16; 1 Chronicles 21:5; 27:1-15; 2 Chronicles 17:12-19; 25:5-6; 26:11-14; Song of Songs 3:7-8). And women and children remained behind when men went to war (Deuteronomy 3:19-20; Joshua 1:14-15).

Third, *God condemned women soldiers as an "abomination"* (Deuteronomy 22:5). In addition to the above texts, the Bible contains an explicit prohibition of women in combat:

> A woman shall not wear a man's garment, nor shall a man put on a woman's cloak, for whoever does these things is an abomination to the LORD your God (Deuteronomy 22:5).

On its face, this verse prohibits men and women dressing like the opposite sex (known as crossdressing or transvestism). This verse requires distinct expressions of masculinity and femininity, as men are to look and act like men and women are to look and act like women (see chapter 2 on this verse condemning "effeminacy"). However, there is a strong case that Deuteronomy 22:5 targets a specific type of transvestite behavior, particularly that of woman wearing a man's combat gear. This is how some ancient Jewish interpreters understood the verse, including 2nd-century rabbi Eliezer ben Jacob in the Babylonian Talmud,[29] as well as Targum Onkelos in its Aramaic translation of the verse. British Bible commentator Adam Clarke (1762–1832) also interpreted this verse to refer to combat gear.[30]

---

29. Sifre Deuteronomy 226, Nazir 59a.
30. Adam Clarke, *Commentary on the Bible*, https://www.studylight.org/

Deuteronomy 22:5 prohibits a man from wearing a woman's "cloak" or "garment" [שִׂמְלַת, *simlat*]. In contrast, a woman is prohibited from wearing a כְלִי־גֶבֶר (*keli-geber*), which is not the normal word for clothing. The ESV translates this as a "man's garment," but there is likely more to this phrase. Rather than use the generic word for "man" [אִישׁ, *ish*] corresponding to the generic word for "woman" [אִשָּׁה, *isha*] used twice in the verse, Deuteronomy 22:5 twice uses a specific word for "man" that can refer to a "warrior" [גֶּבֶר, *geber*]. This is related to the word גבר (*gabar*, "strong/mighty") and גִּבָּר (*gibbar*, "warrior"). The similar הַגִּבֹּרִים (*haggibborim*) is used in Genesis 6:4 to describe "mighty men" and in Joshua 10:2 to describe men as "warriors" [אֲנָשֶׁיהָ גִּבֹּרִים]. The same word for "man" in Deuteronomy 22:5 is also pluralized as גְּבָרִים (*geborrim*) in Exodus 12:37 to refer to soldiers, "men" numbered among the 600,000 on foot. This suggests the word גֶּבֶר (*geber*) is a military reference.

The other word translated "garment" [כְלִי, *keli*] in Deuteronomy 22:5 is never used for clothing in the Old Testament. Rather, it is a generic word used for a variety of containers or utensils. It can also refer to equipment (Isaiah 54:16) and military gear—it is used for "weapons" (Genesis 49:5; Isaiah 13:5; 54:16-17), "weapons of war" (Deuteronomy 1:41), and likely for military "equipment" (2 Kings 7:15). McConville says the word "can have military connotations, which fit here with the word used for 'man' (*geber*, often man as warrior)."[31]

Thus, although כְלִי־גֶבֶר (*keli-geber*) is paralleled with שִׂמְלַת (*simlat*, "cloak/garment") in Deuteronomy 22:5, we see that the two words combine to refer to more than just a man's clothing. כְלִי־גֶבֶר (*keli-geber*) is a specific phrase for a soldier's military gear and is better translated "gear of a warrior" or "implements of a warrior." Therefore, Deuteronomy 22:5

---

commentaries/acc/deuteronomy-22.html: "As the word גבר geber is here used, which properly signifies a strong man or man of war, it is very probable that armor is here intended; especially as we know that in the worship of Venus, to which that of Astarte or Ashtaroth among the Canaanites bore a striking resemblance, the women were accustomed to appear in armor before her."

31. J.G. McConville, *Deuteronomy* (Apollos Old Testament Commentary; Downers Grove, IL: InterVarsity Press, 2002), 337.

specifically prohibits women from dressing for combat. Such behavior is so wicked that it says "whoever does these things is an abomination" [תּוֹעֵבָה, *toevah*] to Yahweh. It is not the behavior that is abominable but the *person* who does this.

The Old Testament Prohibition of Women Soldiers Still Applies

Some will object that the above points concern Israel, including its specific laws and instructions for Canaanite warfare (*herem*), and thus do not apply to the modern day. In response, we must note that the first two arguments against women soldiers are not based in the Mosaic law. There are no examples of women serving in combat even prior to the Mosaic law, and we have Abraham's example of only taking men with him to go to war (Genesis 14:14-15). Further, God's calling of men for combat in Numbers 1:2-4 is not tied to *whom* they were fighting, whether Canaanites as part of *herem* warfare (Deuteronomy 7:1-2) or a defensive war to fend off an invading army. God did not call women to fight Israel's wars because He made only men to fight, not because of some temporary administration.

Thus, this objection is primarily aimed at the case law of Deuteronomy 22:5. In response, we must stress that Mosaic laws still have application to the modern world. The Apostle Paul considers the Ten Commandments to apply to Christians in the new covenant (e.g. Ephesians 6:1-2), and he even applies Mosaic case law to the church (1 Corinthians 9:8-10, citing Deuteronomy 25:4). While the ceremonial laws have been fulfilled in Christ and the civil laws had specific application to Old Testament Israel, this does not mean a law such as Deuteronomy 22:5 can be dismissed out of hand. The question is whether a law is based on the law of nature (and thus has continuing application) or Israel's sacral nature (and thus may not apply directly today). The Westminster Confession of Faith describes the law's application today as the "general equity" of the law.[32] If a law

---

32. WCF 19.4: "To them also, as a body politic, he gave sundry judicial laws, which expired together with the State of that people; not obliging any other now, further than the general equity thereof may require."

was part of the "law of nature, common to all nations" and "universal and permanent," then it still applies.[33] As A.A. Hodge says, "a careful examination of the reason of the law will afford us good ground as to its perpetuity. If the original reason for its enactment is universal and permanent, and the law has never been explicitly repealed, then the law abides in force. If the reason of the law is transient, its binding force is transient also."[34]

When examining the original reason for the enactment of Deuteronomy 22:5, we see it is rooted in the moral law of nature and thus is permanently binding. Deuteronomy 22:5 says Yahweh finds both the man who dresses like a woman and the woman who wears combat gear to be an "abomination" [תּוֹעֵבָה, *toevah*]. While this word can refer to either a moral or ritual offense, it is often used in the context of moral evil, such as sexual sin (Leviticus 18:22-30; 20:13; Deuteronomy 23:18; 24:4). Similar to these passages, Deuteronomy 22:5 involves male and female behavior that deviates from God's design. The one difference is that these passages refer to the *act* as an "abomination," whereas Deuteronomy 22:5 describes the *actor* as an "abomination"—"whoever does these things is an abomination to the LORD." This passage does not concern sacrificial ritual, and there is nothing that suggests it is limited to the Mosaic administration. Deuteronomy 22:5 describes moral evil, and thus it continues to have application today. This is the sort of abominable behavior that Yahweh "hates" (Deuteronomy 12:31; Proverbs 6:16).

All of this evidence from Scripture demonstrates that women should not be soldiers or serve in combat roles, which is consistent with what

---

33. This was the conclusion of the majority report of the *Report of the Committee on Women in the Military and in Combat Presented to the Sixty-eighth (2001) General Assembly of the Orthodox Presbyterian Church*, https://www.opc.org/GA/WomenInMilitary.html. The report concludes that "women in military combat is both contrary to nature and inconsistent with the Word of God." The minority report attempts to make a *reductio ad absurdum* argument that the majority's interpretation would also require the prohibition of women in civil office and the police force. This chapter has argued that such prohibitions are entirely proper.

34. A.A. Hodge, *Commentary on the Confession of Faith: with Questions for Theological Students and Bible Classes* (Philadelphia, PA: Presbyterian Board of Publication and Sabbath-School Work, 1869), 345.

nature teaches about this subject. Combat is part of this fallen world, but when it must be taken up, it is the role and duty of men to protect society. Men are to fight, not women. Of course, this does not mean a woman should not protect herself or use violence when necessary (Judges 4:21; 9:53). The point is that a woman should not seek to fulfill roles requiring the use of force and violence.

By extension, women should not hold positions that require them to use force, such as police officers and security guards. That women are regularly filling such positions is a testament to just how far Western society has strayed from God's design. When women take on the role of protector, it is not just women who are failing, but men are failing to protect their women and keep them from harm's way. Only a weak and effeminate people sends their women into war and intentionally puts them in vulnerable and dangerous positions.

Female Rule Destroys Civilization

The fact is that God has designed men and women differently. Men are to protect women from harm and not vice-versa. God has given men authority, and thus, women are not to serve in positions of civil authority. This principle also extends to other areas of life, including positions of authority in businesses and organizations.

History proves our position right in this matter. Since God has not designed women to rule, it should not surprise us that *a large number of women rulers destroys civilization.* Lieutenant-General Sir John Bagot Glubb (1897–1986), a British soldier and scholar, wrote the following about women in public life destroying civilization in his essay, "The Fate of Empires and Search for Survival":

> An increase in the influence of women in public life has often been associated with national decline. The later Romans complained that, although Rome ruled the world, women ruled Rome. In the tenth century, a similar tendency was observable in the Arab

Empire, the women demanding admission to the professions hitherto monopolised by men. "What," wrote the contemporary historian, Ibn Bessam, "have the professions of clerk, tax-collector or preacher to do with women? These occupations have always been limited to men alone." Many women practised law, while others obtained posts as university professors. There was an agitation for the appointment of female judges, which, however, does not appear to have succeeded.

Soon after this period, government and public order collapsed, and foreign invaders overran the country. The resulting increase in confusion and violence made it unsafe for women to move unescorted in the streets, with the result that this feminist movement collapsed. The disorders following the military takeover in 861, and the loss of the empire, had played havoc with the economy. At such a moment, it might have been expected that everyone would redouble their efforts to save the country from bankruptcy, but nothing of the kind occurred. Instead, at this moment of declining trade and financial stringency, the people of Baghdad introduced a five-day week.

When I first read these contemporary descriptions of tenth-century Baghdad, I could scarcely believe my eyes. I told myself that this must be a joke! The descriptions might have been taken out of The Times today. The resemblance of all the details was especially breathtaking—the break-up of the empire, the abandonment of sexual morality, the 'pop' singers with their guitars, the entry of women into the professions, the five-day week.[35]

History has not been kind to societies that subvert the creation order. When God designs something to work a certain way, it will not flourish

---

35. Sir John Bagot Glubb, *The Fate of Empires and the Search for Survival* (Edinburgh: William Blackwood & Sons Ltd, 1976), 15–16.

when His ways are abandoned. God made man to rule society. A civilization ruled by women awaits the fate of its predecessors.

Toward a Biblical Patriarchy

Relegating biblical gender roles to the home and church only makes Christianity more irrelevant to the unbelieving world. Instead of saying, "God's design for men and women applies to all of life," narrow complementarians say, "You only need to follow God's design for men and women if you become a Christian—and even then, this is only in the home and church." Men like Carl Trueman are part of the problem. Trueman identifies as a complementarian, but then he criticizes a more comprehensive version:

> I rarely read complementarian literature these days. I felt it lost its way when it became an all-embracing view of the world and not simply a matter for church and household. I am a firm believer in a male-only ordained ministry in the church but I find increasingly bizarre the broader cultural crusade which complementarianism has become. It seems now to be more a kind of reaction against feminism than a balanced exposition of the Bible's teaching on the relationships of men and women . . . To borrow a phrase, yes, I guess I am in some sense an accidental feminist.[36]

Trueman's comments are telling. First, he mistakenly charges complementarianism as being too broad when, in reality, most adherents advocate Trueman's own narrow version. Second, he laments complementarianism's "reaction" against feminism, and he then turns around and identifies himself as "an accidental feminist." The irony is that it is actually Trueman's narrow complementarianism that was a reaction against feminism. It was an effort that began in the 1980s to stop the onslaught of feminism in the

---

36. Carl Trueman, "An Accidental Feminist?" *Reformation21.org* (August 18, 2015), http://www.alliancenet.org/mos/postcards-from-palookaville/an-accidental-feminist.

church, seeking to reserve a part of patriarchy for Christians by appealing to the explicit biblical texts on the home and church. As we have seen, the Reformers advocated a broader complementarianism, or patriarchy, which Trueman has abandoned.

Narrow complementarianism fails to take the whole of the Bible into account and apply its teachings to all of life. Narrow complementarians like Trueman want to offer as little offense as possible to the modern secular culture. But this is ineffective. Not only are large portions of the modern church abandoning male rule in the home and church, but Trueman's vision is failing to appeal to the culture at large. He does not offer a biblical alternative to secularism, and he thus ends up identifying himself as a "feminist."

Narrow complementarianism is not attractive, just like a "moderate" political position is not attractive. People want consistency. And in the end, there are only two consistent positions regarding gender roles—egalitarianism and patriarchy. Either men and women are the same in almost every way, or gender differences go deep and play out in every realm of life. Trueman's mushy middle position is going nowhere.

Of course, egalitarianism is not actually consistent. Egalitarians can cry "equality" all they want, but they will never overcome the differences between men's and women's bodies. Women bear children, and their entire lives revolve around this. Men and women will never be the same, and role differences will remain as long as these natural differences remain. Egalitarianism is a revolt against nature.

What the church needs today is a comprehensive and consistent vision of biblical manhood and womanhood. Yet this will not come about by carving out a small piece of the pie reserved for male rule. The feminist movement will not stop until every sphere in society is run by women. Feminists own the society at large. They have won over many families. And they have deceived much of the church. A resistance movement is not enough. What we need is a *counterinsurgency* built upon an alternative worldview rooted in Scripture. Narrow complementarianism does not garner the troops. We need a broader vision. We need masculine Christianity.

Chapter 12

LEAVING A MANLY LEGACY

WE LIVE IN an age of effeminacy, both in the church and society at large. Christians must therefore respond appropriately. What we have been advocating in this book is not a slight corrective to our culture, but an alternative worldview. We are advocating a paradigm shift—a return to the masculine Christianity of the Bible.

The Bible is a "sexist" book by the standards of modern egalitarianism. This is why honest egalitarians have abandoned Christianity, while dishonest egalitarians have sought to reinterpret the Bible according to their own liking. The Bible is the Word of God. It is the standard by which we ought to live. We are not to judge the Bible, but we are to be judged by it. And if the Bible is "sexist" by modern egalitarian standards, then let us embrace such "sexism" as the good.

A Call to Men

What is the alternative to biblical patriarchy? Western society has rejected Christian patriarchy, and the results have been atrocious. Christian men must therefore reject effeminacy and embrace Christian manhood. When we devote our lives to the worship of God and submit to His Word, Jesus makes us the men and women we ought to be.

For men, masculinity means accepting responsibility, exercising godly authority, and developing abilities that aid us in the tasks God has set before us, including providing for and protecting a wife and children. Biblical masculinity begins with taking responsibility for what God has given us. Men are to be strong and courageous, and this means having biblically-based convictions and the spine to uphold them. A true man honors Christ in all aspects of life, and a manly Christianity exercises Christ's dominion over all spheres.

This is a call to the men in the church. The Apostle Paul says, "train yourself for godliness, for while bodily training is of some value, godliness is of value in every way, as it holds promise for the present life and also for the life to come" (1 Timothy 4:7-8). Seek first Christ's kingdom, and devote your entire life to the way of Christ. This is a very practical matter. Let us therefore provide points of application for godly masculine living.

First, *seek spiritual vitality*. The Christian life starts with repentance. A godly man will flee sin and turn to Christ on a regular basis. As Paul says, "But as for you, O man of God, flee these things. Pursue righteousness, godliness, faith, love, steadfastness, gentleness. Fight the good fight of the faith. Take hold of the eternal life to which you were called and about which you made the good confession in the presence of many witnesses" (1 Timothy 6:11-12).

Read your Bible and pray regularly. Seek God, who has revealed Himself to us in His Word. Find a good church and submit to its teaching, ideally a conservative Reformed church. Look for strong male leadership and biblical teaching and preaching. Then serve your church. In particular, seek to disciple younger men. We need to guide the younger men in the faith and so build an army for Christ. But also seek godly friendship. Men need friends to encourage them and support them in life—"Behold, how good and pleasant it is when brothers dwell in unity!" (Psalm 133:1).

Second, *love your wife and lead her in the way of godliness*. Pray with her and read Scripture together, and show her what a godly man looks like. A good start to family worship is to pray before supper and read through a book of the Bible after supper (a small section or chapter each day will do). And if you do not have a wife, seek a godly one (Proverbs 1–9; 31). Proverbs 12:4 says, "An excellent wife is the crown of her husband." So seek an excellent wife and treat her as your queen. The word for "excellent wife" is אֵשֶׁת־חַיִל (*eshet hayil*). It is also used at the end of the book of Proverbs—"An excellent wife who can find? She is far more precious than jewels" (Proverbs 31:10). The only other time that phrase is used in the Bible is to describe Ruth in Ruth 3:11, as her mother-in-law Naomi calls Ruth an אֵשֶׁת חַיִל (*eshet hayil*), an "excellent wife" (the ESV for some reason translates this differently here as "a worthy woman"). And guess which book follows Proverbs in the Hebrew order of the Old Testament? Ruth follows Proverbs 31 in the Hebrew Bible because the wisdom literature presents Ruth as an example of the excellent wife. Seek a woman like Ruth. It matters whom you choose as a spouse, and it matters how you lead your wife once you marry her.

Third, *raise godly children*. This means you first need to have children. You then need to raise them well. God has commanded that Christian parents diligently teach God's words to their children throughout all of life, bringing them up in the "discipline and instruction of the Lord" (Deuteronomy 6:6-8; Ephesians 6:4). Paul addresses this command specifically to "fathers," showing that men have a special place in training up their children in the Christian faith. (There is much more to say on this subject below.)

Fourth, *seek an economic niche*. Work is good, and a man needs to work in order to provide for his family. God has wired each man for a certain task. Find that task, get the training you need for it, and do it. It does not mean you will always have the perfect job or love everything you do, but seek to do something you find fulfilling. Sometimes this takes time, but God in His providence often guides us to the work that fits us best in life. Some men are wired to work with their hands, while others are wired to interact with people or do administration. Some men are fit for pastoral ministry, while others are fit for working in government or the political realm. We need Christians in all walks of life.

Whatever you seek to do, make sure it provides for your family. Seek especially to enable your wife to carry out her role as mother and homemaker. If your wife has to work outside the home, this leaves less time for her primary tasks regarding the home and children. Life is expensive.

But a big reason wives work today is because families live beyond their means. So do not be greedy. Keep your expenses low so your wife can stay at home, and convince her of the goodness of doing this. If you have to live in a smaller house, drive only one car, go on cheaper vacations, and homeschool the kids, then do it. Not every job is going to pay enough for the family to have it all. You have to prioritize in life, and family life and children should be high on your list.

We must not let the idols of comfort and material wealth get in the way of Christian education and godly parenting. We must choose the good of our children over things that will not last. As our Lord says, "No one can serve two masters, for either he will hate the one and love the other, or he will be devoted to the one and despise the other. You cannot serve God and money" (Matthew 6:24).

In addition, seek to return to the home as much as possible. The Industrial Revolution pushed men out of the home by separating the home and work. If you can work from home, do it. If you can work closer to home, do it. Try to be around the home as much as possible. This will support your wife in her role as mother and homemaker, and it will allow you to eat family meals together and save on travel time.

The Women Will Follow

If the men act like men, the women will follow. This is because women are naturally attracted to masculine men, and Christian women are particularly attracted to godly masculinity. God made women to follow. Much of the corruption of women in the church today is due to men not leading their wives and daughters well. Christian women will want to carry out their feminine role if their fathers and mothers train them to do so, if their husbands desire them to do so, and if pastors and the churches expect them to do so. But the opposite is happening—men are enabling and often even encouraging women to trade children for a career outside the home.

This is a call for the women reading this, but it is also a guide for men in dealing with their wives and daughters. Godly women should seek to follow and respect a godly, masculine man. Just as the Spirit leads godly men to love their wives as Christ loved the church, so the Spirit leads godly women to submit to and respect their husbands (Ephesians 5:21-27). A Christian woman should come alongside her husband as his helper. Her work should be primarily homeward and focused on raising godly children.

As seen in the creation account (chapter 5), God made a division of labor between husband and wife. While the husband is to focus on work to provide for his family, the wife is to focus on providing children. Woman is a life-giving being. This is a glorious and special task she carries out, and the Bible ascribes great value to the task of motherhood. As the Psalmist says, "Behold, children are a heritage from the LORD, the fruit of the womb a reward. Like arrows in the hand of a warrior are the children of one's youth. Blessed is the man who fills his quiver with them!" (Psalm 127:3-5). Christians should seek to have many children, as they can be a great blessing. However, such children can also become a curse if parents neglect the task of raising them according to the ways of the Lord. In raising them, we must do our part, while relying on God in the process. For as this same Psalm says, "Unless the Lord builds the house, those who build it labor in vain. Unless the Lord watches over the city, the watchman stays awake in vain" (Psalm 127:1).

God loves children, and we should too. Throughout the Gospels, Jesus blesses children and welcomes them into His kingdom (Matthew 19:13-15; Mark 10:13-16; Luke 18:15-17). Children are part of God's covenant, seen in male children in the old covenant receiving the Abrahamic sign of circumcision (Genesis 17) and new covenant children being told to obey their parents "in the Lord" (Ephesians 6:1; cf. the "household" baptisms in Acts).

Children are part of God's way of growing His kingdom, as He brings a husband and wife together to produce a "godly seed" (Malachi 2:15). God does not only work through missions and evangelism. Sadly, the modern Western church has often focused on world missions while neglecting their own households. We send missionaries to plant churches in foreign countries and then abandon our children to anti-Christian missionaries in the public schools, who make it their goal to indoctrinate them into radical leftist social, religious, and economic thought. This ought not to be. We must get our priorities straight. First get your own household in order, and then worry about others.

The Domestic Woman

One of the chief goals of the Christian household is to bear and raise children to become godly men and women. Christians should order their entire lives around this task. How can such a task be performed if parents are rarely with their children? How can children be nurtured and the house be ordered if the mother is gone all day at work? The Bible does not prohibit women from working outside the home, and the excellent wife of Proverbs 31 even brings in income to aid her family (Proverbs 31:18, 24). However, the wife's primary task is motherhood and working at home (Titus 2:4-5). Such work has a tremendous influence on children.[1]

Women should keep their domestic responsibilities primary. Doing so will leave little time for work outside the home. Not only do children need to be supervised, but they also need to be fed. While the husband can help when not working, there are many tasks around the house that need to be performed throughout the day. For this reason, women, especially those with young children, should not work outside the home because motherhood is just that important. Even when children are grown, the house still needs cared for. Now this is not to say a wife cannot bring in any money. Just as husbands can help around the house, so wives can support their husbands with additional income. Possibilities include selling hand-made goods, providing paid services to friends and neighbors, and online affiliate marketing. There are many ways for families today to make additional income, and there is no reason a wife cannot help. The key is to *keep the home primary*. It is not fair to expect women to work full time

---

1. On the importance of a mother being present with young children in particular, see Erica Komisar, *Being There: Why Prioritizing Motherhood in the First Three Years Matters* (New York: TarcherPerigee, 2017).

outside the home and also care for the home and children. It is asking too much of them. God has designed a division of labor.

The "I can't stay at home" attitude common to many modern women is ungodly, and those who hold it should repent. Many women think staying home with children will be boring and frustrating, or they think their career is more important. Both of these beliefs are false. There is no more important task in the world than raising children for Christ. And raising children is never boring. There is plenty to do. It will be hard at times, but such is life. God has not made life a walk in the park. Childrearing, like all worthy tasks, has challenges that must be overcome.

Feminists have attacked family life, but it really is the best thing for women. As Bavinck says, "When it comes to the bottom line, the woman can nowhere land in a better situation than in the family, at the side of a husband who loves her, surrounded by her children whom she tends and nurtures. Her nature is designed for that, her orientation lies in that direction, there she best fulfills her calling and best reaches her destiny."[2]

For this reason, Bavinck attacks the idea of a mother handing over her weaned children to the community, a criticism that has implications for modern daycare and government schooling—"There is then no more foolish requirement and no more unnatural compulsion than to propose to the wife that in the coming political state, she must give up her children, once they're weaned, to the community. The mother for whom maternal love is the unspeakable mystery and inexhaustible power in her life will never allow herself to be separated from her children in this way; she desires not merely to give them birth, but also to raise them, and she remains bound to them until the hour of her death."[3]

Like men, women should also serve their churches. But this will look somewhat different for the sexes. Some men will serve as elders or deacons, while women's ministry should focus on serving women. Women can lead and attend women's Bible studies, and they should particularly focus on discipling younger women. That is Paul's command in Titus 2, that the

---

2. Bavinck, *The Christian Family*, 145.
3. Ibid.

older women should train the younger women to be good wives, mothers, and homemakers (Titus 2:4-5). Many disparage this role, but it is of vast importance. Part of the reason why so many Christian women have become so career-driven is because older Christian women are not training the younger women in the domestic sphere. Healthy churches will have strong women's ministries geared towards this task. It is not appropriate for men in the church to mentor the younger women. Therefore, this task belongs to the older women in the church.

Parenting Is the Most Important Task on Earth

Christians should desire to leave a godly legacy. This should involve leaving a legacy in a particular field of work or ministry. However, a man's greatest legacy is his children. The fact that so many people are having so few children or forsaking them completely is a sign that men and women today do not care about their legacy. Or at least they only think of legacy in terms of career and material wealth. But what good is material wealth if you have no children to pass it on to when you die? We live in a selfish age. This is further evidenced by the economic disaster prior generations have created by borrowing money from future generations (just consider the national debt).

Godly Christians care about the future of humanity, and they therefore care about children. They care about the children of others, but they have a special care for their own children. In order to inspire you in this task, we can do no better than to quote from R.L. Dabney's 1870 sermon, "Parental Responsibilities":

> Seeing the parental relation is what the Scripture describes it, and seeing Satan has perverted it since the fall for the diffusion and multiplication of depravity and eternal death, the education of children for God is the most important business done on earth. It is the one business for which the earth exists. To it all politics, all war, all literature, all money-making, ought to be subordinated;

and every parent especially ought to feel, every hour of the day, that, next to making his own calling and election sure, this is the end for which he is kept alive by God—this is his task on earth.

On the right training of the generation now arising, turns not only the individual salvation of each member in it, not only the religious hope of the age which is approaching, but the fate of all future generations in a large degree. Train up him who is now a boy for Christ, and you not only sanctify that soul, but you set on foot the best earthly agencies to redeem the whole broadening stream of human beings who shall proceed from him, down to the time when men cease to marry and give in marriage. Until then, the work of education is neverending.

The generation which is trained for heaven is the one that dies; the one that is born into its place is born in enmity and under the curse. Thus the task of training is ever renewed, until the final consummation shall make the race equal to the angels.[4]

Educating children for Christ is "the most important business" on earth. This is the Christian's greatest task next to securing his own salvation. On this training of children today rests "the fate of all future generations." The above quote is worth reading twice. Dabney follows by proclaiming God's purpose for the family—"We hear him declare in Malachi 2:15, long after the fall, that his object in founding the family, in the form of monogamy, was 'to seek a godly seed.' Thus the supreme end of the family institution is as distinctly religious and spiritual as that of the church itself. Civic legislators speak of the well-ordered family as the integer of which the prosperous commonwealth is formed. But God assigns the family a far higher and holier aim. The Christian family is the constituent integer of the church—the kingdom of redemption. The instrumentalities of the family are chosen and ordained of God as the most efficient of all means

---

4. R.L. Dabney, "Parental Responsibilities," in *Discussions*, vol 1 (1890; repr., Harrisonburg, VA: Sprinkle Publications, 1982), 691–692.

of grace—more truly and efficaciously means of saving grace than all the other ordinances of the church. To family piety are given the best promises of the gospel, under the new, as well as under the old dispensation."[5]

Thus, God has brought marriages together to raise "a godly seed." The family is a religious institution and God's means of grace for the salvation of His people. Parents have the great responsibility—and great opportunity—to raise godly men and women.

Ordering Life Around Children

Parenting is the most important task on earth. Thus, a biblical worldview should lead Christians to focus on the natural family and the productive household. Christians should have children and order their lives so as to aid the household. There are three points of application for Christians in this regard.

First, *Christians should seek to have lots of children.* Do not follow the culture and just have one or two. That is not "multiplying," at least not in the sense of increasing the population. God commanded the first humans to "be fruitful and multiply" (Genesis 1:28), which implies that parents should seek to have at least three. However, the primary issue is one's mindset towards children. Seek to have as many as you can possibly support and raise well. This will probably require having more children than you think you can afford, while trusting God to provide for the children He gives you. Think of birth control as the exception rather than the rule. Our society uses birth control as the default in marriage, as if we should only seek children on our own terms. And if you cannot have children (or cannot have as many as you would like), consider adoption. There are many children in the world who do not have parents to raise them.

Second, *Christians should order their household around supporting and raising many children.* This requires the man to seek to bring in enough money to support his family and keep his wife at home to raise them. However, this also means Christians should take radical steps to save

---

5. Ibid., 692–693.

money and sacrifice material wealth for children. We all place value somewhere. Christians must value children more than material possessions or vacations.

Third, *Christians should provide their children with a Christian education.* Having children is not enough. You also need to raise them in the faith. Sending children to daycare and public school—and then giving them unfiltered access to media and technology—does not cut it. Christian children need a Christian education, and this means they need something radically different from what our modern secular culture is giving them. God has commanded Christian parents to teach His Word diligently to their children throughout all of life, bringing them up in the "discipline and instruction of the Lord" (Deuteronomy 6:6-8; Ephesians 6:4).

The atheistic training of the government ("public") schools fosters godlessness. In contrast, a robust Christian education trains children to honor Christ in everything and consider every subject from a biblical perspective. High-quality Christian schools can accomplish this, though homeschooling is much more affordable. Men who seek to provide for their family so the wife can stay at home are in a good position to homeschool their children, especially with the online resources available today. Christian parents should homeschool their children or send them to a good Christian school. Another great option is to start a Christian school, even if it is just a group of homeschoolers meeting for instruction by parents once or twice per week (what is known is hybrid homeschooling). The goal is to raise godly men and women. This is a difficult task, and we must therefore place high value upon it. It takes hard work and sacrifice, often of material comforts.

The way Christians treat the issue of bearing and raising children has a monumental impact on the world. If Christians had more children (say four to five per family instead of one to three as is currently the practice), then we could outpopulate the secularists in a couple generations. However, that is not happening. Many secularists still have a child or two to keep pace. Worse, we are not even maintaining our current numbers. Because of our low fertility rate, the church is dependent upon converts. But for every convert, we lose several children of the covenant to the influences of secularism. This is in large part because Christians hand their children over to the government schools to be trained in another religion. Because of the low fertility rate of the secularists, this is their primary means of proselytization. Leftists seek to propagate through the public schools, and they are proving quite successful in adopting Christian children as their own.

Thus, we see that children are the key players in this battle for the cosmos. And this is all wrapped up in the nuclear family. But because Christians have given up too much to the unbelieving world, we are in for a long slog instead of a quick victory lap. Do not misunderstand—Jesus will win in the end. However, the church may be put through further tribulation because of its failure to keep covenant and steadfast love with the Lord. The Western church has failed to maintain the family unit, failed to raise children in the Lord, failed to worship God according to His ways, and failed to keep God's commands. We are an adulterous people, and it should surprise no one that spiritual adultery leads to societal chaos. Our only hope is repentance through the mercy found in our Lord and Savior Jesus Christ.

Working Hard for Christ

But we should also take heart. We have challenges before us. But Christ has conquered death, and therefore our work on this earth is fruitful. As the Apostle Paul says,

> Death is swallowed up in victory. O death, where is your sting? O Hades, where is your victory? The sting of death is sin, and the power of sin is the law. But thanks be to God, who gives us the victory through our Lord Jesus Christ. Therefore, my beloved brothers, be steadfast, immovable, always abounding [περισσεύοντες] in the work of the Lord, knowing that in the Lord your labor [κόπος] is not in vain (1 Corinthians 15:54-58).

We must note two things. First, it is because ("therefore") Jesus has conquered death and reigns over this world (see 1 Corinthians 15:25-27) that the work we do for Jesus is fruitful and has eternal consequences. As Paul says above, "your labor is not in vain" (cf. 15:14). Second, know that Paul set us an example of hard work for Christ, as he earlier said in this passage, "I worked harder [περισσότερον . . . ἐκοπίασα] than any of them, though it was not I, but the grace of God that is with me" (1 Corinthians 15:10). (Paul uses the same Greek words for "worked harder" that he uses in his call for us to be "abounding" in the work and "labor" of Christ.)

So work hard for Christ. Be the man (or woman) that God created you to be. Uphold His Word. And leave a godly legacy for the future generations. This will likely offend our unbelieving world along the way. But that is not a bad thing. Christianity should look different from the cultural chaos of our day. We must show them a better way. Male rule will upset many progressives. Let it. The husband holds authority over his wife. Only men may be pastors and elders. Only men may be soldiers and civil leaders. And women should help their husbands and have lots of babies. This is masculine Christianity.

SCRIPTURE INDEX

Genesis
Book of 13n18, 103, 115, 239
1 104
1-2 127
1-3 103, 121, 129, 180, 209, 212
1:4 104, 112
1:10 104, 112
1:12 104, 112
1:18 104, 112
1:21 104, 112
1:25 104, 112
1:26 104, 120, 130, 145, 188
1:26-27 223
1:26-28 104, 144
1:27 34, 78, 101, 104, 125, 144
1:28 50, 104, 113, 188, 278
1:31 104
2 106, 113, 122, 125, 130, 180
2-3 163, 191
2:5 106
2:7 120, 122, 130, 144, 179, 180
2:7-8 106
2:8-9 106
2:15 79, 106, 107, 109, 110, 112, 113, 123, 125, 130, 163, 180, 231, 258
2:15-17 129
2:16-17 106, 109, 122, 123, 128, 130
2:17 126
2:18 61, 79, 104, 105, 112, 113, 120, 130, 180
2:18-20 122
2:18-23 120, 130
2:19 124, 180
2:20-24 209n39
2:21-22 122
2:22 122, 124, 144, 179
2:23 120, 122, 124, 130, 180
2:23-24 105
2:24 113, 114, 121n2, 162, 165
3 47, 110, 125, 126, 127, 130, 137, 180
3:1 106, 136, 194
3:1-6 108, 110, 131
3:1-8 127, 127n12, 128
3:1-13 126
3:2-3 123, 130
3:3 126, 129
3:6 108, 120, 125, 129, 130, 179
3:9 79, 111, 120, 125, 129, 130
3:9-13 127
3:12 179
3:13 180, 184n33
3:14 109
3:14-17 127n12
3:15 47, 115
3:16 45, 50, 114, 115, 119, 120, 125, 126, 130, 131, 131n15, 132, 133, 134, 135, 136, 137, 138, 158n35, 182n25, 209
3:17 109, 114, 125, 126, 129, 130
3:17-19 108, 137
3:19 45, 109, 125, 126, 130
3:20 114, 120, 124, 130
3:23 109

---

*Thanks to Douglas Patterson for creating this index.

3:24	106, 135n26	49:9	136, 136n27
4:1-2	114		
4:4	135, 135n26	**Exodus**	
4:7	132, 132n18, 133, 135, 135n26, 136, 137, 138	2:11-12	82n6
		2:11-15	82
4:8	134, 138	2:14	82n6
4:9	106	2:14-15	82n6
4:25	114	3:16	80, 244
5:1-2	78, 79, 104, 120, 121, 125, 130	4:24-26	83
		4:29	80, 244
5:2	34, 104, 121	12:37	261
5:3	121	15:3	259
6:1-4	145n6	15:20	82
6:4	261	18	251n19
8:20-9:17	240	18:4	112
12:2-3	80	18:21	254
14:1-16	82	18:21-26	80n3
14:14-15	260, 262	18:25	252n19
15	240	19:7	235
15:4-5	80	20:12	151, 159
15:16-21	80	20:14	37
17	240, 273	20:17	84
17:4-8	80	21:10	84, 109
17:9	107	22	84n10
17:9-14	80	22:16-17	84, 84n10
17:19-21	80	28-29	81n5
18:11	114	28:1	81
18:12	141	29:14	135n26
22:18	97	32	107n3
25:23	83	32:27-29	167
25:25-26	125		
27:1-40	83	**Leviticus**	
28:13-15	80	1:3	135n26
29:31	50	3:2	135n26
30:22	50	4:4	135n26
30:31	106	4:14	135n26
32:22-32	82	4:21	135n26
34	85	4:23-24	135n26
49	80	8-10	81n5
49:5	261	10:11	235

18:5	107	**Deuteronomy**	
18:22	32, 37, 37n15	1	251n19
18:22-30	263	1:13	252n19, 255
20:13	33, 37, 37n16, 263	1:41	261
		3:19-20	260
Numbers		4:1-14	229
Book of	159	4:19	106
1:2-3	111	5:16	159
1:2-4	259, 262	5:21	84
1:53	107, 167	5:23	80n3
3:3	81	6:6-7	162
3:5-9	81n5	6:6-8	271, 279
3:7-8	107	7:1-2	262
3:8	107	10:18	111
4:23-24	106	12:31	263
4:26	106	13:1-5	96, 205
6:5	32n3	17:8-13	168n1
6:24	107	17:14-20	244
8:26	107	18:20-22	96, 205
11	251n19	20:5-8	260
11:16	80n3, 252n19	21:5	81, 168n1, 171, 232
12:1-15	208	22	84n10
16:8-10	81n5	22:5	41, 42, 51, 111, 242, 260, 261, 262, 263
18:5-6	107		
25:6	107n3	22:28-29	84n10, 160
25:6-8	107n3	23:18	263
25:13	107n3	24:4	263
26:1-51	259	24:5	260
30	84, 96, 146	25:4	262
30:1	159	29:10	80n3
30:2	159	31:1-8	81
30:3-5	84, 143, 160	31:6-7	35
30:5	160	31:23	35
30:6-8	84, 110, 160	31:28	80n3
30:9	161	32:18	77
30:12	161	33:7	112
31:3	260	33:10	81, 171, 232, 235
32:14	134	33:26	112
32:27	259	33:29	112

Joshua

1:6	35
1:14	112
1:14-15	260
5:13-15	259
6:3-9	260
8:3	260
10:2	261
10:4	112
10:6	112
10:25	35
18:7	81n5
24:1	80n3

Judges

Book of	251, 251n19, 252, 252n19, 252n20
2:16	81, 252, 252n20
2:18	252, 252n20
3:9	251, 252
3:10	251
3:15	251, 252
3:31	251, 252
4:1	251
4:4	82, 251, 254
4:4-5	81, 251
4:6-7	252
4:6-9	81
4:8	252
4:9	252
4:21	264
4:21-22	252
5:7	253
5:24	252
6:34	251
7:7	260
8:23	134
9:53	264
10:1	251, 252
10:18	148
11:8	148
11:9	148
11:11	148
11:29	251
13:5	251, 252
13:25	251
14:6	251
14:19	251
15:14	251
20:8-11	260
20:22	35

Ruth

Book of	83, 271
3:11	271

1 Samuel

1:20	125
4:9	35
7:6	81, 252n20
7:15	252n20
8	81, 244
8:11	260
11:8	260
12:11	81, 253
15-17	81
15:9	252n20
15:32-33	252n20
15:33	82
17:1-54	82

2 Samuel

7:7	255
7:12-13	86
22:44	148
23:3	134
23:8-37	260
24:9	260

1 Kings
8:1	80n3
10:1-13	253
11:19-20	253
21:1-29	250

2 Kings
7:15	261
9:1-37	250
9:7	251
11:1-3	251
11:1-20	81, 250
22:14	82, 83
24:14-16	260

1 Chronicles
12:17	112
12:19	112
12:21	112
12:22	112
17:6	255
21:5	260
23:3-4	168n1
27:1-15	260
28:20	35
29:6	95

2 Chronicles
5:2	80n3
9:1-12	253
17:7-9	81, 171, 232, 235
17:9	229
17:12-19	260
22:10-23:15	81, 250
24:7	251
25:5-6	260
26:11-14	260
34:22	82
35:3	81, 171, 232, 235

Ezra
7:10	229

Nehemiah
2:6	253
4:14	260
6:14	82
8:7-9	81, 171, 232, 235
8:8	229

Esther
Book of	83
1:9-17	253
5:2	253
7:1-8	253

Psalms
8:5-6	105
8:6	72n47
30:10	112
33:20	112
68:5	111
104:14-15	6
110:1	72n47
115:9-11	112
123:2	77
124:8	112
127:1	273
127:3-5	273
133:1	270
146:5	112

Proverbs
Book of	271
1-9	270
5:15	165
5:18-20	165
6:16	263
12:4	105, 270
17:2	134

25:15	37	50:37	259
26:22	37	51:30	259
31	116, 270, 271, 274	**Ezekiel**	
31:10	271	12:14	112
31:10-31	117n9	34:2-10	255
31:14-16	116		
31:18	116, 274	**Daniel**	
31:19-24	116	5:10-12	253
31:24	274	7:13	85

Song of Songs
3:7-8	260	**Hosea**	
7:10	133	13:9	112
7:11	133n20		
8:8-10	85	**Joel**	
		2:28-29	95
Isaiah		2:28-32	206
3	256		
3:4	256	**Micah**	
3:12	242, 255, 255n23, 256	5:2	134, 255
13:5	261	5:4	255
30:5	112		
40:10	134	**Nahum**	
42:13	259	3:13	259
49:15	77		
54:16	261	**Zechariah**	
54:16-17	261	6:13	134
56:11	255	9:10	134
63:19	134	10:3	255
66:13	77	11:5-7	255

Jeremiah		**Malachi**	
2:8	255	2:4-7	81, 171, 232, 235
3:15	255	2:14	105
10:21	255	2:15	163, 273, 277
22:22	255		
23:1-4	255	**Matthew**	
25:34-36	255	1:18-19	84n9
31:32	111	1:24	193
50:6	255	2:6	255

5:17-19	33	14:4	179
5:25-26	77	18:15-17	273
5:27-28	33	22:36	163
5:48	77	23:56	179
6:9	77	24:31	86
6:24	272	24:32	152
7:15	233	24:39	86
7:17	33		
7:21	51		
7:28-29	85	**John**	
9:6	85	1:12	97
10:2	87	4:24	77
10:30	147	4:34	72
11:8	37	6:38	72
19:5	162	10:11	255
19:9	12	10:14	255
19:13-15	273	15:18-23	71n46
19:28	87	15:30	71n46
20:25-28	161	19:5	86
20:28	156		
24:10	152	**Acts**	
28:18	87	Book of	80, 187, 198n7, 273
28:18-20	86, 243	1:9-11	86
28:19	248	1:21-22	87
		1:26	87
Mark		2:1-13	206
1:1	85	2:17	96
10:6	34	2:17-21	206
10:13-16	273	2:29	80
11:15-18	85	3:25	97
		6:1	94
Luke		6:1-6	94n27
2:4	97	6:1-7	93, 94
2:15	152	6:2	94
2:36-38	96	6:4	94
2:52	85	6:6	95
7:25	37	7:8-9	80
9:61	175n7	7:23-25	82n6
11:13	77	7:35	82n6
12:1	152	8:27	253

9:3-8	87	1:27	31, 33, 37
11:2	204	2:9-10	157
11:28	211	2:15	30
13:2-4	88	2:21	177
14:4	88	2:27	49
14:14	88	3:28	33, 51
15:11	47	3:29	222
15:22	187	5:9	47
15:25	187	5:12	79, 126
15:27	187	5:12-21	120, 122, 126, 130
15:32	187	5:15	79
16:1	93n24	5:17	79, 126
18:24-26	186	5:18	126
20:17	168n1	5:18-19	86
20:27	27	8:14	97
20:28	168n1, 232	9:5	80
20:28-30	233	9:26	97
21:9	96, 211	10:12	157
21:9-11	211	10:14-15	232
21:10-11	206n34	11:13	87
21:11	206, 206n34	12:4-8	228
21:14	179	12:7-8	168n1
21:17	206n34	13:1	151
21:27	206n34	13:1-2	247
21:30	206n34	15:4	259
21:32	206n34	15:8	80
21:33	206n34	15:25	93
22:2	178, 179	15:31	93
22:29	206n34	16:1	93
28:17	206n34	16:1-3	95
		16:2	95
Romans		16:3	95
1:1	87	16:7	88n13, 89, 90
1:16	157	16:21	89
1:18-20	242		
1:20	30	**1 Corinthians**	
1:24	33	Book of	35, 200, 201, 221
1:24-27	31	2:4	49
1:26	31, 34	3:15	47
1:26-27	31, 32	4:6-9	88

5:9-10	39	11:6	143
6:1	210	11:7	99, 144, 145
6:9	36, 38, 39, 39n22, 40n23, 41, 44	11:7-9	223
		11:7-10	68, 98
6:9-10	35, 40	11:8	209n39
6:11	40	11:8-9	99, 113, 123, 124, 144, 180
6:12	221	11:8-10	99, 209
7:1	221	11:9	117, 120, 130, 209n39, 238
7:1b	221	11:9-10	149
7:2-3	165	11:10	99, 124. 143, 145, 146n7
7:3-4	62	11:13	143
7:4	165	11:14	32, 145
7:5	165	11:14-15	32, 32n3, 144n2, 189
7:7	51n43	11:15	145
7:8-9	51n43	11:16	209, 214, 215
7:14	163	11:17	210
7:15	12	11:17-18	210, 215
7:25	221	11:17-34	214, 215
8:1	221	11:18	210, 215
8:1b	221	11:20	210
9:6	88n13	11:21	6
9:8-10	262	11:31	204
10:7-8	38	11:33	152, 210
10:23-33	210	11:34	210
11	142, 143, 143n2, 145n4, 146, 149, 189, 190, 200n16, 209, 210	12:1	221
		12:28	96, 168n1, 205
		12:28-30	186
11:2-15	215	14	169, 195, 197, 199n11, 200n16, 203, 221, 250
11:2-16	123, 129, 142, 149, 172, 189, 190, 210, 214, 215, 222, 223	14:1-33	202
		14:2	202
11:3	72n46, 96, 100, 110, 124, 143, 147, 148, 149	14:4	202
		14:5	202
11:4	143	14:6	202
11:4-6	124	14:13	202
11:5	143, 145, 195, 196, 197, 198, 199n11, 199n12, 200, 200n12, 200n14, 200n15, 202, 207, 208, 209, 215, 216, 217, 219, 220, 221, 222, 223, 225	14:14	210
		14:18	202
		14:19	210
		14:23	202, 210
		14:23-29	213

14:26	204, 210, 215, 217	15:24-28	71n46
14:26-28	197	15:25	72n47
14:26ff	208	15:25-27	281
14:27	202, 204	15:27	72n47
14:28	202n26, 208, 210	15:28	72, 72n47
14:29	197, 202, 204, 205	15:40-41	145
14:30	202n26, 208	15:45-49	120, 130
14:30-35	197	15:49	144
14:31	203	15:54-58	280
14:33	195n1	16:1	221
14:33-35	196n3	16:12	221
14:33b	208, 214, 221	16:13	35
14:33b-35	195		
14:33b-36	214	**2 Corinthians**	
14:34	68, 175n7, 193, 199n12, 200n12, 202, 203, 208, 212, 212n44	1:1	88
		8:23	90, 90n18
		11:3	180
14:34-35	ix, 56, 57, 96n32, 193, 195n1, 196, 197, 198, 200n16, 201, 202, 203, 204, 207, 208, 209, 211, 212, 212n43, 213, 217, 218, 219, 220, 221, 222, 223, 224, 225, 227, 228	**Galatians**	
		1:19	88, 90
		2:3	157
		2:9	88n13
		2:14	157
		2:16	33, 157
14:34-36	191, 192	3:7	157
14:35	193, 203, 210, 212, 216, 217	3:25-29	157
		3:26	97, 157, 157n34
14:36	214, 221, 222	3:28	155, 156, 157, 157n34
14:36-40	203	3:29	157
14:37	203, 208	4:6-7	97
14:37-38	216n48	4:19	77
14:39-40	203	5:13	154, 156
14:40	218	5:22-23	43
15:2	47	6:2	152
15:5-7	88		
15:7	88, 90	**Ephesians**	
15:10	281	1:20-22	148, 150
15:14	281	1:22	147, 148
15:20-23	72n47	2:20	33, 96, 205, 205n33
15:21	87	3:5	96, 205
15:22	120, 126, 130		

3:14-15	97
4:11	171, 186, 205n33, 232
4:11-13	87
4:13	87
4:15	87, 147, 148
5	73, 117, 143, 152, 243
5:18	150, 152
5:19-21	150
5:21	121n2, 150, 151, 152n19, 154, 155, 156
5:21-27	273
5:21-6:9	155
5:22	96, 121, 148, 150, 151, 157n34
5:22-23	145n4
5:22-24	61, 140, 141, 149
5:22-33	111, 148, 172
5:22-6:9	152n19
5:23	62, 96, 110, 140, 147, 148, 156, 243
5:24	96, 140, 149, 150, 151, 156, 244, 247
5:25	43, 87, 96, 110, 117, 156, 164
5:25-27	140
5:31	121n2, 193
5:31-32	158n35
5:32	156
5:33	117
6	158, 159, 243
6:1	151, 158, 163n37, 273
6:1-2	243, 262
6:1-4	163
6:2	159, 163n37
6:4	158, 162, 163n37, 172, 271, 279
6:5	151, 157n34
6:9	158
6:12	167

Philippians

1:1	88, 92, 92n22, 94, 168n1
2:12	49, 51
2:15	97
2:25	90, 90n18

Colossians

1:1	88
1:7	93
1:18	147, 148
2:10	147, 148, 150
3:5	33
3:11	157
3:16	186
3:18	61, 96, 148, 152n19, 172
3:18-19	140, 152
3:18-4:1	155
3:19	117
4:1	158
4:10	89

1 Thessalonians

1:1	88
1:5	242
2:6-7	88
2:7-8	52
2:11-12	52
4:3-4	165
4:11	109, 179
5:12	116, 172
5:20-21	205

2 Thessalonians

3:12	178, 179

1 Timothy

Book of	48
1:3	187
1:9-10	37
1:10	37

1:18	167	2:15	44, 46, 47, 48, 48n39, 49, 50, 51, 115, 174, 187, 191
1:19-20	188		
2	vii, 45, 117, 123, 169, 171, 189, 190, 191, 192, 193, 194, 195, 212n43, 225, 226, 235, 239, 250	3	92, 92n22, 168n1, 169, 173, 235
		3:1	168n1
		3:1-2	232
2:2	178, 179	3:1-7	170, 173
2:4	45	3:2	91, 93, 94, 110, 168n1, 170, 171, 230, 232
2:5	87		
2:8	174, 174n6, 185, 192, 193, 210	3:4	110, 111, 172
		3:4-5	92, 94, 116, 171, 232
2:8-10	174, 185, 191, 192	3:5	168n1
2:8-15	48n39, 56, 173, 174, 174n6, 186, 187, 191, 193, 209, 211, 212, 213, 217, 225, 227, 231	3:8	92, 168n1, 172
		3:8-10	92, 173
		3:8-13	91, 172, 172n5
		3:11	92, 93, 93n24, 94, 172, 172n5
2:9	48n39, 174n6, 210		
2:9-10	191, 193	3:12	91, 93, 94, 116, 172
2:9-15	44	3:12-13	92, 173
2:10	48, 48n39, 49, 50, 51	3:14-15	186
2:10-12	45	4:1-3	187
2:11	48n39, 174, 179, 184n33, 212	4:6	93
		4:7-8	180, 270
2:11-12	174, 179, 191, 211	4:13	229
2:11-14	59, 91, 98, 221	4:14	49
2:12	48, 48n39, 49, 50, 57, 68, 92, 129, 171, 174, 175n7, 175n10, 176, 176n14, 177, 177n14, 178, 179, 180n20, 184n33, 185, 186, 188, 189, 190, 192, 193, 196, 199n11, 212, 212n44, 216, 228, 239, 248	4:16	45, 46, 180
		5	171
		5:3-16	109
		5:4	180
		5:8	109, 110
		5:9	91, 110, 170, 171
		5:10-16	171
2:12-13	111, 128, 190	5:11	180
2:12-14	129, 238	5:14	51, 115, 116
2:13	48n39, 63, 118, 120, 122, 123, 130, 179, 180, 184n33	5:14-15	46, 50, 187
		5:15	46, 180
2:13-14	44, 174, 179, 180n20, 181, 185, 188, 191, 193, 209, 212, 233	5:17	116, 168n1, 171, 172, 177, 230, 232
		5:18	180
2:13-15	47	6:11-12	270
2:14	45, 46, 47, 48n39, 180, 182, 184, 184n33, 188		

6:12	167	5:10	86
6:16	176n14, 177n14	6:20	86
		7:4	80
2 Timothy		7:17	86
1:6-7	180	7:26-28	86
2:3	167	7:27	234
2:7	180	8:1	86
2:16	180	11:23	162n37
2:17-18	188	11:32	81, 253
3:5-6	180	12	164
3:16	259	12:5	163n37
4:1-2	230	12:7	163n37
4:3	180	12:7-11	164, 172
4:5-6	180	12:8	163n37
4:9-10	180	12:11	163n37, 164
4:11	180	12:14	51
4:15	180	13:4	164
		13:17	151
Titus		13:20	255
1	168n1, 169, 235		
1:5-7	168n1	**James**	
1:5-9	170	4:7	151
1:6	91, 110, 170		
1:7	232	**1 Peter**	
1:9	171, 232	2:25	255
1:12	216n48	3	191, 193
2	275	3:1	96, 141, 148, 152, 193
2:3-5	51, 172, 178, 186	3:1-6	172
2:4-5	44, 111, 115, 140, 152, 245, 274, 276	3:1-7	141, 192
		3:4	179
2:5	101, 115, 148	3:4-5	141
3:1-3	180	3:5	148
3:9	180	3:6	141, 149
3:12	180	3:7	96, 111, 117, 141, 164, 165n38, 182, 192, 238
Hebrews		3:20	47
Book of	80, 239	5:1-2	168n1
3:1-6	86	5:2	232
4:14	234		
5:6	86		

Jude
3	233

Revelation
Book of	13n18
2:14	178
2:20	251
6:4	152
7:17	255
19:11-20:15	87
21:14	87

RECOMMENDED READING

Bavinck, Herman. *The Christian Family*. Translated by Nelson D. Kloosterman. Grand Rapids, MI: Christian's Library Press, 2012. Bavinck was one of the great theologians of the 19th and 20th centuries. This short work does not disappoint.

Gouge, William. *Building a Godly Home: A Holy Vision for a Happy Marriage*. Volume 2. Edited by Scott Brown and Joel R. Beeke. Grand Rapids: Reformation Heritage Books, 2013. A practical work by a Puritan minister and member of the Westminster Assembly, edited and in modern English.

Hughes, R. Kent. *Disciplines of a Godly Man*. Wheaton, IL: Crossway, 2001. An excellent practical book on developing godly character.

Köstenberger, Andreas J., and Thomas R. Schreiner, editors. *Women in the Church: An Interpretation and Application of 1 Timothy 2:9-15*. 3rd ed. Wheaton: Crossway, 2016. This is a technical treatment of one of the most controversial and important passages on gender roles. Highly recommended for those wanting more in-depth study.

Merkle, Rebekah. *Eve in Exile: And the Restoration of Femininity*. Moscow, ID: Canon Press, 2016. This book is aimed at women, surveying the history of feminism and showing God's design for femininity.

Neuer, Werner. *Man and Woman in Christian Perspective*. Translated by Gordon J. Wenham. Wheaton: Crossway, 1991. This is a helpful theological work on men and women that is more conservative than most complementarian writings. It is unfortunately out of print.

Wilson, Douglas. *Father Hunger: Why God Calls Men to Love and Lead Their Families*. Nashville, TN: Thomas Nelson, 2012. An excellent work on the importance of fathers.

www.ingramcontent.com/pod-product-compliance
Lightning Source LLC
Chambersburg PA
CBHW071953070526
44583CB00015B/1179